*"LATEST CHELSEA FOOTBALL FANZINE
IT'S ONLY A POUND NOW HURRY UP"*

Chelsea Football Fanzine
the best of cfcuk

volume one

Gate 17
5 Weir Road
Kibworth Beauchamp
Leicester LE8 0LQ, UK
Tel: (+44) 116 279 2299
Fax: (+44) 116 279 2277
Email: enquiries@overlandandsea.net
Web: www.overlandandsea.net

ISBN 978 095574 5942

British Library Cataloguing in Publication Data.
A catalogue record for this book is available from the British Library.

Typeset in 11pt Arial by Troubador Publishing Ltd, Leicester, UK
Printed in the UK by T J International Ltd, Padstow, Cornwall

Gate 17 is an imprint of Troubador Publishing Ltd

ACKNOWLEDGEMENTS

Martin Knight, The Sheditor, Porca Troia, Baba Cracka, Blue Daze, Ross Eccles, Rayners Blue, Chels Guevara, The Guy Who Blagged Me, Chief Inspector Moody, Chris Tarant, Johnny Jackal, Emu, Paul the Bookie, Tom Traveller, Juvenile D, Merlin, Blue Bear, Dog, Smiffy, Slim Jim, The Politician, Natasha, Euro Blue, The Bar Steward, Chelsea Sven, The Independent, Tommy Ticket, The Joker, Neil Smith, The Financier, Urchin D, Alan Corfield, Cool Blue, John King, Billy Bookworm, Norvern Muppet, Technical Terry, Bacchanalian Blue, Stanic Worship, The Visionary, The Reporter, Blue Berry, Famous CFC, Hocus McPocus, Harri Hemi, Dicko, Don Dilemma, Quique 21, El Russo, The Chelsea Advocate, Emma H, Chopper, Local Boy, Martin W, Wally Otton, John Terry's Barmy Army, Peter Hain MP, Jack Slade, Dave Mac, The Striker, Luke Turner, Peter Caton, True Blue, John Drewitt, Mickey Microphone, Joe Cole, CFC Andrew, Harry Moss, Bruce Buck, Alan Hudson, Kelvin Barker, Mark Worrall, Gate 17.

cfcuk is available on matchdays from the cfcuk stall directly opposite the main entrance to Fulham Broadway Station or by subscription from cfcuk, PO Box 26066, London, SW10 0XP. www.cfcuk.net

FOREWORD

by MARTIN KNIGHT

I first became aware of the Matthew Harding's Blue And White Army fanzine around the early part of 2000. It was a different world then. The founder, proprietor and sole salesman had a mop of corkscrew hair, for starters. He looked like one of the blokes you'd see loitering in the Harlequin record shop in the early 70s forensically examining the cover of the latest Incredible String Band album.

Chelsea won the last FA Cup Final to be staged at Wembley courtesy of a goal scored by Robert Di Matteo while I was doing my flies up in the toilets of the Lillie Langtry pub. Musty old political stalwarts like John Major and Michael Heseltine were withdrawing from the bear-pit and Gordon Brown was only in the early stages of sabotaging the economy. Bono was whining about a beautiful day and Kevin Spacey made an American Beauty of a film.

I remember being introduced to the (now named) cfcuk fanzine man at an event for Alan Hudson at Ealing Studios. My diary tells me it was April of that year. The place was full of legends. Besides Mr Hudson there was Danny Harkins and Johnny Haynes to name but two. The fanzine man was sorry. Sorry for being introduced. Sorry for talking to me. Sorry for buying a drink. Sorry for being sorry. He told me about the publication - Matthew Harding's Blue And White Army - and how he had reviewed the Hoolifan book I had co-authored.

My initial reaction was that he was mad.

As I got to know him over the next decade my suspicions were confirmed. But mad, maverick people are what make the world an interesting place. If everyone was "normal" it would drive you mad. This man and his fanzine (and to me you cannot separate the two) have provided me with many of my Chelsea adventures over the years. They were instrumental in getting the Peter Osgood book off the ground and toured the pubs and clubs with Ossie and us, in one of the best years of my life. Later we reprised it all with Charlie Cooke. The fanzine man arranged for me to have tea with Gianluca Vialli and set up most of the interviews with the players for The Special Ones book. Who else can bring Frank Lampard, John Terry and Gianfranco Zola to the table while forgetting to put food on his own?

cfcuk / MHBAWA is Chelsea's conscience. It is one of the few assets that club cannot buy, though some think they may have tried. It is the custodian of the past and the keeper of that CFC unique spirit that has been all but ethnically cleansed from Stamford Bridge. Yet, its orginators look forward, their love of Chelsea driving them on and they bear only goodwill. When the fanzine was embroiled in a potentially life-ruining legal dispute with the most powerful man at Chelsea at the time I suggested they change the name of the fanzine (with one eye on Fulham's offering) to THERE'S ONLY ONE C AT CHELSEA - they would have none of it. The fanzine is infuriating. It is responsible for more Chelsea supporters having to wear glasses than any other factor. It refuses to embrace the march of technology, still looking like it has been cranked out on an old Gestetner machine in a greenhouse on some allotment. It still only costs a pound. But it is an institution with the cfcuk stall, a haunt of old players, old hooligans, old guffers and old spice, an essential destination on match days. And yet when cfcuk has gone, God forbid, Chelsea Football Club will have finally died. The business will continue, but so what?

cfcuk HISTORY

With the sad and premature demise of the previously long established bastion of the supporters' cause that was the Chelsea Independent fanzine looming, the first issue of Matthew Harding's Blue And White Army appeared in February 1999 and two issues were published during the 98/99 season.

Named in memory of Matthew Harding, as well as to remind then Chairman Ken Bates that there were still Chelsea supporters who cared about what was happening to their club, it also carried the title because most of the people who submitted articles sat in the lower tier of the Matthew Harding Stand.

From the outset, all who wrote for the fanzine agreed to use pseudonyms in order to retain anonymity. The last edition of the 08/09 season was the 100th, and while the majority of people of people who buy it might know some of the faces associated with the fanzine, they still aren't quite sure exactly who writes what. After all, it isn't the writers themselves that are important and it's not about being the 'daddy of opinions', it is the subject itself … Chelsea Football Club … that matters most of all.

As well as that, at the time when the first issue went to print, Bates' libel team were working overtime in an effort to stem the tide of criticism from fanzines such as ours, the Chelsea Action Group website and opponents in the media. Those writing for the fanzine were more than happy to play their part in confusing the enemy!

Although there are several writers who do use their real names, the majority are more than happy to use an a.k.a. and the principle has served its purpose well. From its inception, most of the Chelsea supporters who contributed to the fanzine were radically opposed to Ken Bates' involvement at the club, however, the fanzine always offered space to those who wanted to express supporting viewpoints. Over the years, there were a few articles published that were pro-Bates, though the majority were, when the former Chairman was the subject, vociferously anti.

cfcuk set out to establish a pool of regular writers, a practice still employed today, with each giving their own particular slant on one topic or another. All who contributed to issue 1 had previously written for the Chelsea Independent. By issue 4, they were supplemented by other contributors, including those involved in the Carefree 92/93 fanzine. Matthew Harding's Blue And White Army always encouraged new writers and some who joined the fanzine in the early days are still writing for it today, as well as for other media outlets, notably bawa.net.

The fanzine's aim was to stand true to the ideals of Chelsea Fundamentalism, an unwritten mantra that was subsequently put into words and appeared via The Visionary in later editions of cfcuk. At all costs, it set out to take the fight to Ken Bates and become the natural ally of those who could, even then, foresee both the demise of the genuine supporter and, in certain cases, their own financially related exile. The 99/00 season saw six editions published with one, issue 6, having its front cover reproduced in the News Of The World. The fanzine was given help from many quarters, including established authors such as John King, Martin Knight and Martin King, all of whom have not only featured in interviews but have also contributed many articles, albeit under their chosen pen names.

After just four issues, the Matthew Harding's Blue And White Army fanzine was approached by Chrysalis Records, parent company of the fledgling Rivals web network, to host a Chelsea website under the banner Blue And White Army … bawa.net … and a contract was signed in December 1999.

At the end of the season, to mark Chelsea's FA Cup Final appearance against Aston Villa, Matthew Harding's Blue And White Army, along with the Man In The Brown Suede Jacket and Emu, jointly produced a free giveaway mini fanzine entitled "Luca Vialli's Blue And White Army", each featuring an A3 sized colour poster of the Blue Flag. 20,000 were distributed and, to this day, many a wall is still decorated with what, for several months in May 2000, became an iconic symbol in and around South and West London.

During the course of the following season, the fortunes of Matthew

Harding's Blue And White Army were boosted when a benefactor … a long-time supporter both of Chelsea Football Club and of our cause who, for several reasons, including magnanimity, wishes to remain nameless … donated a cheque for several thousand pounds, some of which went towards the cost of two season tickets. Had it not been for his intervention, the fanzine would not have survived and the Lower Matthew Harding Stand would have been short of two of its supporters!

The fanzine has also received financial backing from other individuals and those fighting for the same ideals the fanzine espoused. When a leading member of the fanzine's staff began defamation proceedings against Ken Bates, another loyal Chelsea supporter who goes by the name of 'Local Boy' gave him help with the initial costs of bringing the case to Court.

At this point, while mentioning the case, thanks are also due to media law specialists David Price Solicitors and Advocates, in particular David Price and Kathryn van Gelder, for their help in agreeing to take on the case and in bringing about a successful conclusion to the libel proceedings. During the litigation, Local Boy was always on hand to provide the help and necessary preparation required in mounting an action that took several years to resolve. Thanks, too, to the Chelsea supporters who also gave their help by agreeing to provide witness statements and, if necessary, Court appearances.

Over the course of its publication, especially at the outset, the fanzine has received various financial donations from Local Boy as well as many, much appreciated kind and inspirational words and a listening ear for guidance. As in the case of the previously mentioned benefactor, Local Boy has always wished to remain anonymous. That said, cfcuk, on behalf of all Chelsea Fundamentalists, would like to thank him for his assistance to not only our purposes but also on behalf of those of the Chelsea Independent, Chelsea Action Group and to all supporters who have ever flown, seen or sung about the Blue Flag.

The first edition of the 00/01 season, issue 9, featured a front-page picture of Luca Vialli with the caption "Come On Luca, Let's Win The League!" It was still on sale when Luca was sacked, so the remaining copies that were sold had a message ink-stamped over Luca's photo that read, "Cancelled – By Order Of Ken Bates!" By the end of the season, another five editions, six in all, had been published … the readership was expanding. This was the first season that the fanzine writers could air their views to the web and, with the sacking of Vialli, both the sales of Matthew Harding's Blue And White Army and the hit count on the website shot to record levels, with all subsequent issues of the fanzine selling out, and the website achieving nearly 15,000 hits over two days.

The following season, another six issues, numbers 15 to 20, were produced and, in issue 16, a souvenir pull-out marking Chelsea's 25th consecutive game against Sp*rs without defeat was given away as part of the fanzine. At the end of the season, Matthew Harding's Blue And White Army was behind the production of a programme for a benefit match in aid of Peter Osgood between the Chelsea Allstars and the SKY One Dream Team.

When Chelsea reached the FA Cup Semi Final against Fulham at Villa Park, it was cfcuk who negotiated and organised the flying of the Blue Flag before the game. Even as the flag was being unfurled, Chelsea supporters began to applaud its appearance. Carried proudly over the heads of the Chelsea faithful, it eventually reached those taking part in CFCnet's "Mission Celery" campaign and, for a few seconds at least, there were hundreds of lumps of the sublimely tasty green vegetable covering the top of the flag.

The appearance of the Blue Flag was given a mention in the following Chelsea home programme after it prompted manager Claudio Ranieri to comment upon the fact that its sight had inspired him … a photo of the Blue Flag in flight was featured alongside this article. Supporters who enjoyed seeing it that evening should know that is was there through the kind cooperation of Matthew Harding's son Luke (and his Chelsea mates) and his mother Ruth.

Season 02/03 began with issue 21, but by the time that campaign had ended with issue 27, the design of the front cover had changed and now appeared with a solid blue header along with information, a photograph below, and below that a headline. Within the fanzine, the 'Times New Roman' font was replaced by 'Arial', a change for the better attributable to long-time Chelsea stalwart Neil Beard, a Chelsea Fundamentalist and solid supporter of our fanzine.

Issue 28, the first of 9 published for the 03/04 term, featured a photograph of Mr Abramovich with the headline, "Roman's Conquest – Hail Caesar!" Whilst this issue was full of articles about the Russian himself, it was more significant for the fact that the name cfcuk replaced the title Matthew Harding's Blue And White Army.

Patrons to Matthew's cause should have no fear. "cfcuk – published in memory of Matthew Harding" is at the head of most of the pages, it is also printed within the fanzine's information section on page 3. As well as the change of title, readers also found a new 'extra' supplement containing accounts of the latest Chelsea matches (at time of going to print) but with added information such as the songs that were sung and the pubs and bars that were visited.

In Issue 32, January 2004, cfcuk began a campaign to reinstate the 1970s crest. The return of the badge was one of a number of principles from which the fanzine drew its inspiration and a print of it featured on the front cover. Within the fanzine, a petition was launched with a middle page pull-out comprising on one side a form and open appeal to Roman Abramovich to answer our pleas and on the other a print of the full 1950s Lord Cadogan crest. Above the badge was written, "Dear Roman," and below came the words, "Please … bring me back!"

The campaign secured over 20,000 signatories, each adding their individual voice to over 800 petition forms (each form contained sufficient space for 25 names). Of these, hundreds were forwarded on to Chelsea Football Club having been collected by the fanzine sellers or returned to cfcuk's Fulham Rd stall … many more were sent direct to Stamford Bridge. To quote Chelsea Football Club Chairman Bruce Buck, "The club was inundated with them …"

The timing of issue 35, April 2004, coincided with Chelsea's pitch having recently been turned into a quagmire due to bad weather and extensive use. In it, Technical Terry debated whether football should be played on grass or plastic. News that the 'old badge' would be returning to Chelsea was broken first by way of "The Thoughts Of Chels Guevara" in issue 37, the first edition of the 04/05 season whose cover featured a smiling John Terry. Later during that season, Chelsea Football Club officially announced that from the start of the 05/06 campaign, it would be changing the official crest from the one that Ken Bates had imposed upon the Club in 1986 to a close approximation of the 1950s badge.

In issue 40, another fleeting appearance of a column entitled "Dong's Diary" raised a few eyebrows. The self-penned account of Dong's sexual exploits and gigantic 'love-truncheon' wowed and worried female Blues fans in equal measure as they perused his journal. Whilst many who read Dong's column were flummoxed by his subsequent unannounced disappearance, others who read John King's novel 'Skinheads' were relieved to find that Dong … now DJ Dong … was alive and well (page 200) and playing the best of Punk Rock and New Wave to punters frequenting the "London Calling" gigs run by well known London live gig promoter Barnet, a man also renowned as the lead singer and founder of Punk Elvis tribute band 'Viva Las Vegas'.

cfcuk accepted a kind and generous invitation to attend the press announcement regarding the new crest from Simon Arthur (former Group Operations Director) and Simon Greenberg (former Communications and Public Affairs Director) of Chelsea Football Club … recognition perhaps of the role played by cfcuk and all those who had signed the petitions for a return to the favoured badge. The official club announcement was marked on the front cover of issue 41 with an image of the 'new' badge … underneath, the headline "Welcome Home!"

In issue 47, published in May 2005, the Chelsea Supporters Group published their Draft Constitution. The group, established to represent the majority of Chelsea supporters, were then invited by the club to take up a permanent position on the Club's Fans' Forum.

At the end of the 03/04 Season, cfcuk produced a special edition of the fanzine entitled "cfcuk – The Football Factory". After being given unique and exclusive access during the course of the making of the film, which was based on the John King novel The Football Factory, Mickey Microphone went on to produce a publication that featured interviews with the stars of the film. John King co-edited this issue that also featured articles from, amongst others, Stephen Menary, Rayners Blue, Martin Knight, Juvenile D, Mark Wyeth and Chels Guevara. It has been subsequently acknowledged as the 'definitive' read about the film.

Credit must go to John King for his help and assistance in every matter pertaining to the "cfcuk – The Football Factory" fanzine appearing 'on the streets'. While the idea was always there, it would never have actually happened without his help. Within weeks, even though it was the close season, it soon became sought-after cult reading for those interested in terrace culture, and the original print run of 1500 copies soon sold out.

Fresh from the success that The Football Factory special edition fanzine had been, Juvenile D was then Herculean in his efforts to produce the vast majority of material for a second special edition of cfcuk published that summer, entitled "cfcuk – Zola The Legend". Published as soon as the date for a special game for Gianfranco Zola between

Chelsea and Real Zaragoza was announced, it was on sale at the cfcuk stall on the morning of the match. Like the Football Factory edition, it also sold out quickly and proved to be a great success. Others who also submitted material to the Zola special were Chels Guevara, Dutch Blue, Famous CFC and EuroBlue.

Whilst meeting the great man at the dinner marking his career at Chelsea, Juvenile D presented Gianfranco with a copy of his work and, in return, received autographed copies of the fanzine for himself. Now, whether Gianfranco treasures his memento from Juvenile as much as Juvenile does his from Gianfranco is another question, but from our perspective, both The Football Factory and the "Zola – The Legend" special editions of cfcuk are highly ranked amongst what we consider our finest achievements.

The 04/05 Season ended with issue 48, an edition that was produced in time to mark the celebratory Premiership parade through the streets of Chelsea and Fulham in May 2005. cfcuk had mirrored Chelsea's success on the pitch in breaking all records by publishing 12 editions of the regular fanzine plus the two specials. Subscribers to cfcuk that season got excellent value for money; each receiving the 14 fanzines published in addition to a regulatory cfcuk tshirt.

05/06 began with Chelsea, as Champions, playing the Goons for the Charity (Community) Shield at Cardiff's Millennium Stadium. As ever, cfcuk sellers were there and issue 49 was on sale before, during and after the game … the first edition of the season. As in previous campaigns, the fanzine continued with its format of regular columnists and features, including the popular "Frankie Says" page, music articles, Chelsea or football related book and film reviews, Smiffy's quiz page and, perhaps most crucially, correspondence from our readership.

The 50th edition, published in September 2005, featured an interview with Joe Cole, who is generally acknowledged as being the greatest Chelsea footballer of all time by many at cfcuk.

For those associated with the fanzine, reaching the half-century mark was considered to be a landmark achievement and we sincerely hope that this 'best of' collection of articles from those first 50 editions will provide an entertaining and interesting snapshot of what it was like supporting Chelsea during one of the most turbulent and ultimately triumphant periods in the Club's history.

Now, after over 100 editions plus three special publications and a

Peter Osgood programme, it seems we'd finally managed to convince our harshest critics ... ourselves and those who care about cfcuk ... that we might have got it right!

Whether the cfcuk fanzine will reach issue 200 remains to be seen, whilst on the other hand, the future might see the reincarnation of cfcuk in its own right via the internet. Whatever is to come, Chelsea Fundamentalists and those who wish to see an 'ideal' Chelsea Football Club, can find all they need to know within the pages of the issues already published.

THE SHEDITOR
LONDON 2010

ISSUE 1 February 1999

The Sheditorial

Welcome to the first – and hopefully not last – issue of Matthew Harding's Blue and White Army.

Why that name?

Well, firstly, this new fanzine is primarily written by people who sit in the Matthew Harding Stand. And no offence to those sitting elsewhere, but the Matthew seems to be the only part of the ground prepared to make any noise; it's the only part of our ground that seems to remember what football should be about. And, of course, the name Matthew Harding carries with it certain ideas. We're not trying to canonise the man, but with Matthew the football club came first. As it stands, there's a very real danger that the West Stand will not be completed because it's tied in with planning permission for a 900 capacity nightclub. That would not have happened if Matthew was here. And thirdly, it's one of the few songs left at Chelsea with more than three syllables.

One thing I'd like to make clear from the start is that just because we bear the Harding name, does not necessarily mean we're out to slag off Ken or the Village, although when you read Baba Cracka's piece you might get a different impression. We just want proper supporter representation. We're called on to get involved and help fight Chelsea's cause in the planning enquiry, but no bugger turned up. If we had supporter representation and worked with the club, it could have been different.

I spoke to the local residents, and apparently the pre-enquiry meeting was full of 'Chelsea fans' with professionally produced placards who, according to Cherie Finger-Uparse, were paid for their morning's work. There was no sign of them at the start of the enquiry proper.

I also spoke to Hammersmith and Fulham's representatives, and their attitude (between you and me) was that they're prepared to be flexible to help the club, but, as one of them put it: "What we're worried about is giving permission for a museum and then find the fuckers have built another bloody hotel." Quite.

There is general acceptance amongst the locals that if you have 35,000 fans at the ground 25 times a year, then another 10,000 doesn't make much difference. My grandmother lives nearby and says yes, it's hassle, but so are lots of things about living in central London. If the good doesn't outweigh the bad then move somewhere else.

But nightclubs are a different story. That's more likely to create problems and nuisance for locals. They'd object to any new nightclub in the area – and it's not as if the area isn't well served already – whether it's Chelsea's or not. It is a sign of Ken's ability to turn on the charm and play the affable rogue that, even after all this time, the councils and residents still want to see Chelsea do well. Just think, if he'd given local schools free tickets for games that were never in danger of selling out, how much goodwill would Chelsea have built up?

We're not here to rival Red Card or the Chelsea Independent (mainly cos we want to sell off their stalls), and this fanzine will not be coming out every month.

The Chelsea Fanatical and Curious Blue sadly came and went, but they were one-man bands. We've hopefully got the numbers to meet our target of four issues this season.

Just about everyone you'll read in this magazine is contributing to a fanzine for the first time – although we have poached Independent regular Chels Guevara – so hopefully we'll have a fresh slant on things.

Getting Chels was a bit like tracking down Kendo Nagasaki, the mysterious British wrestler. Rumours abound: it's Wolfie out of Citizen Smith's girlfriend's dad; it's Colin Hutchinson's paper boy; he won't talk to you unless you're wearing a beret. Whether you like him or loathe him, he's never dull. Or that's what he says.

Finally, apparently even glancing at Alan Collis means you'll get the sack from Chelsea.

Also, if your name has appeared in the Independent's contributors list you're banned from writing for the official magazine (although this might be because if you've written for it, you're probably not very good).

In the hope that this curse will spread by default to Matthew Harding's Blue And White Army, can I thank the following people:

⬜⬜The management of Canaletto's for providing me with a delicious meal without wine cos you haven't got a licence.

⬜⬜The ham-fisted git who designed the YMCA End for giving me a nose bleed at the Helsingborg game (when people look at it and say "that's a bit steep", do they mean the stand or the hotel?).

⬜⬜Whoever writes those God-awful match reports and 'Chelsea Choir' bits in Onside, which piss me off every month.

We are Matthew Harding's Blue And White Army – and so are you.

Porca Troia

*****

Reasons to be Fearful (Part One)

Chelsea Village is fast becoming a thriving metropolis. Manchester United are our inspiration, both on and off the pitch, and we 'are driving them hard'. At least, according to Ken Bates we are. All in the Village garden is rosy, and the supporters have nothing to complain or worry about.

Sound familiar? If the above reads like a Ken Bates column in the match programme, I make no apology. That opening paragraph quite succinctly sums up the opinion that seems to be coming out of the club. It also appears to be a view shared by a large proportion of Chelsea fans. Is it an accurate picture, though?

'Come on', I hear people cry, 'We've got world class players galore, we're playing quite well and we've won four cups in the past 18 months. How can you find something to worry about?'

An acknowledgment of high prices and a concern about a lack of atmosphere apart, most fans see the present time as a time of unprecedented success for the club. Yes, but at what cost? All football fans have been forced to accept changes in our game as inevitable. These changes, though, are being made and the supporters' interest is not always very high up on the list of priorities. This is particularly apparent at Chelsea.

In this two-part article we'll look at the various issues to worry about.

Ticket pricing and the changing faces amongst the support

Ticket prices seem to rise by £1 or £2 per season. Not a great amount over one year, but it continues from year to year. Bear in mind that in 1991 you could stand for £7 and sit for anything between £8 and £20. These prices were accessible to almost everyone.

Now you'll be paying between £22 and £28. It is not even possible to get into some areas, as they are reserved exclusively for season ticket holders. How much longer can normal fans sustain this kind of financial outlay every week? Whilst everything on the pitch is attractive, Chelsea will have few problems selling out for most games. Supporters who take the risk of getting tickets on a match-to-match basis will inevitably lose out occasionally. Picking and choosing games is becoming more common, with the less attractive matches (see Helsingborg) not selling out.

The only way to guarantee a seat is to get a season ticket, but these too have gone through the roof. This year saw a well documented 15% increase in cost in most parts of the ground. The East Middle is now the most expensive season ticket in the land, going from £887 to £1,027.

The biggest jump was in the Matthew Lower. Tickets here rose 50%, from £370 to £545. Granted, a few cup matches were included, but to ask people to stump up that kind of cash is incredible.

By including the Worthington Cup games, Bates knows he has the fans over a barrel. These games were the chance for the penny-pinching supporter to take a break. Now we have to pay for unattractive matches as part of the total cost. Bates, rather than rewarding loyalty, seems to see it as a weakness to exploit at every turn.

You can buy a season ticket at Man U for £380, £374 for Villa and £377 at Arsenal. A matchday ticket at Arsenal can be bought for £14. Arsenal even make a reduction on the renewal if the previous year's SEVEN cup ties aren't fulfilled. In an exploitative league, where everything is about money, we are the most exploited. Why?

Many other clubs allow season tickets to be bought on a direct debit system so that the fan can balance out the cost over a year. Chelsea?

No. It has to be renewed/taken out several months before the start of the season. This allows Bates to have all the money gaining interest in his account before the customers even see the product.

So we're still paying more, with less benefits and less flexibility than our rivals. Do you still think Bates cares? 'If you don't like it, don't come', is the sympathy we get from our chairman. While things are good, this emotional stranglehold he has us in means we will continue to renew. If we don't pay, we can't see our Chelsea. He is testing the patience and pocket of many of Chelsea's old faithful. There are a significant number of old Chelsea fans who can no longer afford to go. Take a look around you next time: how many pensioners do you see? There are also fewer children than at our rivals. Lack of youth development does not only apply to the playing side. Add to these groups the fans who feel marginalised by the changes and the price increases and we have a significant disenfranchised minority.

Does Bates care? No, he's happy as long as the seats are filled. I welcome the new fans, but not at the expense of the old guard. Whilst we are successful, the new fans will come, but success has to be sustained to keep their interest. In a game of highs and lows, that's impossible. Fans who have been going for years will still go, even if we slipped into the First Division. Have a look around you: how many of the people near you would do the same?

The French players in the World Cup made a plea for tickets to go to real fans and not men in suits. They were worried about a lack of passion. At Chelsea we still have the passion, but less than in the past. In the long term, Chelsea's pricing policy will damage the fan base.

A fairer and more accessible pricing policy is needed. The fans are not another tool to exploit. They are an integral part of the club, and its future depends on them. A more understanding policy is needed. Changing the fan base is a potentially destructive measure. Whether Bates is doing it as a strategy or if it is a side effect, we don't know.

One thing is certain though, the repercussions of high pricing in football will have a long-term effect on football supporting culture. In his programme notes, Bates wrote: 'Our successful future is based on maximising returns from our 70,000 supporter database.' I think that says it all.

Baba Cracka

Matthew Harding's Blue And White Army
Issue 2 - £1.00
April 1999
"HARDING BELIEVED THAT CHELSEA WAS DOING FAR MORE FOR BATES THAN BATES HAD EVER DONE FOR CHELSEA"
(T REDDITION, BUSINESS AGE, FEB 99, NO86, PG8)

ISSUE 2 April 1999

Dazed and Confused

Am I the only one who gets really hacked off at people doing the 4.40 quickstep at Chelsea these days? Considering the amount of late goals we have scored this season, if you partake in this regular second Saturday pastime you must have missed at least six Chelsea goals this season. When you go to the cinema, you never leave before the end of the film, because you want to see what happens at the end, so why should football be any different? My Lord! We used to give home fans all over the country stick when we could see them sneaking out, but our support for the Man United game was pathetic. Yes, we were 2-0 down and there were only ten minutes to go, but seeing so many seats empty so quickly throughout the ground, showed some of our fans as the glory hunting, Johnny come lately's so many other clubs now think we are.

UEFA, being miserable stick in the muds, with Ken Bates' sensible suggestion that the game should be moved to Wembley, have shown that they have learnt nothing from the Stockholm fiasco of last year. Even when last year's final was decided, Chelsea did ask about moving the venue because of the lack of accommodation in the city, but UEFA dug their heels in. Lo and behold, they are doing exactly the same now. If it is Lazio, will the city infrastructure of Birmingham, on a midweek night, cope with thirty thousand Chelsea fans and ten thousand Lazio fans flying, bussing and training their way towards Villa Park? Our semi final fiasco at Villa Park is still fresh in many people's minds, when many fans missed the start of the game against Man United, and that kicked off early on a Sunday morning, when the roads are meant to be quiet. What is the M6/M40 going to be like in the middle of the Birmingham rush hour? Wake up, UEFA!

Some Chelsea fans, though, were disappointed about the thought of a trip to Villa Park, and word has reached Blue Daze of some imaginative fans who wanted a trip abroad for the final. Already some fans have provisionally booked to fly to Dublin before the game and then fly to Birmingham on the day, so it feels like you have left the country. Others are considering Amsterdam or Paris before flying back to Brum. Perhaps a potential money maker EDT missed out on then, Gary?

So season tickets have gone up again. Quel surprise! With the Hammersmith and Fulham saga rolling on, Bates still has the convenient excuse of the West Stand not being built. A line he has recycled so many times over the years, from the ground not being complete to the West Stand now not being complete. When the extra six thousand seats get put in some time next year, does anyone actually expect there to be some form of price freeze for at least one or two years? You do – dream on, suckers, and start getting ready for the £700 Matthew Harding season ticket.

He has got us by the balls, hasn't he? Who? Ken Bates, that's who. In a previous home programme he raised the question of where we should play our Champions League games next year (if we qualify) – Wembley or the Bridge? I have not met a single soul yet who has said Wembley. Yes, it was a great PR exercise for Arsenal this year, allowing 70,000 fans to see each of their games, but did they qualify? Nope. So £10 a ticket was a right result, but at what price – failure! So when Ken turns round next year and tells us that our capacity for Champions League games will only be just over 30,000, as we will lose several thousand seats in perimeter advertising, and it's going to cost £30 minimum to get in, when we all start moaning how outrageous it is, what will he say? Well, I did ask you to choose Wembley or the Bridge, and you chose the Bridge – it's down to you.

Blue Daze

ISSUE 3 August 1999

Business Age – Magazine Review

Hmm… it amazes us all here at MHBAWA when people visit our stall and ask us why we give Ken Bates so much grief. Why, they say, when Ken has given us four trophies and a team full of world class stars, do we persist in slagging him off? Good point, but I'd ask you to take your blindfolds off and take a close look at reality. It may well surprise you. You see, the simple fact is that nothing is what it seems and there are uncanny parallels between what Bates has built at Chelsea, and the empire Robert Maxwell built a decade ago. We all know what happened to Maxwell, as tens of thousands of ripped off pensioners will testify.

And it's not just MHBAWA that is saying this. Tom Rubython, editor of *Business Age*, has recently devoted four pages and a front cover to a story that rips open the myth of Bates as a businessman. Rubython is a highly respected journalist, with no axe to grind against Bates or Chelsea, so when he attacks Bates it's time to sit up and listen. So, are you sitting comfortably? Read on…

Firstly, Rubython investigated why Bates did not become chairman of the FA. After all, Ken would have been able to clean out the old guard and bring in a dynamic, fresh approach, wouldn't he? Perhaps, but Bates is, quote, 'personally reviled by many directors on the FA Council because of his continued attacks on the memory of the late Matthew Harding.' Strong stuff, and it continues: 'Many (of the FA Council) believe that Bates has had little to do with the success of Chelsea as a football club or a business and that the architect of the current success was actually Harding. It was certainly Harding's money.' Now, that is not MHBAWA saying this, it is members of the FA Council – people who know intimate financial details of all the Premier League Clubs, including Chelsea.

But of course, Bates has got nothing to hide, has he? Well, as Rubython puts it, 'This article was originally intended as a friendly profile based on his views, but [Bates] replied "no" and hid behind his lawyers.' I wonder why, don't you? After all, if you've got nothing to hide, what's the problem? A friend of mine, an ex City financier, told me once that if people have got something to hide, it's because they need to keep it hidden. What you've got to understand is that the rumours suggest Bates does not own Chelsea – he merely represents 'mystery men' who own shares in Chelsea through a remote network of offshore companies.

So who actually owns Chelsea? No-one is quite sure and that is why, it is said, Chelsea Village shares are a scam, pure and simple. If you are one of those people who owns shares in Chelsea Village, you are either mad, blindingly loyal or plain stupid. No-one in the City ever buys shares in a company where the identity of the owner is not known. Chelsea Village shares are essentially 'junk bonds'.

It is all very reminiscent of Robert Maxwell, and at the age of 67 Bates is not too far from popping his clogs himself (his ashes to be sold to season ticket holders at £200 per gram, along with a signed, framed death certificate and a money off voucher to visit his gravestone). Believe me, if Bates is going to the pearly gates, not only will he be asked by St Peter to wait a very long time, but the finances of Chelsea Village will unravel faster than it takes me to throw up after eating a dodgy prawn at Fishnets.

But, I hear you say, you are being too harsh on the old geezer. Hmm, perhaps I need to remind you of the time Bates moved to Dublin, where a bank he founded went into voluntary liquidation. Or the time he was chairman of Oldham Athletic, where one director not so fondly remembers him and says, quote, 'Bates believes in being part of a committee of two, with one member absent.' Does Robert Maxwell spring to mind or have you still got that blindfold on?

Rubython's article also goes into great detail about the time when Bates made a serious mistake of not purchasing the property of Stamford Bridge, when he did the deal to buy the club in the first place. Bates was offered the freehold to the ground at £1million, but offered £600,000 because he felt Mears wouldn't be able to sell it to anyone else. But Mears found that Marler Estates would buy it for £1.2million and sold it, not for reasons of just profit, but 'in revenge for what Bates had said about Mears in public.' The end result was a battle that cost 'millions in legal and professional fees' and a future option to buy the club for £16.5million in

2012. And you still think Bates is a good businessman? He could have bought the ground for £1million. Please, take those blindfolds off.

Worse still is, who do you think foots the bill for all this? And you wonder why we have the most expensive season tickets in the Premier League? You think it's only because of the world class players? As Rubython says of Bates: 'Undoubtedly, his own hubris cost him tens of millions' – and if it costs Bates, who does he pass it on to? Please, take those blindfolds off. It's beginning to make you look really stupid.

Rubython's article goes on to talk about Harding and his involvement with Bates. It's all been written about before, but I found Rubython's conclusion that 'there is little doubt that Harding made Chelsea' uncannily accurate, as was Rubython's assertion that: 'As soon as anyone else's contribution is publicly recognised at Chelsea, Bates turns against them. The same happened with Harding, although the real venom would not spring from Bates' lips until Harding was dead.'

And what of the Harding/Bates feud? Rubython simply says: 'Bates saw the Club as a business with a fiduciary duty to the shareholders, whereas Harding wanted the players and the team to be a top priority.' That makes sense when one considers that Chelsea Village is now finished and includes an upmarket, 130-bedroom hotel, five conference rooms, a piano bar, three restaurants and 38 apartments… yet in all this, the West Stand has been conveniently forgotten. Another season goes by with 6,000 fans getting soaked.

And what of the current finances of Chelsea, run by that business wizard that is Ken Bates? Chelsea Village has, quote, 'Obligations in excess of £50million.' To you and me, that means a debt of £50million. If I had Chelsea Village shares, I'd be running for that phone if I were you. And what about Bates? When Harding died, Bates said publicly that he would 'miss his personality and sense of humour.' A year later, Bates said: "This is a much happier ship now he's not around… I don't believe evil should triumph, and he was an evil man." And you still trust Bates?

So, there you have it. We here at MHBAWA took our blindfolds off long ago and are waiting for the day when Chelsea Village implodes on itself, leaving a legacy of worthless shares, bankruptcy, a relegated team and an empty Chelsea Village that no-one wanted in the first place. Well done, Ken.

Ross Eccles

The article reviewed by Ross was entitled 'Is Chelsea's Ken Bates Headed for a Fall?' by Tom Rubython, and was featured in *Business Age* No.86, Feb 1999.

*****

Football, Kids and Now

I was born in 67, I can't remember how and when I became a Chelsea supporter, I just know that I've never supported anyone else (except Wealdstone, my local non-league team).

My earliest recollections of Chelsea are around 1972. I was taken to my first football match, but can't remember who was playing. My cousins lived in Bolton, I think it was a match up there. What I can remember was that my brother and cousins got pennants for the Chelsea/Stoke cup final and I didn't, cos I was too young. I wanted one and moaned.

The next memory I can recollect of Chelsea was a game on the Big Match, Chelsea versus Bolton. Bolton won 2-1, but Chelsea scored all three goals, an early Graham Wilkins own goal included! I remember my dad teasing me about it, it was around 1975. I finally got taken to my first match, Oldham Athletic at home, October 1976, and we won 4-3. It should have been 6-2! We were all over them. I remember a kid sitting near me, he was shouting his head off all through the match. I wasn't, I was quiet, maybe nervous? I don't know.

My dad took me to three more matches that season: Millwall at home (1-1), Fulham away (lost 3-1) and Hull City at home, we won 4-0 and there were mass promotion celebrations! I remember Millwall taking the Shed, then being led out and seeing the Chelsea fans in the Shed close ranks and attack the remaining Millwall in the Shed. In the streets I remember the roar of 'Chelsea' followed by the roar of 'Millwall'; it left an impression. Hull City, like all the early games my dad took me to, I was in the West Stand. By now I had learnt to cheer and shout! It was an amazing game, with three pitch invasions. My dad continued to take me to three or four matches a year until he died in April 1979. For the 1979/80 season, my brother took me to couple of matches, but he wasn't really a Chelsea fan.

1980/81, I didn't see a match. Early in 1981/82, I was 14 now, going down the park and playing football etc. One Saturday afternoon a few of us thought 'fuck it', jumped on the Tube and went down to Stamford Bridge to see Chelsea.

From the first match back, in December, it became every home match from January 1982. It wasn't always the same crowd every week – sometimes a couple of us, sometimes half a dozen. Our mums found out later, but weren't too bothered as we were going together, not on our own. Though I did a few times, when others couldn't make it. Then, though, you could. It was about 50p-£1 for kids to get into the Shed. We were getting around £3 paper round money a week; train fares were about 20p return (remember Ken Livingstone's Fares Fair policy?). There were no membership schemes, few all-ticket matches – it was just pay at the turnstiles.

Inside the ground, the Shed was full of like-minded youngsters. When we started going as 14 year olds, there were plenty of others in our age group; the eldest boys in the Shed were in their early twenties. The real nutters had transferred over to the North Stand. We used to watch them and cheer them on when they attacked the away supporters.

From those early days, I met Chelsea fans from all over London, mainly South London. I was a West London boy. I met others, of course, along the Piccadilly Line route that I took.

Though Chelsea weren't winning anything, there was still a young base. Most of us were too young to see Chelsea win the Cup in 1970 but kept alive the dream it would happen again. It took a bloody long time to happen again, though, but we had fun along the way. In later years, some of the South London boys from Balham, Tooting and Mitcham, who we had met up with in the Shed, met with us on away trips, as we organised our own minibuses. The away support in the 1980s was great with Chelsea.

My worries now? Many a Chelsea fan at a young age was once given the opportunity to watch Chelsea. Now they can't. There is no child admission anymore, if you want to get in at a reduced rate, you have to be a 'child member' first, and after that you can only go in the 'Reserve Family Enclosure', if it is available. The days when a group of kids met down the park and said 'Let's go and see Chelsea play' are long gone. The days of a group of two thousand 12-18 year olds doing a serious Knees Up Mother Brown in the Shed are long gone.

Kids still love football, but they don't have the independence at football matches anymore. They are prevented from the bonding and socialising we had as youngsters, to build up a great Chelsea support.

Nowadays I get pissed off with the quiet atmosphere at Chelsea. I know a few in the Harding Stand and others dotted around do try to create an atmosphere, but it's not quite the same.

Me? I still get up and shout my head off. I get pissed off with other so-called Chelsea fans around me, who don't sing and tell me to sit down. I think it's brilliant that plenty of kids are wearing Chelsea shirts these days. Maybe they are glory hunters; maybe I was in 1972? I have no complaints with kids supporting Chelsea, as long as they stick with it. Once you start supporting Chelsea, it's for life, whether you like it or not.

I do have complaints with some of our new thirty-somethings and corporates, etc – people who have never bothered with football before, but now fill the seats up, keeping prices high and denying true fans the opportunity to carry on watching Chelsea. People who have never been before, but go now cos it's fashionable. People who don't sing and dance, people who really know fuck all about football and Chelsea. I hate them. Sometimes I wish our 'hooligan' days were back, if only to drive them away and keep the true supporters. Then again, if they all got behind the team and sang and danced for ninety minutes, I might like them.

Rayners Blue

ISSUE 4 October 1999

The Thoughts of Chels Guevara

In the Sunderland programme, Bates yet again displayed his caring nature, by describing the victim of the fire in the West Stand as a 'nutcase'. However, one of the latest rumours circulating is that the poor unfortunate was, in fact, a homeless down and out. Apparently, the guy had been trying to make some kind of shelter out of the unused turf boxes that were surplus, after the disaster that was the pitch sale. Bates then goes on to intimate that the victim was a criminal. There is, though, a fair chance that had the person been discovered before the fire, the police would have taken no more action other than removing the 'offender' from the premises without any charges being brought. It is typical of Bates, once described by Graham Kelly as a 'renowned litigant', to use words and language to 'label' a person who is unable to answer back (Editor's note: This appears to be contradicted by Chris Tarant's interview with Chief Inspector Moody, which can be found on page 22).

In the same programme, Bates writes about a 'second criminal' who was caught trying to 'steal a replica shirt by stuffing it down his trousers.' This is, as far as I'm aware, the first reported incident of a shoplifter being caught. This, to me, says one of two things: either the security staff are no good at their job or, and most likely, the merchandise isn't worth nicking! Any half decent shoplifter knows that it's not worth stealing anything that can't be sold. The trouble with stuff from the Megastore is, no sooner have you stolen it than you'll find that it has been reduced in price anyway! Perhaps this is a true reflection of the perceived 'desire' for souvenirs and merchandise a la the Village.

It's nice to see the BBC have given Mellor, once described by Radio 5 Live's Nicky (I like Chelsea) Campbell as 'the ugly face of football', demotion from the 6.06 Show to the Wednesday night slot. On his first night in charge, Mellor's replacement, Richard Littlejohn, received a call from a Chelsea supporter, who enlightened the listening nation as to the reason for the empty stands during the home leg against Skonto Riga. The caller correctly pointed out that the pricing structure at Stamford Bridge is far beyond the means of many Chelsea supporters. He went on to mention Bates' programme notes and the fact that the current chairman was moaning about the demand for tickets for the big games and the lack of demand for the 'minor' games, such as the Champions League qualifier. Correctly saying that the admission price could, and should, have been reduced in order to achieve a full house, the caller neglected to point out that, on the page opposite Bates' notes, was an advert for a reduction in the price of a meal at all three Village restaurants. '£10 per person buys a 2-course meal' reads the ad. It is obvious that the strategy employed by the Village in reducing the price of meals is because the restaurants are not achieving the required turnover. Isn't it about time that the same reasoning was applied to the FOOTBALL CLUB?

The above mentioned Mellor's first appearance in his new slot was also quite interesting, because of the 'announcement' made by the presenter that the Task Force had met and would be publishing a report on what was to be done about the ever spiralling cost of attending games. However, the thought of a prominent name attached to Chelsea making such statements on-air reminded me of Bates' appearance on the 6.06 Show on 21 February 1998. Mellor had asked Bates about the justification for the massive increase in the price of season tickets in 1998. Bates blamed the massive 40% increase in Matthew Harding Stand supporters' season tickets on the fact that we only had a 34,000 capacity and that there was a problem gaining permission to build the West Stand. Referring to the Council's objections, Bates promised that: "… on Monday (23/2/98), having wasted 13 months of my life, we're going to appeal against every application and go direct to the Government." After a bit more waffling, Bates went on to say: "We're being obstructed by a bunch of small minded, mean attitude, petty civil servants who vet every issue possible." The civil servants in question were, of course, Hammersmith and Fulham officers and employees. Bates finally got to the end of this particular rant and finished with the immortal statement: "They're just playing silly buggers. These are playing like ping pong. We've had enough of it. We're going to the Government."

I might be wrong on this one, Chelsea supporters, but the latest statement concerning the 'governmental approach' was in the August 1999 edition of Onside (Page 13). The current chairman states: 'I've just entertained a top Government quango member at King's Brasserie in Chelsea Village Hotel, and the bill came to £31 each including service. We had a vintage bottle of wine, bottle of water, starters, main course and coffee.' Typical of Bates to eat in a gaff where the service charge is included (Editor's note: no chance of getting a tip out of him!). Let us hope that somewhere between the menu, vintage wine and the 'entertainment', some time was found for talking about finishing the ground. Considering the above mentioned 'ping pong' remark, it might have been prudent for someone to remind Bates that there is still a question mark hanging over the exact relationship between beef and BSE. On the other hand … it seems like it's too late!

In the Villa programme, Bates resumed his attack on those who are watching Chelsea from above. He described the well-respected Joe Mears as 'craven', meaning cowardly, because of his failure to stand up to the FA in 1955, when they advised Chelsea Football Club not to enter the European Cup. On the scale of importance in matters concerning the meaning of life, I should imagine that to most football fans, the FA as an organisation is higher than that of any type of governmental body. Never mind craven, I think it's pretty sad that the present chairman, while moaning about one of his predecessors having trouble with the FA, can't even get himself past Hammersmith and Fulham Council. Couple this with Bates' total compliance with UEFA's requirements for the Champions League matches, meaning that many season ticket holders will have to move from their own seats, and it is yet more proof that he has more bluster than balls.

Finally, while mentioning the 'Villains', I must give credit to Chelsea supporter and Villa star Paul Merson for an interview he gave recently to Match of the Day. When asked why he thought Villa Park was not full, he replied quite simply: "Five games in three weeks, the supporters can't afford it. Even the players realise that!" Go on, you Blue Boys.

Chels Guevara

*****

The Sheditorial

Here we are at issue four and things seem to be going well for us at MHBAWA. A lot of people have said they like the content etc, as well as the style. I don't want to sound like Ken, but the list of subscribers is growing monthly. We have been getting good support sales wise, and we have achieved (limited) recognition in the national press. A common 'complaint' we have had, however, is the extent to which MHBAWA concentrates on the 'political' side of things at Chelsea. More than a few people have commented that there are too many articles slagging off Ken Bates, and that the articles themselves are of a similar nature.

Although this is the first time I have had the honour of being editor, I know for a fact that most of the letters and articles that this publication has received have been of the type that have been published. Although editorial control has been used on a couple of occasions, we have only had one letter sticking up for what is going on at Chelsea (Issue 3, page 16). Perhaps the positive side of all this is that on the pitch, we haven't got much to complain about and, after all, Chelsea's results are the things that really matter.

However, the well documented attempts by certain supporters or fans representatives to have a dialogue with the board at Chelsea have failed. Bates, for what he could have achieved, would have been given hero status. Instead, he joined the ever-growing band of individuals, as well as corporate organisations, who see football as a tool with which to etch out a fortune.

Maybe I'm looking back through rose-tinted specs, but most of the chaps that I see at Chelsea have an affinity with the days of the 70s – Osgood, Lion, Shed and all – the days when going to Chelsea was a much less complicated process than it is today. Many feel that anything Bates does now would never make up for some of the things he has done and said. He'll never be a hero to them.

This, perhaps, is why we publish what we do. After all, this is your fanzine, just as much as Chelsea is your chosen team. We at MHBAWA will continue to be a platform upon which those who are not happy with certain aspects of 'Village Life' can express their opinions.

Up the Chelsea!

The Guy Who Blagged Me

*****

Chief Inspector Moody

Ever wanted to know the time? Had your collar felt at Chelsea? Chief Inspector Moody is the man in overall charge of those 'other' boys in blue, Hammersmith and Fulham Police's Football Unit.

MHBAWA sent Chris Tarant to ask the questions.

MHBAWA: Are you a football supporter? CIM: I used to be. I like all sport. My main sport in my private life is rugby union. I'm generally interested in all sports and I like to see British teams do well.

MHBAWA: How long have you been attached to Fulham? CIM: I've been attached to Fulham and Hammersmith Borough for about a year and a half.

MHBAWA: So, do you deal with QPR and Fulham, as well as Chelsea? CIM: It's my responsibility to effect liaison and plan the operations for all three clubs.

MHBAWA: Which is the easiest? CIM: Ease wise, they're all the same. They've all got their own unique demands. They've all got their own individual Safety Officer and team structures. It's my job to work with them.

MHBAWA: Has policing football games become easier over the past few years? CIM: I would say, from my own experience, that it is getting easier. Technology such as CCTV and electronic counters on turnstiles etc, help us make objective decisions concerning crowd movements. Crowd crushing is less of a worry. We can monitor the situation and, if needs be, deploy officers to deal with any situations that might arise.

MHBAWA: Chelsea's reputation has got better, hasn't it? I can remember years ago thinking I'd hate to be an away fan coming to Chelsea. CIM: I don't think hooliganism has been eradicated. I think all the clubs are now working towards trying to get a family type of atmosphere.

MHBAWA: How closely do you work with Chelsea? CIM: My main link is with the Safety Officer.

MHBAWA: How do you feel about the way it's going at Chelsea?
CIM: In what respect?

MHBAWA: Chelsea Village as opposed to Chelsea Football Club.
CIM: If you're investing in building a huge, modern stadium, you've got to be able to make money from things other than football.

MHBAWA: I'd disagree with you there, but it brings me round to another point. When the ground is finished, it will hold about 42,000. Personally I would like to see a 50/55,000 capacity. CIM: I think the chairman would want that as well, but he's having trouble with the local authority.

MHBAWA: We won't get into the politics of that one! CIM: (laughs) I agree!

MHBWA: Could you foresee trouble policing Chelsea if they had a 50/55,000 crowd? CIM: No!

MHBAWA: None whatsoever? CIM: We'd need more resources. We train with the people who run Wembley Stadium. That used to hold 100,000 but is now down to 70,000 because of the Safety at Sports Grounds Act. We share our expertise and we have regular meetings with the other ground commanders in the whole of the London area. We share our intelligence and our experiences, both good and bad.

MHBAWA: What about touts? CIM: Touts are a problem. I'm not worried about the Private Walker type (Editor's note: Pte Walker was a character in BBC TV's *Dad's Army*) or the Del Boys who are trying to make a few bob on the side. I'm worried about fans sitting in the wrong section. Did you see the photo and article about the trouble at the Leicester/Sp*rs cup final at Wembley? It was in the Daily Telegraph the other week. There was a picture of a big looking guy punching a diminutive looking woman on the jaw. If fans are sitting in wrong places and their team score, the other fans might not share their feeling of euphoria.

MHBAWA: There was trouble here a couple of times last season.

Man United springs to mind. CIM: We haven't eliminated trouble. It's a passionate game, what we try to do is minimise the risk.

MHBAWA: How do you feel about having less of a presence within the ground? CIM: We do a risk assessment. We evaluate all the information coming in from the other club. They tell us how many fans they think will travel, ticket sales etc. If we think that there might be a problem historically, or we have special intelligence, we'll negotiate a bigger presence with the club.

MHBAWA: Going back to that Man United game, the police seemed to let both sets of fans out at the same time. If that had been played at Old Trafford, there would have been a fair chance that Chelsea supporters would have been kept in. That didn't seem to happen here. CIM: No, it didn't. We've been advised by solicitors that we have to take the decision to retain fans after the games very objectively. In effect, by keeping supporters in we're detaining them. If someone didn't like it, decided that we'd arrested them and decided to sue, they might have a case. The fact that we are acting for their own interests doesn't seem to come into it. We would have to have very sound intelligence to justify it. Most of the fans, when they mingle, have a bit of banter. That's part of the game. As a result of the Man United incident, both the stadium rules and the condition of entry to the ground have been changed. Now, if we think that there might be trouble, we retain the right to detain fans.

MHBAWA: Do you have an arrest quota? CIM: No. What we do have, though, for the whole borough is a positive arrest policy. If someone turns up drunk we don't say "Just go home, mate, and sober up". We'll nick them, make no bones about it!

MHBAWA: What do you call drunk? CIM: I'm talking about the guy who turns up staggeringly drunk and is likely to fall asleep across a gangway when we're trying to get people out, or who is abusive to either stewards or other fans. We're not talking about people trying to have a good time. We don't mind a bit of banter. If the stewards have a problem with anyone, they'll identify them to us and they will be arrested, taken to court and, if convicted, we will apply for an order banning them from the ground. That goes for anyone convicted of any disorderly behaviour.

MHBAWA: Within the ground, would you prefer to police the games yourself or are you happy with the job that the stewards do? CIM: We have a meeting before and after every game, as well as a 'wash up' meeting at the end of the season. That goes for all the borough. At this, we review all the games and look for areas of improvement, as well as at what went wrong. If we find that things haven't gone according to plan, we try to work out why. We debrief after every game anyway and, if there has been a problem during the game, I'll get in touch with the club straight away. As far as the performance of the stewards is concerned, the clubs themselves have a pretty robust policy.

MHBAWA: Do you ever have any complaints regarding the behaviour of stewards? I mean, if a policeman came up to me and told me to sit down or whatever, I'd be more likely to take notice of him than if a steward told me to do it! CIM: The stewards do have a very hard role. They're now trained to minimum GNVQ level. But you're quite right, people are more likely to respond if it is a police officer giving them instructions rather than a steward. Quite often, the steward is in the same place every week, but the copper might be different. Perhaps it is a bit daunting.

MHBAWA: Football has now started to cater for a money orientated, middle class spectator. Has that changed your perspective of what the average supporter is now like? It might be that the working class can't afford to come. Whatever it is, something has changed. CIM: Football is a business, right across the board. You can't attract support unless you have a successful team, and selecting that team costs money. That's market forces for you, I'm afraid.

MHBAWA: Changing the subject slightly, a little bird tells me you've just come back from Berlin. CIM: Berlin? No, I haven't just come back. It was some of the other officers that went out there.

MHBAWA: I got that wrong! CIM: You did – I've just come back from Galatasaray!

MHBAWA: Just as good then! CIM: (laughs) Long old journey. It's very hard work actually.

MHBWA: Is it? How do you go about working abroad? It seems like a lot of the time, when English teams are abroad, things go wrong. Whether it's not enough tickets, the other fans starting trouble, or the foreign police themselves picking on English supporters, I don't know. How much of an input do you have as regards trying to stop any trouble? How do you get on with the foreign police? CIM: That's part of our role. Although we have no powers of arrest over there, we try to give the local police commander a perspective on how we try to police games over here. We advise them how to go about such things as crowd segregation etc. You know, the sort of things that have come in over here since the implementation of the Taylor Report. If we know that hardcore trouble makers – category C's – are in the crowd or intend travelling to the game, we let the local police know. We offer the use of spotters to identify these people. This enables them to monitor the behaviour of individual trouble makers.

MHBAWA: When foreign fans come over here, there's never any trouble. They seem to have a good laugh and it seems like the local police just let them get on with it. CIM: That's right. It's part of the exchange of information. We let the other police know what their supporters can expect over here.

MHBAWA: How are we going to get on in Turkey? Their fans have got quite a reputation. CIM: They have. As well as that, the stadium facilities aren't as good as they are at Stamford Bridge. In fairness to them, their stadium is awaiting development. (Editors note: An ideal opportunity for a certain Chairman, not a million miles away).

MHBAWA: The facilities aren't as good in what respect? From your perspective or the supporters'? CIM: From both, in as much that British supporters now expect a certain minimum standard in terms of comfort and facilities on hand, and it's likely that it's not going to be available.

MHBAWA: We can't complain about the water anymore, we have to complain about the football facilities! CIM: Exactly! People are forking out a lot of money and they expect to have both a good trip and enjoy themselves.

MHBAWA: Arsenal had a bad time out there, didn't they? CIM: And Man United did. If you remember, a couple of their players got involved with the police in the tunnel. Robson and Cantona got shoved about a bit but, since then, after negotiations with UEFA, things have calmed down out there. At the end of the day, it's their country and they police it how they like. I respect their laws. I hope that supporters travelling out there will respect their laws. I wouldn't like to get nicked out there!

MHBAWA: I wouldn't either, I've read Midnight Express! CIM: (laughs) Maybe they should show some extracts of the film to travelling fans!

MHBAWA: How do you feel about the '10-day' rule on Cup replays? Chelsea, being one of the other 91 league clubs, couldn't have a replay the next week, after the first tie, like Manchester United did a year or two ago. CIM: There is an impact on the local community. I have to get extra officers in to deal with it.

MHBAWA: How did you manage before, when the replays always used to be on the Tuesday or Wednesday after the first game? CIM: Before, we had a more generous budget. Now, I have to make sure that my budget doesn't interfere with the budget that nicks the burglars and the robbers.

MHBAWA: Is that why you're happy for Chelsea to have their own stewards within the ground? It saves your unit money. CIM: Well, today I'll have a lot of police officers outside, ready to go in. They'll be ready to respond and I'll have them patrolling outside for the benefit of the local community. They aren't just sitting there, drinking tea. The public are paying for them and they will be working.

MHBAWA: How many officers will be on duty today? CIM: 70: two in the control room and the rest placed in areas such as the corner between the East Stand and the Matthew Harding Stand.

MHBAWA: No trouble today with the Geordies, then? They're usually alright, aren't they? CIM: Yes, they're alright. They'll be coming down here to see Bobby Robson's first game in charge.

MHBAWA: We better get the Kleenex out for them, then! CIM: (says nothing)

MHBAWA: Do you ever get a chance to go and watch the game? CIM: No.

MHBAWA: Don't you? Too busy? CIM: We have a control box in Stamford Bridge.

MHBAWA: That's above the Shed End, isn't it? CIM: That's right. The Taylor Report says that the Commander must have a view of the pitch, but most of the time we'll be watching the crowd. We have men in and around the ground, and the information coming in over the radio is constant. Before, during and after the match, there is a high level of information being exchanged and it's very busy. Very hard work.

MHBAWA: Would the ideal situation, from your point of view, be just to keep rival supporters segregated and to keep a lid on any trouble? CIM: We will try to contain any disorder. My policy is, if there is any disorder, if we've got the resources I'll send my officers in to arrest the trouble makers. Those people shouldn't be there fighting, it's as simple as that. If there were problems going on elsewhere as well, my policy would be to isolate the trouble using both police and stewards. If there is ever a disturbance, the crowd usually settle down quickly anyway. It is my job to facilitate the safe arrival of fans, hand them over to the club and ensure they get away safely after the game. If they want to go and have a few pints afterwards and moan about the ref and then go home, that's fine. They've had a cracking day out.

MHBAWA: A couple of years ago, though, the pubs were shut before a victory parade. CIM: That was because of information received.

MHBAWA: I don't think there would have been trouble at that, do you? Everyone would have been in a good mood anyway, and there weren't any rival fans coming, so what was the problem? CIM: There was a possibility of not being able to cope with the numbers. Yes, everybody was on a high but, as we mentioned earlier, once people have had too much to drink, the red mist starts to cloud their judgement. You know, the bloke walking down the road with a traffic sign etc. It might not be a major crime to him but, to the local residents, when they find debris like that in their gardens, or people are urinating against their walls, it's not very nice.

MHBAWA: Do you have any community links with the club or the residents? CIM: We do, we have a Borough Youth Office and they work quite closely with the clubs. The clubs themselves have community links. Chelsea pays for the Fulham Road to be swept twice on match days, once at half time and [again] after the game, when the crowd has dispersed. That is so the local residents aren't wading around in all the muck and litter.

MHBAWA: Did the police object to the licensing of Bates' intended 900- capacity disco? CIM: We do have a licensing officer here at Fulham. He presented information at the licensing application but it was the local residents that objected. They're quite well organised. It's funny you should mention that, because the club and the local residents' committee have recently met to discuss forging better links.

MHBAWA: Concerning the fire at the beginning of the season, there are various rumours going about. One is that it was a disgruntled Chelsea fan, another is that the person who died was just dossing down for the night. Obviously I wouldn't expect you to comment or go into the specific details, but had the person just been an old tramp or whatever, would he have been charged with anything? CIM: I should imagine, in a case with similar circumstances, that the man, had he lived, would have been charged with arson. That would be my impression anyway. At the moment, though, the case concerning the fire at Chelsea is a matter of sub-judice. The case hasn't come before Her Majesty's Coroner.

MHBAWA: Getting back to the stadium in general, do you think the facilities have improved? CIM: I think all the grounds within the United Kingdom have improved.

MHBAWA: What about the return of terraces? Football is a passionate game. All week you get fired up and want to come down

here, shout at the ref and sing a few songs. Don't get me wrong, I'm a convert to sitting down, but there is always someone who stands up in the corner, and once that happens, everybody else stands up. Why not bring back terraces for those who want them? CIM: It's all a question of learning the lessons from history. I've got figures here for all the people who've died in the dim and distant past. Not just at Hillsborough. Crush barriers have broken because there weren't enough minimum standards etc. People tend to forget that. I've been at Chelsea and kids have fainted and had to be passed over people's heads, hand over hand, down to the front. That was quite a common occurrence. I remember one game, I think it was Sheffield Wednesday in 1960, that there were loads of kids getting passed down to the front. You don't see that now. That nostalgia thing, people shouldn't forget the line of bodies at Hillsborough. Things are definitely better today.

MHBAWA: What about Chelsea's chances then? CIM: I hope they do well – I hope all our teams do well. I'd be foolish if I didn't. I used to go to Stamford Bridge in the Sixties.

MHBAWA: Are you a local lad? CIM: I'm a Londoner. I didn't live locally, though.

MHBAWA: How is it you came to watch Chelsea, then? CIM: Because they were the best team! I started coming in about 1964 and went all through the Sixties, until I joined the police.

MHBAWA: Stand in the Shed and all that? CIM: Yeah, I used to stand in the Shed. I used to go when there was the greyhound track running round the pitch and Bobby Tambling was dribbling the ball everywhere and Charlie Cooke was whizzing around. One of the best games I saw was the 5-5 draw with West Ham. Peter Bonetti was in goal. He let a howler in!

MHBAWA: Did he? CIM: Yeah, but most of the time he was springing everywhere. He was brilliant.

MHBAWA: Getting back to now, so it's Chelsea for the league then, is it? CIM: And the European Cup! They'll do alright.

MHBAWA: Cheers, mate. That's what we want to hear! MHBAWA extends its thanks to Chief Inspector Moody and Hammersmith and Fulham Police Service for arranging this interview.

Chris Tarant

ISSUE 5 December 1999

Game for a Laugh

It is said that Dennis Wise was always hard, even as a kid. His mother recalls him coming home from a school match one day with a broken leg. She made him take it back straight away!

A young merchant seaman from South Shields was shipwrecked on a beautiful tropical island. On the first evening, he watched the sun set over the palm-covered beach as he leaned on a rock. Suddenly the most beautiful of native girls appeared, carrying a silver tray, upon which was an ice-cold bottle of Newcastle Brown Ale. He drank it greedily as she disappeared. The next night, at the same time and in the same place, she appeared again. This time she had upon her tray a huge plate of fish, chips, mushy peas, bread and butter, and a pot of tea. Again, he greedily scoffed the lot. The following night, the scene was the same. This time she appeared without a tray and came up beside him as he leaned on a rock. She squeezed up to him and asked in a very attractive and seductive accent: "Would you like to come down to the beach with me where we can play a little game?" The young Geordie looked at her, eyes popping, and replied: "Don't tell me you've got a football an' all!"

There was the referee whose wife informed the press that he had been a premature baby – he was born before his parents were married. A motorist stopped outside Fulham Broadway Tube Station and asked the quickest way to the Chelsea and Kensington Hospital. A pedestrian pointed out the White Hart pub and said: "Nip in there and shout 'Vialli's a wanker!'" "Have you thought of anything to say about this disgraceful act of hooliganism?" asked the judge of the thuggish-looking Chelsea fan. "Fuck all", replied the fan. "What did he say?" the judge asked the Clerk of Court. He said "Fuck all, your Worship." "Funny," said the judge, "I could have sworn I saw his lips move."

A little boy was lost in the Matthew Harding Stand and was crying his eyes out. When a policeman approached him, he told the officer: "I've lost my dad." "What's your dad like?" asked the copper. "Chelsea, beer, women and the odd bet", said the little lad.

You can tell an Arsenal fan – but you can't tell him much.

At the World Cup, two international footballers were having a chat. One asked the other: "Where's the best place to go and get stoned on just one spliff?" The other replied: "Iran".

Why won't a rattlesnake bite Ken Bates? Professional courtesy.

What's the difference between Arsene Wenger and Hitler? Both wasted millions but Hitler got further in Europe.

A T*ttenham fan was charged with attacking an Arsenal fan with a razor, but was acquitted because he hadn't plugged it in.

A certain Mr Dixon is apparently skint. He's given all the hundreds of thousands he has earned to sick animals. He just didn't know they were sick when he backed them!

Luca, the famous football manager, had just died and was not even buried yet. The ambitious trainer, Mr Rix, went to see the chairman. "Mr Chairman", he asked, "I was wondering whether you would have any objection to me taking Luca's place?" "Not at all", said the chairman, "I have no objections if the undertaker hasn't."

On the chairman's farm, two cows were looking over the fence and one said to the other: "What do you make of this Mad Cow Disease?" The other one said: "Nothing to do with me – I'm a duck!"

*****

Lion Rampant Regardant Holding Golden Crozier in Annulet

When I was but a lad, there were several reasons to be proud to be a Chelsea supporter. We had a marvellous, skilful, exciting team of local heroes (Osgood, Hudson etc), huge crowds and a fanatical support. We also had style, a style best exemplified by our rich royal blue kit (including our unique – for England – white stripe and number on the shorts) all rounded off with our classy and classic badge. The 1971 version, with the two adjoining stars (representing the two cups recently won) being my particular favourite.

As we all know, the man with the soup stains on his beard and a scruffy suit, who is our chairman, dumped the much-loved lion for, well… for our current badge. It is a lump of nothing, representative of nothing, and the version with the yellow trim used on the backdrop of ITV's Champions League coverage looks like a piece of cauliflower cheese that has fallen on the kitchen floor. So why did we get rid of something patently very good, and replace it with something patently very bad?

The official explanation from the club-footed one was that the old badge was not available for copyright, so 'all the spivs up the Fulham Road can rip it off' (as opposed to a spiv a bit further up the Fulham Road from ripping us all off, I suppose). A reasonable explanation perhaps – at least it would be if it was true.

A couple of years ago, I did some research into the matter. This involved a trip to Trademark House to determine the truth of the matter. They informed me that as a badge was a heraldic symbol, copyright was held by the Royal College of Arms.

A brief history lesson: as we all know, Henry VIII was a fat, bearded man with a bad temper and no scruples (sounds familiar!). As well as carrying out the reformation, he established the Royal College of Arms by Royal Charter, and this gave them the sole right of use and distribution of heraldic symbols. I expect that you are all impressed by my knowledge of Tudor England but, in truth, this was all explained to me by the Master of the RCA, a friendly and helpful man (despite putting half a pound of plums in his mouth every time he spoke) named Mr Parr-Jones. I sent him a copy of the CISA badge and he identified it as a Lion (a large feline with sharp teeth and claws) Rampant (standing upright) Regardant (looking back over the shoulder) holding Golden Crozier (the staff) in Annulet (the decorative scroll around the design).

Now, here comes the interesting bit. Yes, it is true that you cannot copyright a heraldic symbol unless it is incorporated in a wider design. Any such design would have to satisfy the RCA that it was sufficiently different to the original symbol. It would be possible to contest a negative response in the courts, because as Mr Parr-Jones conceded, applying 16th-century laws to the present day is a fairly arbitrary process.

However, in the early Sixties, the RCA received an enquiry from the Football League about the status of the usage of heraldic symbols by some of their members – Chelsea, Villa, Middlesbrough etc. They assessed the situation and granted special dispensation for the six clubs concerned to copyright their heraldic symbol (with embellishments like club name etc) for their own commercial purposes. One of these clubs was Chelsea.

As we all know, when the last seven-year dispensation ended, Chelsea did not seek to renew the copyright on our badge, as they could have done as a formality. So there you have it. The only organisation in the world that can copyright our badge is our club.

I will leave you to decide why we have ended up with a bit of cauliflower cheese on our shirts instead of the mighty lion, but you should know that it is there by choice and not by accident.

Johnny Jackal

ISSUE 6 February 2000

Greenaway Passed Away
Micky Greenaway: Mr Chelsea has died

My final conversation with Micky Greenaway was in August of last year. I had given him an old computer so he could pen his memoirs, and periodically I would go to his house, tutor him in word processing basics and troubleshoot his latest problem. He was forever accidentally deleting files, spilling coffee into his keyboard and generally getting frustrated with the technology. This final time, I was at work and Mick demanded that I decamp to Catford immediately to sort out his latest computer crisis. When I told him it was not possible he berated me.

I now know that Mick died within days of this call. I knew he was ill. He had serious circulation problems with his legs and was walking with the aid of crutches for a while. I believe he had also suffered some sort of stroke. He ignored medical advice to cut out his 100-a-day cigarette habit and his mobility problems caused him to neglect himself in many other ways. One day when I was around his place I was heartened to see some fiftysomething- old Shed Boys trying to make sense of the jungle that his back garden had become.

But don't think that the charisma and sheer presence that made Mick what he was – the most famous football fan of all time – had gone. It hadn't. We all got a glimpse of it when Greenaway stood up at the launch party for a recent book on Chelsea culture and regaled us with what was probably his last *Zigger Zagger*.

This prematurely aged man in the Bud Flanagan coat gripped the hand rail and summoned from deep within an earth-shattering Zigger after Punky Al had counted him down. For a few minutes he was back up there playing to his people. The leader of the Shed rallying his first Shed boys. Him in his fifties and them all forties and downwards, straining their vocal chords to offer back to him a heartfelt *Oy-Oy-Oy*. He seemed genuinely touched that the autograph most people wanted that night was his.

Mick was raised in Billing Street, just a bottle's throw from Stamford Bridge, by adoptive parents. He told me proudly that they picked him out from the children's home because of his cheeky smile. His father was Chelsea mad and managed to get a young Mick in as a mascot before one home game in the glorious 1955 season. He carried with him sometimes the coin that had been tossed by the referee at that game.

In the early Sixties, after watching coverage of the 1962 World Cup and a newly-launched *Match of the Day* on TV, he noticed that some clubs backed their teams through enthusiastic singing. Mick decided to start a Chelsea choir, firstly down the side terrace where him and other young boys gathered, but soon moved to the Fulham Road end, where Mick figured that the tin roof would give them some much needed amplification. Noting that Liverpool's end had been christened the Spion Kop, between him, the Webb brothers and Eccles, they eventually christened the end The Shed. The rest, as they say, is history.

He was vague when asked if he actually wrote *Zigger Zagger*. There was a play in the early Sixties with the same name. Maybe Mick had borrowed something from that. But did Bing Crosby pen *White Christmas*? The chant was used in the mid-Sixties, when not so many travelled to away grounds, as a way of calling disparate Chelsea fans together on the sometimes hostile Northern terraces. It soon became his trademark, as *One Man Went to Mow* also did in later years.

At what point an urban myth grew around Mick, that transformed him from cheerleader extraordinaire to leader of the notorious Shed, I don't know. Probably about the same time the Shed got demonised in the media. Mick was firstly appalled about this shift in perception, and wrote to the official programme more than once about his efforts to stamp out the bad language and bad behaviour in the Shed. Or was he having a laugh? Who knows? He was an enigma. Only those close to him in those formative skinhead years can tell us what role Mick played, if any, in Chelsea fans establishing their terrace credentials.

Once the legend had been established, though, it would have been impossible for Mick to live it down even if he had wanted to. For a time he was as famous by name as any media celebrity. Rival supporters up and down the country ritually chanted 'Greenaway, where are you?', and on many occasions he himself was clapped into the seats by his own younger supporters. He refused to think ill of any of them. If they were true blue that was enough for Mick. Chelsea was his family. And, generally, people stick by their families whatever they do.

But all the hero-worship and myths had its downside, and Mick's face bore the scars of some vicious beatings; but more damagingly, the press set him up and effectively ruined his life. A Sunday tabloid splashed his face all over and labelled him falsely as a right-wing thug, and they distorted some words he had given them unwittingly in a pub. As a result, Mick lost his much-loved, lifetime job on the railways, and his fortunes entered a period of decline.

Just a few seasons ago, some of the lads organised a benefit night in his honour which was fittingly held in one of the new Stamford Bridge bars. They had raised some money and bought him a season ticket for this ground that was barely recognisable from the one where he had first galvanised the Chelsea support. He shuffled in in an old suit and baseball cap. But it was unmistakably Mick who beamed as friends old and new queued to press his flesh. "Do you think he'll do a *Zigger Zagger*?" I whispered to my pal Ian. "Do you go to see Sinatra and he doesn't do *My Way*? Course he will." As it happens, once he started, they couldn't stop him.

When I started to talk to him regularly, some four years ago, about the possibility of him doing a book, he was naturally very suspicious. Who was Chelsea's reserve centre-half in the 1962 season? Who scored first in the Moscow Dynamos match? Did I know him? Can I have another pint of Smooth? I was no match for his encyclopaedic knowledge of Chelsea but he did eventually open up, showing me his massive collection of memorabilia. I hope someone has rescued that.

I heard a rumour recently that Ken Bates was considering loaning one of the new bars for a party in his memory, and that he was even looking at naming a new room or bar after him. I hope so. Such an act would show that Ken does appreciate the role played by terrace supporters in our famous club over the century, and more importantly, it would be what Mick wanted. He craved recognition from Chelsea Football Club and, better late than never, CFC should acknowledge their most famous and loyal supporter ever.

Emu

ISSUE 7 March 2000 DISCLAIMER

The backers, sponsors and editorial staff of this publication wish to make the following statement:

In the event of the 'Village' or any connected business/company taking any form of legal action against this publication, the backers, sponsors and editorial staff are willing to strike any kind of deal with Bates in order to avoid prosecution. This will include grassing on all contributors and subscribers by way of providing Bates' legal team with any information they require, including all real names, addresses and contact numbers.

All who contribute to this publication do so at their own risk and in the full knowledge of the above contingency plan. We will also change the name of this publication to that of 'Kenny Bates' Visa Card Army', and will increase the cover price to £4.50. To avoid any unnecessary paperwork etc, all proceeds from sales etc will be paid direct to Bates at the hotel after every game, by way of a brown paper envelope.

The aforementioned contributors will no longer be required, as the pages of this fanzine will be full of adverts proclaiming the benefits of the wonderful Chelsea Village complex, as well as a Bring Back Village Racing campaign. We know you, the reader, will understand, because when the shit hits the fan (sic), like you, all associated with this publication will wish success to all of Bates' business ventures, and wish to see Chelsea's name riding high at the top of the financial league tables.

THANK YOU FOR YOUR SUPPORT

*****

True Blue

Has anyone heard this story? It is the Sunday morning after Chelsea have won the FA Cup for the first time in nearly thirty years. The pubs along the Fulham Road are opening their doors to let the first of the revellers in, as they anticipate a very busy day. Fathers and sons in replica shirts soon start to fill the bars.

The Imperial is doing a roaring trade in Sunday lunches. A crowd gathers outside and elbows nudge each other, as a man with a shock of grey hair and a grey beard, dressed in a suit and flanked by two bigger men, is walking towards the pub on the other side of the road. He is waving at the growing crowds. Some move over to shake his hand. The king has come to acknowledge his subjects.

King Silver has delivered the silverware and now wants to spend some minutes basking in their gratitude. But, as he draws level with the Imperial and glances over with an expectant grin, someone starts the chant: *"One Matthew Harding, there's only one Matthew Harding..."*

The silver smile freezes as the chant is picked up by everyone in the pub. There is a crush at the door as more people sing at him, challenging – *"One Matthew Harding."*

He shakes his head and laughs dismissively, and continues his walk up towards the Beer Engine. One man, who has no tattoos and does not wear a baseball cap, quietly returns his glass to the bar and walks purposefully out of the pub. Seconds later, on the bridge, Silverbeard is on his arse, having taken a right-hander off this determined individual. He gets to his feet and clumps the guy straight back, but he does not even rock.

True? Urban myth? Exaggerated? I'm sure this can't be true – can it?

Hudson Barred

On the subject of our favourite person, if the following story is true it proves he does not lack a sense of humour.

It was a few seasons back, when the ground redevelopment was in full swing. King Silver and ex-player Alan Hudson are enjoying one of their rare periods of talking to one another.

"See that over there" says King Silver pointing, "that's going to be Tambling's bar, and over there will be Drake's". Alan nods. "And over there, Alan, that's where I'm going to put a bar called Huddies." Alan is surprised and flattered. Is the old bastard lightening up at last? "Yes, that's right Alan. I've always been a great fan of Roy Hudd" he adds.

Emu

*****

Joking Apart

Chelsea are due to play T*ttenh*m – it's Saturday morning and the reserves are playing at Ipswich. Wisey trots into Stamford Bridge, where he's met by Vialli, who tells him the entire first team squad are injured and he'll have to call off the game. Hearing this, Dennis replies: "We can take them on, boss, just you and me." Luca is a bit reluctant at first, but Wise soon talks him into it, so off Vialli goes to ask the ref, who agrees, much to Wisey's delight.

Chelsea kick off, and it's a pleasure to watch as they take the piss out of the sub-standard players from north London. It's all one-touch football. In their first attack, Chelsea win a corner. Wise takes it, and there at the back post is Vialli, completely unmarked! He rises like the proverbial salmon to bullet it in. For the rest of the first half Chelsea are all over them, with Sp*rs hardly touching the ball, and T*ttenh*m are very lucky to go in at half-time only one down.

The second half starts as the first finished, with Sp*rs on the ropes, and it's not long before Chelsea go further ahead. Wisey picks the ball up in his own penalty area and beats all eleven T*ttenh*m players, before walking the ball into the net – a truly great goal (even better than the one in the San Siro!). As the crowd are still celebrating, a message goes out on the electronic scoreboard: "Would Mr Vialli please make his way to Ken Bates' office." Big Luca tells Dennis he's got to go, and asks him to hold the fort for the rest of the match. When he hears the final whistle, Vialli tells Bates he's got to go and see how Wisey got on. Gianluca gets down to the tunnel just as Dennis walks in; his head bowed and his face tripping him. Luca fears the worst, and shouts:

"Did we get beaten, Wisey?" "No boss, we won 3-0" "Well, what's the long face for?" "Well boss, I got sent off with 15 minutes left."

A bloke walks into a boozer and sees a dog riding a unicycle. He's amazed. He grabs a pint of beer and goes over to the dog's owner. "That's brilliant" he says. The dog's owner, looking very modest, says: "That's nothing, mate. When Chelsea win he sings *Carefree*, while playing the piano; and when Liverpool win he juggles four eggs without breaking them." The bloke is very impressed, but curious. "And what does he do when West Ham win?" he asks. "I dunno, mate. I've only had him four years!"

A really ugly female T*ttenh*m fan with a speech impediment, couldn't get a man. To relieve her frustration she took to reading the classical erotic literature featuring the Nordic Gods (that's even before Tore Andre Flo's time). One night, after a particularly steamy read, she fell asleep and dreamt that a big, blond man burst into her bedroom, ripped off her nightdress and repeatedly made love to her. In the morning, the big, blond Viking God got up, dressed and left, saying: "I'm off to Valhalla, and by the way, I'm Thor." "Tho am I" replied the girl, "but it wath wonderful, wathn't it?"

A Leeds fan goes to his solicitor and says: "I want a divorce." "Why?", asks the solicitor. "I can't tell you", came the reply. "If you won't tell me, there'll be no divorce", said the solicitor. "OK, OK", said the Leeds fan, "I'll tell you. I want a divorce because of my wife's disgusting habits." "What sort of disgusting habits?" asked the legal eagle. "I can't tell you, it's so disgusting", the Leeds fan replied. "Look, if you won't tell me, there'll be no divorce", said the solicitor. "OK, OK", the dirty northern Leeds fan replied. "Every time I go for a pee in the sink, there's a pile of dirty dishes in there!"

*****

Wage Rage

It was quite refreshing to read a confession from a pro footballer that, in his opinion, modern day soccer stars are being paid 'over the top' salaries. The footballer in question, Chelsea supporter Paul Merson, made the comments in an interview with a national newspaper. The points raised from the interview have far reaching consequences and provide evidence as to why the huge amounts of money swilling around the trough are slowly erasing the grass root supporters by pricing them out of the game. Merson, to his credit, acknowledged his own involvement in the equation when he said: 'I know how lucky I am to be playing this sport and I know I earn a lot of money, but how much money do you really need?'

Quite! Especially when you consider that young men playing professional football are now capable of hitting millionaire's row before they leave their teens. The problems that can follow have been well chronicled – gambling, drugs, alcohol – in Merson's case it was all three! All brought on by having too much money and not knowing what to do with it. Once you've bought a big house, your fifth top of the range motor and enough tomfoolery for the 'Ron Atkinson Collection', what else is there to aim for? All this, and in some cases not a Premiership or Cup winner's medal in sight! As Merson points out: 'I don't think it's down to medals anymore, as far as players are concerned.' He goes on: 'It's got to the stage where kids can't go to football matches anymore because they are paying the professionals too much. That can't be right.' Spot on, Merse.

Footballers have always been well paid, following the scrapping of the maximum wage in the early 1960s. During the 1990s, the wages spiralled out of control, as money flooded into the English game and the desire to succeed in the Champions League called for bigger squads and fatter pay cheques. Consequently, the cost of watching live football has shot up in price. A recent survey by Premier League researchers claimed the average amount required by a fan annually came to £862. Chelsea supporters, as most of you must surely know, top the Premiership outlay league, forking out an average £1,306 per year! (Editor's note: I hope my girlfriend doesn't read that last bit. That calculation probably doesn't include beer money etc. In the interests of keeping the peace amongst the families of Chelsea supporters, our advice is to cut out the previous sentence. Failing that, a deft stroke with a black, permanent marker pen will suffice!). Furthermore, the next few years could mean digging deeper into your pockets in order to follow the Chels.

One of the main reasons for the increase in players' wages is the Bosman ruling. Pre-Bosman, clubs had to wheel and deal on the transfer market instead of looking for freebies. A greater financial responsibility meant lower costs and lower entrance fees. The pattern emerging after Bosman seems to be that clubs are breaking their pay structures, not only to encourage players to sign on but also to keep their own players happy. Keane's deal with Manchester United, worth a reported £52,000 a week, springs to mind. If he had gone on a free transfer this summer, how much would it have cost to replace him? 15 or 20 million pounds at least. Instead, by upping the wages by £20,000 a week on a five-year contract, it costs the club £5-6 million. The kickback is obvious. Once a player earns the pay rise, the rest of the squad want more (£100,000 a week, wasn't it, Mrs Beckham?) and the wage bill rises dramatically. How is it funded? TV, sponsorship, changing strips every season, increasing ticket prices etc, etc. Who pays for it? You do.

Recent press reports suggest Paulo Maldini, 33 years old, wants to move to Chelsea on a free transfer after Euro 2000. This is a player who has often belittled English football in the past, but obviously the lure of £30,000 a week and the chance to meet up with a few old friends is tempting. If he comes, his shelf life will be limited and could result in another promising youngster, 20- year-old John Harley, losing his first team place. The worst scenario would be if he sought a transfer. Call me nostalgic, but wouldn't it be nice if we could see a return to when players wanted to play for the club because they loved the team they played for, and the financial considerations came second. Ron Harris, John Hollins and Peter Bonetti played nearly 1,700 games for Chelsea between them! In terms of service and loyalty, it is doubtful whether we will see their like again. If we do, you never know, but football might become accessible to the traditional supporter once more. It might not cost an arm and a leg to visit the Bridge, and the club shirt on your back might still be the one being worn by the players by the time you get it home from the Megastore!

Paul the Bookie

ISSUE 8 APRIL 2000

A Night at the Bridge

Following on from Sven's rundown of all the Chelsea songs in a game on tour in the last copy of MHBAWA, I am including a home version, via the television. Well, I haven't been able to get away much lately, even down to the Bridge, so the TV was the best I could do (part-time supporter). This is the Marseilles home game, where for reasons best known only to myself, I began to write down the songs as they were sung. Before I knew it, I had written a song list of 'A Night at the Bridge', presented by the Matthew Harding Stand and the Shed (with occasional work by the West Stand, and occasional contributions by the East Stand Stocks and Shares Department gratefully received).

The number one song of the night, as ever, in terms of volume and times sung (nine complete choruses) was *'Carefree.'* This is THE Chelsea song, isn't it? Any ideas where it first came from? It wasn't a 70s song as far as I can remember. Have you noticed how lots of other clubs have their versions of it now? The Geordies sang theirs at Wembley. I tried to note the lyrics, but you can't understand a word they say anyway, let alone what they sing. An all time classic.

Number two was *'Chelsea, Chelsea, Chelsea'* (four choruses). Now, this was a 70s song – great lyrics, great tune. I remember with pride the times it took off at away games, and just didn't stop. Ten minutes, fifteen, ebbing and rising, never stopping until, at last, another song took over. You almost became lost in the words. Erm, you had to be there!

Number three: *'One Man Went to Mow'* (three choruses). Another 70s song, I remember the first time in the Shed, some dull, empty midweek game, when you were told to sit down by those at the back and everyone got nearly on their knees and bobbed until we all jumped up for ten men.

41

It isn't quite the same from seats but is still a sight. It always makes the fans look over, the only choreographed song of the Premiership, I believe. Unless you know different. And no one has tried to copy it. Who would?

Number four, equal on two choruses each, were *'Come on Chelsea'* – always nice when the team are down – and *'Oh Dennis Wise'*, an excellent recent addition to our repertoire which, to be honest, has been getting rather stale lately. It is hard to get a new song going nowadays, when so much of the ground has never heard the old ones before, let alone considered actually joining in.

Also equal with two choruses each were *'Blue Flag'* and *'John Harley'*. *'Blue Flag'*, has been sung in earnest, as far as I can recall, since the 1994 cup run, but it must be older than that. Wicked lyrics – 'we are supreme.' Nicked left, right and centre by other choirs, but will those Hammers ever get it out of their arses? John Harley: it might have been Vialli, though. Even Harley himself wasn't sure when we first sang his name. A star in the making.

The following were all equal at number five, having been heard just once. You may disagree if you were there, but this is what came over on my TV: *'We All Follow the Chelsea'* – a nice old song, which everyone has their own version of. The over land and sea bit has a bit more meaning of late.

'You Don't Know What You're Doing' – a nice addition. *'Oh My, What a Referee'* was never bitter enough.

'West Stand/East Stand/Shed End Give Us a Song' – yes please, this song was really taking off at the end of last year. We need it more. Can't wait 'til the West Stand is finished and it does really go all the way round.

'Stand Up If You Hate Man U' – as others have said, this gives them too much attention. Roll on the day they all sing it about Chelsea.

'Booooo' – my personal favourite of the night, heard when the announcer spoke in French to pass on a message about leaving. I love that xenophobia. How dare you speak French at the Bridge, you twat.

So there it was, all the songs on the night. Any trainspotters out there can get out their video and check. It might not look a lot, and, well, it isn't. We are not singing as we have done in the past. What can we do about it? Who knows? The commentator said several times how quiet it was. At least we are not at the stage of Cold Trafford, where they had to put out a special call for some atmosphere; and we will never be the Library. One thing at least from watching it on TV was the little titbits that the commentators have researched for you. For instance, did you know that in our eleven European games until Marseilles, we had eleven different goalscorers? Or that we had conceded only five goals, the joint best in the competition, and had the best disciplinary record of any team left in? And, more trainspotterly but interesting nonetheless, when Marseilles played Southampton, they lost 4-0. And who scored the last? One Peter Osgood. Not a lot of people know that.

Tom Traveller

*****

On A Quiet English Summers Day

How many of you can put your hand on your heart and say that you love the English summer? I hate it! No footy, a sweaty, sore arse and poncy bloody tennis on the box. How can the close season last so long, with each week seeming like an eternity? Saturday comes and goes with no footy, but just the sound of leather on willow, and the chinless wonders scoffing on overpriced strawberries in south London.

Don't you just long for something to do? Something to eat away the hours and minutes, to ease the monotony of no Chelsea. Well, last summer I had a particularly rude awakening. My Doris works overtime most Saturday afternoons, helping to swell the family coffers, and Juvenile D looks after the sprogs. This particular summer's afternoon, the eldest sprogs were running amok down the local park and the youngest sprog was fast asleep upstairs. I was bored rigid. The Test match was on and English willow was definitely not hitting foreign leather; and the bookmakers were fleecing Juvenile D on Channel Four. What could I do to pass the time? The choices were awe inspiring. Mow the lawn, hang the washing out, wash the car or do a little housework. What a choice! After pondering over the matter for a few hours, it was decided that if I ignored my male chauvinistic attitude and did the housework, it might well enhance my chances of getting my end away later that evening with Doris. Venturing into 'womansland' or, as the new man would put it, the kitchen, I eventually located the polish and a duster. By this time the television had been turned off and the stereo cranked up. 'Sod the neighbours – we're moving soon anyway, and little sprog always sleeps through anything. Being male, I applied a little logic and started in the far corner of the room. After a few minutes I realised what a p*ss easy job this was. No wonder women spend half their life with their feet up watching *Neighbours* and *Home and Away*!

I carefully manoeuvred my way past the lava lamp, glided along the top of the television, across the top of the gas fire and down towards the phone, pausing only to dismiss any thoughts of getting the vacuum out. This was cushy, man! The dust soon disappeared off of the phone, along with a multitude of grubby fingerprints. 'That's it', I thought, 'job well done. I'll surely be giving the meat and two veg a good time when Doris sees what I've done.'

What happened next was like your worst nightmare. As I moved towards the stereo, my past flashed before me as a uniformed police officer came bursting through the front door and landed face down on the carpet. Now, Juvenile D has been no angel in the past, and has several skeletons in his cupboard, but surely not now! I'd been a good boy for several seasons, and I had a Doris and three sprogs to look after. Why now?

As I gathered my senses together, another two officers walked in through the door. The door-busting officer casually picked himself up and angrily pointed at the dodgy step he had tripped on and, as a consequence, subsequently head-butted the door and unintentionally gained premature entry. As I glanced outside, I could see more plod: two patrol cars with blue lights flashing. What sort of sh*t was I in? Who had fingered me? Was this a frame-up? All these thoughts rushed through my head. Then common sense clicked in. Why was I still standing, and not spread eagled on the floor, face down in the carpet and hands cuffed? 'This is a wind-up', I thought, 'Beadle will pop his head round the door in a minute.' But he didn't, and the nightmare was to move on.

It seemed like an age, but it was probably only a minute, before plod broke the silence and glared menacingly towards me:

"Reports of a disturbance, young man", he barked. 'Which one?' I thought. I can remember a good two dozen I had been involved in over the years. "Operator traced your phone line and reported a major domestic disturbance, young man." "What?" I muttered. "I'm on my own apart from a sprog upstairs." "Are you sure, sir? Can we take a look around?" "Do I have any choice?" I hissed under my breath.

That was it – the signal for a mass invasion of plod outside. Two car loads piled in through the door and dispersed to all corners of my house.

What planet were they on, and what did they hope to find? My Doris butchered, carcass in the freezer and head in the washing machine? Sprogs hung up on meat hooks from the ceiling? This was unreal. The search moved into the garden, as helmeted heads peered down the passageway. It was like having an episode of *The Sweeney* in my own house!

After ten minutes, the humble climbdown came. Plod had gone back to their cars and a sole officer remained, his eyes not willing to make contact with mine.

"Looks like there has been a mistake, sir. Probably a fault on the phone line" he muttered. 'Sir?' I thought, 'Ten minutes ago I was young man.' How attitudes change!

Then, without another word, they were gone. I peered out of the front door and all the neighbours were pointing and chatting. 'You're not worth it', I thought, and slammed the door shut.

Once the colour had returned to my cheeks, I sat and pondered over the latest escapade in the life of Juvenile D. Then it hit me. I realised what I had done. It was the dusting, the Mr Sheen and the telephone. Whilst cleaning it I distinctly remembered lifting the receiver, squirting in the polish and rubbing the buttons with the duster. Somehow I must have got through to the operator, and the domestic crisis overheard was the receiver dangling and banging against the table the lava lamp sits on. As for the commotion, that was the music on the stereo. What a prat I felt.

Then I looked around. What a mess! Plod had rampaged through my house and there was mud all over the carpets. Doris will kill me! All that poncy effort doing the dusting, with a view to getting my end away, and now she'll lynch me when she sees the carpets. How I hate the fucking summer!

That night, as I lay in bed, I couldn't help reflecting on the day's events. At one stage, I had visions of laying on a bed in a cell, but here I was, laying next to Doris, still a free man. As tired as I was, I couldn't sleep. I just could not get rid of the image of that officer tripping over the step and crashing head first through the door, and ending up spread-eagled, face down on the carpet. Poor old plod. Perhaps summer ain't that bad after all!

Juvenile D

*****

Letter from Al Fayed

In an attempt to get some free legal advice on the libel law, we wrote to Mohamed Al Fayed. We have, with kind permission, printed the main man at Harrods' reply:

Dear MHBAWA,

Mohamed Al Fayed has asked me to thank you for your recent letter. Mohamed is about as big a fan of Mr Bates as he is of Chelsea! He was sorry to learn about your spot of bother with Ken but has quite enough of his own battles to fight without taking on more. The only advice he can offer is that you switch your allegiance to Fulham – a club you can afford, with a chairman who really does care about the fans. Nothing would get up Ken's nose more!

With best wishes.

Yours sincerely,

Laurie Meyer
Director of Public Affairs

Thanks very much for showing an interest in our affairs, and for taking the trouble to reply to our letter. As far as leaving Chelsea and becoming a Cottager goes, to quote Suggs' song: 'Our blood is blue, and we will leave you never!' However, your letter proves that to be a Fulham fan, you definitely do require a sense of humour!

*****

Palaces and Myths

Emu recalls his first live sightings of the Chelsea crowd home and away

Chelsea had a big reputation as *the* skinhead club. We'd been raised on folklore about Chelsea and the football hooligans, as they were already being called. One story that did the rounds at our school was so obviously

46

an urban myth, but at the time we believed it: a mother takes her young son to Stamford Bridge. He wants to go to the toilet and she waits outside for him. After a while she becomes concerned that he has not reappeared, so she goes in the toilet to find him. Inside she sees her little boy in a pool of blood on the floor. He is alive, but some Chelsea skinheads have cut his testicles out with a knife and had been rolling them around on the floor like marbles. How these ridiculous urban myths start and built is baffling. They were always told in confiding tones, and the teller always knew the person who knew the victim. These stories were never told jocularly. It was as if we'd been let into a terrible secret. As impressionable eleven, twelve and thirteen year olds, we never wondered why these stories never made the papers, and we passed them on with equal authority.

This particular day, the famous Chelsea were playing a local club, Crystal Palace, and the local rail network was awash with blue and white woollen scarves streaming from the train windows. The Chelsea boys sang songs with uncompromising words, like:

With hatchets and hammers, Carving knives and spanners, We'll show those T*tt*nh*m bastards how to fight.

And:

We don't carry hatchets, We don't carry lead, We only carry pick-axes, To bury in your head.

Vic and I were in no doubt these people meant what they said. We knew that people were routinely hit with axes and iron bars at Chelsea. That's what the papers said, so it must be true. We'd even heard that at Millwall there was a bloke that carried, and occasionally used, a shotgun.

At Selhurst station, we alighted and tagged along with the Chelsea mob towards the ground. I was looking for the leaders. We'd heard so much in the playground about Eccles, the fearsome warrior, and Greenaway, the so-called Leader of the Shed. I was so excited at the prospect of just clapping eyes on one of these mythical characters that I failed to notice that two older boys fell into step with me and Vic, on either side of us. We knew something was up. They veered us off into a side road as the mob continued onward. "Give us your jacket", said one menacingly. He was eyeing Vic's Budgie jacket. This was his pride and joy. A black and purple thing with a long pointed collar, which had been made popular by Adam Faith in the TV series Budgie, about a cockney wide boy. "And I'll have your sheepskin", said the other, nodding at my dirty but much prized coat.

Time seemed frozen for several seconds. We were, of course, shitting bricks, but giving up our precious items of clothing was something else. Seeing that we needed convincing, one of the boys turned the side of his leg towards us and tugged slightly on his Levis. Tucked inside the woolly grey sock that was visible above his Dr Marten boot, was what looked like the top of a sheath knife. I began to unbutton my coat.

"Alright Terry?" shouted Vic. He had spotted Terry Baker from the estate at the top of the road, passing along with the moving crowd.

"Vic, John – what you doing down there? Come with us", and he beckoned us towards him. We stepped away from the older boys and hurried up to join Terry and his mates. Our would-be muggers pressed on ahead of us. For some reason, we didn't even mention to Terry what had happened.

Despite the scare, we had the bug and decided next that we could visit the famous Shed at Stamford Bridge. Chelsea were playing Sheffield United, who were far from being a glamour team. They had Tony Currie, who was being hailed as a creative midfield genius, but the player that impressed me was their winger Alan Woodward. I think a couple of seasons watching Don Rogers had conditioned me to focus on the wingers in any side. I believed they were the most important players on the pitch. Because they didn't get as many goals as the other forwards, they didn't get as much glory, but I got more pleasure from watching them than any of the others. Most of the big clubs had them, and they all had their unique styles: Dave Wagstaffe at Wolves, who they said could cross a ball on to a sixpence, Peter Thompson at Liverpool, George Armstrong at Arsenal, Alan Hinton at Derby, Eddie Gray at Leeds, and Manchester City's Mike Summerbee to name but a few.

We gingerly joined the cauldron of young bodies that was the Shed. I still couldn't believe that we could just walk in. Who were we? Five-foot nobodies, yet we were able to become members of the most notorious football crowd in London just by turning up. To be inside was exhilarating. It had a force of its own. Vic said to get as near to the middle as possible, which wasn't easy when ten thousand other boys were trying to do the same. You ended up lost in a mass of bodies, and during the course of the game, the natural movement to them caused you to be gradually carried all over. Bobble-hatted teenagers just smiled at you as you came crashing into them after the latest surge. They were loving it as much as you were. There were no adults around, and the police rarely intervened.

It was like on the school field, when we would shout 'BUNDLE', and all go charging in to one another and start rolling around the grass. The only difference was that this was on a massive scale.

If I catch you winking, I'll saw your legs right off, Knees up, knees up, don't get the breeze up, Knees up Mother Brown.

This strange ditty always triggered a mass, friendly free-for-all, whereby you pushed and shoved the people in front of you as they did the same. From a distance it looked like a landslide. From close up it was a lot of innocent fun. There didn't seem to be an obvious cheerleader, but the songs came thick and fast. Who made them up? Some of them had detailed words and rhythms. They couldn't have just tumbled out of someone's brain and mouth during a match. I tried to picture some big skinhead sitting in his study, sucking on his pen and waiting for inspiration.

Up at the back of the Shed, I got a hint of the darker side. The back row was raised up, and this is where the older boys stood and sat, draped over the crash barrier, looking down on the dark walkway that was a chicken run through the end. They were not watching the game, they couldn't possibly see. I found it frightening walking along, my head level with thousands upon thousands of shiny leather Dr Marten boots and all eyes on you. That's how it seemed. But there was more police here, mingling in with the crowd. The youths didn't wear bobble-hats, nor were they flourishing scarves or singing. They sported sideboards, and many were covered in tattoos along their muscular arms. Unlike most of us, their tattoos were not in the first flush of their colour.

I sneaked glances up at their hard faces, wondering which ones might be Greenaway or Eccles. But for the time being, I was content to grab my pie and return to the carnival atmosphere that was the middle of the Shed.

Emu

ISSUE 9 AUGUST 2000

Boring! Boring! Boring!

No, not Arsenal but the weeks between the end of Euro 2000 and the start of the new season. Firstly I must apologise for pinching the title of a famous Young Ones episode, but it accurately sums up how I feel. I couldn't give a toss about the state of the weather. I want my football back and I want it back now! Every year I feel the same. It doesn't get any better as you get older – life without football is live living in a void.

What is there to do when there is no football? Watch Wimbledon – no thanks. Too many chinless wonders. Watch the cricket? Well, it's okay for a couple of hours but five days, it's a bloody eternity. Talk to 'er indoors – blimey, that would be taking it a little too far!

To kill time, I went to the pictures. I hadn't been for years and what a disappointment. I paid a fiver to see Chicken Run, and all I got for my money was a bloody cartoon. What happened to our loveable claret and blue friends from Upton Park? I could have sworn I read that it was a documentary about the ICF. Got home and picked up the paper and got another shock. Leeds were above us in the hooligan stakes! Come on lads, what is going on? In my heyday, we used to romp home, miles clear of the others. I guess things are changing more than we ever imagined. A human failing I suppose, clinging on to our misspent youth.

Saturdays come round once a week, as they do, with nothing to look forward to. No bustling crowd on the Fulham Road, no excuse for a lunchtime drink or an early start after the match. No euphoria after a glorious win, no kicking the cat after a defeat. What a sad life it is in the summer. Desperately thinking up excuses as to why you can't go shopping; mowing the lawn as quick as you can or decorating and getting splattered in paint – and so the monotony goes on.

This year, the gap might only have been a few weeks but it wasn't any less painful. Kingstonian and Oxford away followed by the Charity Shield. Quite meaningless games usually, but for some strange reason I've got that buzz. Something is stirring in the deepest inner passages. This season ain't gonna be like any other, this is gonna be our season, I just know it. So come on boys, do it for yourselves, your wives, your grannies; but most of all do it for us. Us who have never seen Chelsea at the top of the pile when the season is all wrapped up. Us who are not old enough to remember 1955 and all that went with it.

Come on Chelsea, this is our year… but don't I always say that!

Merlin

ISSUE 10 OCTOBER 2000

The Thoughts of Chels Guevara

The sacking of Gianluca Vialli was nothing short of scandalous. Although the dismissal was being put down to player dissent, the removal of Luca highlights both the Village board's lack of football knowledge and the fact that they are totally out of touch with Chelsea supporters.

Vialli was not only Chelsea's most successful manager – he was probably the most liked. Even though the start to the season could have been better, there didn't appear to be a lack of faith from the supporters. Generally speaking, most appeared happy.

It seems incredulous that, with only five games gone and on the eve of a European tie, the board would have acted in a manner that would only cause chaos. If the sacking had come at the end of the season, or indeed during the summer break, although not being acceptable to a large section of support, it would have made more sense from a football perspective.

After allowing Vialli a figure in the region of £54m to spend, one would have thought that the board would have allowed the manager time to mould his team. But no, and this is where the flaws in Bates appear, the man responsible for the Village complex wanted instant success.

Vialli would, had he been given time, have gone on to become a great manager. However, only winning the FA Cup last season was, for Bates, a disappointment. His ill thought out plan to turn Chelsea Football Club into a leisure complex is apparently badly short of money. He required a run in the Champions League to bring in much needed finance.

The current chairman's burning ambition is for Chelsea Football Club to be put 'up there' amongst the elite of Europe. However, at this rate, the credibility of Chelsea, as reflected by Bates' actions, will be brought into serious doubt. Vialli, in just over two years, brought Chelsea the following: an FA Cup, Coca Cola Cup, Cup Winners Cup, Super Cup, a Charity Shield plus a taste of the Champions League. If that isn't success, I don't know what is.

Within the football fraternity, Vialli was loved by Chelsea supporters and admired by the rest – even those who support other teams. In a world of moaners, whingers and cry babies, both his eloquence and apparent sportsmanship when being interviewed was refreshing.

It is said that Bates is an admirer of the achievements of those who helped to build the Roman Empire. Perhaps he should have remembered that, as in the case of a successful football team, Rome wasn't built in a day.

Good luck, Luca, and thanks for everything – we will miss you!

Bates gave no clue to us, the faithful. The last programme to be printed before the dismissal was for the Arsenal game. Even in that, Bates – the master tactician – wrote of the press speculation concerning Vialli's future.

His programme notes read:

'Then next, it was Vialli had pleaded for an extension to his contract. He hasn't, Luca doesn't plead for anything. His job is supposed to be under threat from our so-called indifferent start to the season. Now that Tony Adams has advised us that Luca will probably leave at the end of the season, I am totally confused.' As usual, he signed off with 'Viva Vialli'.

Even on the day before the announcement of Ranieri's appointment, another 'high profile' but out of work manager was also believed to have been in the crowd for the St Gallen game. Ironically, it was Ranieri's successor at Valencia, Hector Cuper. If true, was this part of a plan to hurry Ranieri into making a decision on whether to take the job?

Of course, the following Sunday that 'good old read' – and general all round voice of the public – The People newspaper had the 'exclusive' on Bates' reasons for the dismissal.

Claudio Ranieri might well prove to be the man to take his team forward – we'll have to wait and see. However, in one of his first interviews, he seems to have rejected Chelsea's so-called continental outlook. Flying in the face of Bates' recent demolition of young, home bred talent, Ranieri stated that he would like to see the Chelsea side have an English backbone.

He was also honest enough to admit that he couldn't promise to bring success. Good luck to you, Claudio – what you're saying sounds good. I hope you can make it work. Whatever happens, things will be interesting! As far as Chelsea supporters are concerned however, the future ahead could suddenly look brighter. If it works, we'll be laughing. Although I would still like Chelsea to be interested in winning cups, Ranieri says he's here to win a league title. That would be good.

However, if it does all go wrong, as it might, there's only going to be one man to blame …

Chels Guevara

*****

Another Sunday and Sweet FA
What the fuck is going on at this club, Bates?

You get rid of the most successful manager in the history of Chelsea Football Club and replace him with an out of work (sorry, I mean 'in between jobs at the moment') unknown, who can't speak a word of English! Ferguson and Wenger must be taking the piss out of us right now, and having a good laugh at our expense… and that hurts.

Do you know what you're doing, Bates? I only hope for your sake that you do. Coming away from Stamford Bridge after the Leicester game, I felt depressed, sick and suicidal (I hate Sunday games to start with, I mean it's just not natural, is it?) but I really felt angry and let down by that shower of shite that called themselves Chelsea on that day. I felt that I had gone back in time to the dark days of the late-Seventies and early-Eighties, when we were gutless, clueless and shite. I don't know about you but I thought that those days were long gone. But here we are again, playing without the passion and pride our blue shirt demands. At least in the Seventies and Eighties we didn't expect to win much, because we had a team made up of youngsters still on the tit and players that were well past their sell-by date. This was due to lack of funds and the fact that no decent player would be seen dead in a Chelsea shirt! However, this can't be used as an excuse any more. We now seem to have more funds than we need, and players want to come to Chelsea. So just what is the problem with these players, Bates? Just tell us, we really do need to know. I mean, you're still in charge, remember? Or are you?

When are we going to see some grit in this team, and some will to win? All we seem to have at this moment is a team of prima donnas on enormous egotrips, and preoccupied with only high wages. Their effort rate on the pitch so far this season has been hopeless, and most seem to be infatuated with elaborate short passing across the park, which ends as soon as we make any effort to penetrate our opposition. Every team we have played so far this season has sussed us out. They allow us to play our fancy football across the midfield because they know that we aren't going anywhere with it. They crowd midfield positions in their own half and when we try to move forward, we are hustled off the ball by the more aggressive players like the Keowns' and Elliotts' of this world. Our marking in defence has been horrendous, and heads drop when the pressure is on. Let's face it, we are just too soft. It's a long way home when we get beat, Bates. It would be nice if we could just walk round the back of the Shed Stand and make our way up to our luxurious penthouse, but some of us have a few hundred miles to travel home. Anyway, the post-mortem examination of the Leicester game will show that it would be premature to say that our season is over after just six games. We still have plenty of time to sort this out but this will be down to Ranieri. I just hope you are big enough for this job. Let's not give up, we must fight for every ball with grit and determination. We will come good again, but for now the party is over and it's time to fight for the right to be at the top. Ranieri can start by sorting the men from the boys, and to all those fans who left as soon as Leicester scored their second… do us all a favour and stay away. Don't come back, because we don't need you.

However, if these recent problems aren't sorted out within the next three weeks, then we will just kiss the title goodbye again. Consistency wins titles, and we just haven't got it. Hey, maybe The Sun was right, and we are just a team full of 'bottlers'.

Blue Bear

*****

Bumming Up Ken Bates!

Remember the 'good old days'? A ten-minute struggle to get out of the

Shed, down the stairs and a quick sprint to the gents. The need to reach it growing more urgent by the second. Relief at last! Well, almost. There is a wall of bodies before you, with five or six similar walls before them, all grinning and bearing it, as it were.

Wet weather was worse, for there was no roof, but at least the rain served to dilute the often ankle deep urine in which we stood to serve our weekly penance for over indulging in pre-match refreshments. It was much better for the ladies of course – they had roofs! There was one by the Britannia Gate and one by the main office. Oh, and by the way, I do mean two toilets and not two toilet blocks. Not that many women attended in those days, and the majority seemed to prefer the rickety stands to the Spartan delights of the terraces.

You could get a beer of course. Remember that little bar tucked under the old East Stand? The one just past the old garden shed that served as the club shop (they sold scarves, badges and very little else as I remember). Open to the elements, of course, but you could get a beer, and if you didn't mind joining the throng that was the queue, midway through the first half, you'd be lucky if you were served midway through the second! One could become quite a minor celebrity if you were spotted clutching your lukewarm glass of (st)ale by your contemporaries.

Mind you, we had the team – and Sexton and Mears. Charlie Cooke, Ossie, Chopper... the glory days were here at last. "Silverware! Silverware!" Two cups in the cupboard and runners up in a third! Third place in the league! I would gladly endure anything for that. Then suddenly it happened, SHOCK HORROR!

There's been a row in the dressing room. Hudson's gone, Osgood on the list. This can't be happening. Handbags at dawn, and half the best team Chelsea have ever had, were to go to the highest bidders. What's Mears doing? Surely he must intervene. Talk about out of the frying pan and in to the fire! Not only did he allow Dave Sexton to do his dirty deeds and then flee; he sold Chelsea to a property developer at that. Still, never mind, we might do well out of this. Look how much room there is behind the new East Stand. Lose the dog track, three more stands like that and in-fill with flats. We get a brand new ground, developer sells flats for a fat profit and everybody's happy.

I first saw it in the old Evening News: 'Stamford Bridge... new development plans'. Eagerly I scanned the papers and found the artist's impression. Wow! It certainly was impressive: shops, restaurants, fountains, plazas, penthouses. I wouldn't mind one of those, and right next to the ground as well. Hold on, where is the ground? Perhaps it's below the development, indoors, like the Astrodome in Houston. That'll be a first, and it'll certainly give us a home advantage. Then the penny dropped, play at Craven Cottage, ground sharing with Fulham and QPR. P*ss off! I'd rather die! We'll soon put a stop to that! Action groups, petitions, fund raising. They all came and went, but nothing changed. Except the ground, of course.

With no money being spent on maintenance, it went from bad to worse, the team faring little better. The same old Chelsea, really: beat the best and lose to the rest. We can take it, though. We are Chelsea. We are hard.

The fateful day arrived. Chelsea FC were up for sale. Asking price £1 – I can afford that. So can you, so can a ten year old kid. Just imagine me, the guvnor, the manager too if I like. Best seats in the house on match days, feet up, guzzling free champagne with the lads. Free admission for them, obviously. None of them ponces in suits. They're too much like Mears: snakey b*stards. The bubble bursts, I haven't got the bottle. Nobody in their right mind would have. The club was skint and probably couldn't have got a half of lager on tick using the name of Chelsea. Some enterprising scrap dealer would step in and make a nice few quid selling the corrugated iron from the Shed. It would take a madman or a genius.

Salvation cometh! Ken Bates. Who? Ken Bates, comes from Oldham, I think. A northerner. Probably made a fortune running the abattoir, and selling tripe and cow heel pie to the TNCs. Got a lot to say for himself – now let's see if he puts his money where his mouth is.

The ground needed urgent attention. How could the club have any self esteem if we presented ourselves to the rest of the football world like that? Apprentices were pressed into decorating the stadium in the close season. Why pay professional decorators when all these fit young lads are lounging around and being paid by the club to do so. The stadium may not even exist soon. Still, he's got to spend a few bob. So what's in it for him? What's his angle?

Time and again I have heard this question asked, even now, all these years later. Why the doubt? The next time you visit the Bridge take a good look. Read the team sheet. You've never had it so good! It's football luxury. It's a bit pricey, admittedly, but when you think that I paid £27 to sit in the pouring rain at Watford and then had to queue for a toilet which was about half the size of our bathroom (my wife told me that the ladies was even smaller, with no sign of a mirror). West Ham was similar, very basic facilities and that was £32.

Old Trafford, I hadn't been there for years, it was always a good ground. Last season I went there, I spent all night on a coach and arrived there at 5am on a rainy bank holiday Monday. The Theatre of Dreams – it'll be well worth it. What a let down! Basic facilities and no sign of a TV screen. And the state of the pitch!

I have heard a lot of criticism about the comparative size of the stadium, to the amount of land available at Chelsea. Build wider and build higher is the demand, just like at United. But let's not forget one of the basic laws of nature: grass needs adequate amounts of sunlight in order to photosynthesise, and likewise a good airflow is essential to dry wet soil and promotes good strong root growth. I suspect the grass grows faster at Old Trafford during a floodlit game than it does on a summer's day. Likewise Liverpool, Leeds, Arsenal and Tottenham were all basic. At Spurs, they even contrived to run out of beer an hour before the game kicked off. I don't know what the away facilities are like at Chelsea, but presumably they are akin to those enjoyed by us home fans.

I am not aware of any complaints relating to value for money, despite what you may read in the press. They're always ready to put the knife in, and they constantly quote the most expensive season ticket prices, irrespective of what may be on offer for the money. The only valid criticism can be regarding child concessions, a situation that one would expect to be reviewed with the advent of the West Stand. After all, the club must have a youth policy off the pitch as well as on it. Catch them young and they're yours for life. Ask any member with kids. No, Ken Bates is merely doing what any businessman worth his salt would do: identifying and exploiting the market. The fact is, the club lies in the heart of one of the most fashionable and affluent areas of London. Young, mega rich corporate types, most of whom have money to burn. The type of fan so often despised by the rank and file supporter.

From the outside, the complex would not look out of place in the City or Canary Wharf. You would hardly know that the ground was there at all. It's just the sort of place the City types like to eat, drink and party in – expense no object. It's just the sort of place they like to brag about and bring friends to: "One of the finest stadiums in Europe, you know".

Don't get me wrong, though. Wealth doesn't make you any less a supporter. I've seen them all in the Imperial after matches, cracking open the bubbly and joining in all the songs. Thoroughly enjoying it. We need these people. If your seat price is not actually being subsidised by their money, it probably will be, and to a growing extent, as Chelsea Village reaches completion. At a game a couple of seasons back, I got well out of order. I had too much to drink beforehand and some over-enthusiastic support led to several complaints from surrounding fans. A subsequent ban ensued, for the rest of the current season and the whole of the next. Friends thought it was hilarious: "It's the wet stand for you next year, that's if you can get a ticket!" they laughed, "No-one ever gets off a ban, so it's no use appealing." I was sick. One mistake surely didn't warrant draconian treatment like this. To appeal, futile though it seemed, was my only option. I spent hours on the letter, apologising and attempting to relate the circumstance of the event. "I am not a bad fan, just a stupid, inconsiderate one." I pointed out my previous good character, even relating an incident after the Real Betis match, when my son and I threw our shirts across the players' tunnel in exchange for those of two Betis fans (rather impetuous, as it cost £100 to replace them). We heard shouts and, looking up, we found ourselves being applauded by the Chairman and his partner. He shouted an invitation to my wife and I to join them for drinks in the Shed Bar.

Unfortunately we couldn't attend, being in the company of two juveniles. A missed opportunity I shall always regret. That is the closest I have sat to him at a match, and the look of sheer joy and elation on his face after that game dispelled any misgivings I may have held previously about his motives. What's in it for him? The same as you, the same as me, the same as any Chelsea-mad schoolkid who has never been to a game.

Anyway, back to the ban. What have I got to offer, I thought. It's easy to expect them to forgive and forget, but what was in it for them? I would be a model citizen, offering to forfeit the right to appeal should I be a nuisance on any future occasion. A kind of self-imposed suspended sentence. I was on tenterhooks for weeks. Talk about 'you don't know what you've got until it's gone'. I gave away my seats for the rest of the season. Better a casual fan than an empty seat, I reasoned.

They took their time in answering. Strangely enough, this gave me hope. At least there hadn't been a flat rejection. The reply arrived in due course. 'After consultation with others', it read, 'it has been decided not to impose the ban past the end of the current season.'

I was reprieved! After consultation with others!!! Ken Bates must have been called upon, both to authenticate my claims, and possibly to adjudicate. I felt honoured. He had given me the benefit of the doubt. Me, a mere fan. Rigid, inflexible, unapproachable. Never!

What has he given us? Hoddle, Gullit, Vialli, Dennis Wise, possibly one of the best teams in Europe, certainly the finest group of players ever assembled at the Bridge. And what if he hadn't spent his quid in the bargain basement? We could all still be watching Chelsea, albeit on some glorified park pitch, possibly in the lower reaches of the Ryman League. Ask Aldershot, and they kept their ground!

Dog

*****

Chelsea Action Group A Short Interview

The growing sense of unease that is appearing amongst the chaotic state that Chelsea have got themselves into, comes as no surprise to fast growing cyber supporters organisation Chelsea Action Group. Founded last year, the CAG seeks to provide an alternative view of Ken Bates' empire from both a supporters' and a shareholders' perspective.

The main focus of their interest is the financial side of Chelsea Village, and their website is a useful reference source for all Chelsea fans. For example, did you know that it takes thirty nine companies to run our club? Well it does – check it out for yourselves. They also run an e-zine called 'Village Eye', which is updated monthly.

We contacted CAG and asked them what their main concerns were.

Spokesman Joe Walton cited the enormous Eurobond debt as the major worry:

"The bond runs out on 12th December 2007, at which time Chelsea Village will have to pay the £75,000,000 back. The interest is £6,850,000 a year, which means that Chelsea Village has to pay out £124,662,500 over the next seven and a quarter years – over £28,000 every single day. Where is that money supposed to come

from? If anyone has passed by Chelsea Village on a non-match day will tell you that the restaurants and bars are failing. The bond was taken out to pay for Bates' property development on Chelsea's land, but repaying the bond will be left to the fans in the long run."

The CAG has worked with a number of journalists to spread their message.

"When we wrote to Adam Crozier at the FA last year, asking how they could allow a large proportion of Chelsea Village's shares to be held anonymously, while at the same time upholding their regulation on multi-club ownership, we expected a serious reply from the game's ruling body. But when he just refused to answer the question, we decided to ask journalists the same thing instead. At some point the pressure will force Crozier to answer, and I would like to think that the CAG has had a hand in that. We are currently working with a couple of radio stations who are keen to pursue certain leads that we have given them."

Who are the CAG? They said that they are True Blues who are concerned about the future that will be left after Bates has gone. They have members who sit on all sides of the ground, including inside the executive areas. Some live overseas, and they are well represented in the City, as their well researched financial site shows. Why the exclusively cyber set-up? Walton answered:

"Criticising Bates is a risky activity, especially if you happen to sit in the same part of the ground as him. This makes anonymity important. What is important is what we say – not who we are."

Although Bates is a controversial figure, many Blues appreciate what he has done for the club. Shouldn't CAG remember that when they are criticising him? Walton continued:

"Bates says that he saved the club, we say that he seized it. Chelsea Football Club was £800,000 in debt when he took over – if he died tomorrow he would be leaving us a debt of over £100,000,000. Work it out yourself."

*****

Liquidator Fund Bubbles Over

Not for one minute did I dream that my article in the last issue of MHBAWA would generate such interest and support. I told you all about my good fortune in selling my Mickey Mouse football programme and souvenir business, Rosette.net, to an internet incubator fund for £1m and my efforts to use that money to kick off a fund that could be built up with the intention of mounting a takeover of Chelsea Football Club and returning it to the real fans.

Well, as I expected, Rosette.net went tits up (the cost of the office in Knightsbridge instead of my bedroom in Hounslow not helping things) and Charles Stand-Offish, the venture capitalist, had to fall on his Filofax. However, the Liquidator Fund goes from strength to strength. Donations have been flowing in from all and sundry, and the fund now stands at just shy of £3m. My stockbroker tells me that I have a long way to go before we can mount any sort of assault on Bates and the myriad of other invisible shareholders in Chelsea Village. "You'll have to hope your fund keeps going up and that the team starts to muck up and the company's value starts coming down", he said.

Lo and behold, Bates plays right into our hands. He sacks Vialli, the only manager to deliver any serious trophies (besides Ruud, who he also sacked) for nearly thirty years all because Mohammed Al Fayed rang him up and jeered "I've got maximum points – you haven't." Now we have a serious opportunity of relegation and the collapse in share price that goes with it. Therefore this will allow us to charge in, pick up our club and return it to the true supporters. Keep your fingers crossed.

Some of you have written and asked us to detail what changes we will make once control has been seized. Whilst we are always open to suggestions, our plans, so far, can be summarised as follows:

1. To reintroduce *The Liquidator* as the pre-match song at Stamford Bridge. 2. To reinstate Eddie McCreadie as manager. 3. To give him a company car. 4. To rebuild The Shed and allow entrance on that gate on a first come, first served basis. 5. To convert one of the hotels into 'Greenaway's', a bar where supporters will be encouraged to dress scruffily, smoke, drink and vomit whilst singing songs with inexplicable lyrics in hoarse voices. 6. To appoint Hickey as Police Liaison Officer. 7.

To ban celebrity 'fans', including those who aren't famous yet and those who used to be famous, like David Mellor. 8. Only accept sponsorship from British companies. 9. Limit the number of foreign players in the side to eleven. 10.To make Ian Hutchinson Hospitality Director, and allow him to humiliate Ken Bates by asking him to leave the executive bar.

Keep the money rolling in! The result against Leicester has convinced me we could be on the brink of something big at last!

Emu

ISSUE 11 December 2000

Great Expectations

I must admit it felt good coming out of Stamford Bridge after stuffing T*tte*ham – not just because we had just extended our run against them to over ten years, but also knowing the match stats would state that out of four shots on target, we had netted three times! Hey, remember the days when we used to have twenty consecutive shots on goal and fail to score with any? You know, when we were always the glorious losers.

As it turned out, it was no great conquest defeating Spurs, as they were, in the main, clueless, hopeless and, well, at times just hapless. However, on the back of a 6-1 destruction of Coventry and a tidy 3-0 victory over Liverpool, we may have found a bit of consistency. Well, at home at least. We still have time to sort out our dreadful away form. If we could only duplicate our home results on our travels then we could still be in with a shout. However, back in the real world we are still a good few points behind the likes of United.

One thing is sure, and that is that it is going to be a long hard season for us. If we are going to achieve something this season (and I still hope it is going to be the Premiership) then we are going to need more firepower than the impressive Hasselbaink. More goals are needed from the likes of Wise, Poyet and Flo. Zola to date has been a sensation. His creative play puts him on a higher level than others and he is loved by us all. Grown men will cry on their knees the day Franco leaves Chelsea (or when Bates sacks him!).

Let's be honest, we have made some sh*te signings during the summer, and it would be an understatement to say that some of our regular players have been a great disappointment. Christine Panucci must be the worst Chelsea Number Two in the history of the club. "Hang on, what about Gareth Hall?" some might shout. Well, at least Gareth had heart and passion. Panucci, you're just a waste of space. No skill, no pride, no heart… just go. We'll even pay your plane fare home! Just who did you have to sleep with to get in the side in the first place?

Talking about bad players, what about Bogarde? Is he really a footballer? I mean, is it just me, or do you think he is sh*te as well? No, I mean really, really sh*te. Who the hell signed him? Is it just a joke that Luca played on us all before he got the sack? Talk about clueless. You know, it's an embarrassment to even have you on the bench. Just go home!

Ambrosetti, Lambourde and Babayaro all need to go as well. In fact, any player who cries, whinges or just talks gibberish to the press – we don't need you at Chelsea.

Bates needs to spend some more serious money to increase our firepower. We need to become a very difficult side to break down if we are to become winners. We all know that one defensive lapse nowadays could cost us all three points. Our midfield must cause more problems and score more goals if we are to be a better side. Our forwards must look at Hasselbaink and follow his goal-scoring example by finishing off the chances we create.

The league is still there for the taking. United don't have the right to win it every season; this could still be our year. Don't give up Chelsea – you still owe us this after all these years of inconsistency… and it's time to pay up.

Bluebear

*****

The Last Zigga Zagga

This article was originally written in April 1999, for the Hoolifan book launch. It was submitted to the Chelsea Magazine – they didn't use it! It's a bit out of date but I think it's relevant, as Mick sadly passed away four months later. Will a Zigga Zagga be required? It was the afternoon of the launch party, and Mick Greenaway, Chelsea living legend and all-time anorak, was trying to ascertain they type of crowd that was expected that evening. He knew that John King and Gary Armstrong (authors) would be there, and Frank Skinner, but was unsure of what to expect.

By 8.30pm the landlord of the Old Father Thames pub on the Albert Embankment was feeling distinctly uneasy. All that he knew was that it was a private party to celebrate the launch of a new sports book and the drinks were paid for. 'It must be a new book on boxing', he thought, 'or rugby.' He had watched the hosts, Martin Knight and Martin King, warmly greeting their guests for the last hour, and there seemed to be quite a few largish men present.

Admittedly they seemed to be getting on a bit, but they still looked quite a daunting prospect! He also observed that there didn't seem to be many women present. By 9pm the crowd was swaying to the strains of The Liquidator, and he was overcome with curiosity.

Under the pretext of collecting glasses, he worked his way round to the pile of books on display and, casually picking one up, he glanced at the cover and then rather more hurriedly at the synopsis on the back. Even in his worst dreams he couldn't have imagined this!

The book was called Hoolifan, and it tells the story of a boy who grew up with Chelsea, from just after the advent of the Shed in the mid-Sixties, until the present day. His gaze was drawn to the word 'Headhunters' (a term that was invented by the same newspapers that still stick the knife into Chelsea at every opportunity, but was never adopted by the people it was directed at). The most notorious football gang ever – and they appeared to be holding a reunion in his pub!

By 11pm everyone was partying, and then suddenly the music stopped. The landlord was feeling a little easier by now. Vast amounts of beer had been consumed and everyone was dancing; barely a word had been spoken about football. Mostly, it seemed, people were renewing old acquaintances and catching up on gossip with long lost friends (in my own case, people I had not seen for twenty-odd years. My wife had initially been apprehensive about going, but after I reassured her that she would meet most of the people who started the Shed, she was swayed, and she thoroughly enjoyed the evening, along with my 15-year-old son).

A balding, middle-aged man stood on a chair. *"Zigga Zagga, Zigga Zagga."* *"Oi Oi Oi"*, responded the crowd.

"Oh when the Blues go steaming in", *"Greenaway's our leader, we shall not be moved."* It was a trip back in time. The words said it all. Long before the days of organised travel for fans, there had been a 'hard core' of ardent supporters who, despite the many problems involved, followed

Chelsea everywhere. When you played a League Cup game in Sheffield on a wet Tuesday night, and the Chelsea support was struggling to reach double figures, they were there. Zigga Zagga – the rallying cry. Such was the power of Greenaway's voice that it could be heard at all points in the ground. You knew where the Chelsea were, and headed in that direction. Unfortunately, so did the opposition! A friend once entered a near-empty Chelsea section at Goodison with Mick, only to hear about five thousand Scousers chanting: *"Greenaway, where are you?"*

"Greenaway's our leader, we shall not be moved." We are in your end and we are laughing at you! That was the trouble: no matter how uneven the numbers, Chelsea never ran. Therein grew a reputation which, owing to the nature of young men, attracted a following, fuelled by massive amounts of publicity, attempting to outdo that which had been done before. Greenaway actually conducted a poll at one away game, and was appalled to find that something like 70% of the group were there for the confrontation rather than the football.

The evening continued much as before, although I was disappointed that more of the original Shed members were not in evidence; people such as the Webb brothers, the eldest of whom, Cliff, wrote most of the songs we now (still) sing, and actually christened the Shed. Pip Mitchell, Dave Stevens, Primo and Pat Wooten – unfortunately they were still in Majorca, being part of that group who were so warmly praised by Ken Bates in his programme notes. It would appear that the original travelling hard core are still the travelling hard core.

At around 1.30 am it all ended, having been thoroughly enjoyed by all in attendance. During the course of the evening, I spotted Johnny Vaughan and the boxer Andy Till. I spent what seemed like an hour, engrossed deeply in conversation with Irvine Welsh (Trainspotting), and all that I could remember the following day was that he supports Hibs (I think!). Another conversation I recall, though not the content, was with Micky Fillery and Gary Chivers. Lovely blokes (I think).

The landlord spoke to the two Martins afterwards and told them of his thoughts earlier that evening. Not only had his worst fears proved unfounded, but he went so far as to say that it was the best behaved crowd that he had every played host to, in their behaviour both during and after the event. He was especially impressed with the way they left in a quiet and orderly manner, and called a credit to Chelsea FC. Perhaps Mr Bates could have asked him to give evidence at the Planning Enquiry, as to the behaviour of (even the most miscreant) Chelsea fans, when leaving a late night venue whilst well under the influence!

Many thanks to the two Martins for hurling me back in time, both in the pages of their book and at the celebration of it.

Within four months Mick sadly passed away. He had been ill for some time and had spent most of the evening sitting signing copies of the book. He could not stand for too long, as he was suffering from fluid retention in his legs. There are plans underway for a benefit evening to raise money for a memorial; and possibly shame Chelsea into publicly acknowledging perhaps the most famous non-celebrity football fan in the country.

Dog

*****

You Must Be Joking

Becks goes down town to buy a pair of trainers. Upon returning home, he tries to put them on to show Posh. "These don't fit proper any more", he complains. "Take them back then", replies Posh. Back at the shop, Becks looks bemused when the salesman informs him that he's got the shoes on the wrong feet. "Well, sir, it's perfectly simple", explains the assistant, "there's a special code underneath: L for left shoe and R for right." Becks puts them on again and, surprise surprise, they fit perfectly. Becks returns home and explains to Posh that there is a special code to tell which is left and which is right. "I could have told you that, you moron", replies Posh angrily, "why do you think I've got C and A in my knickers?"

The mystery surrounding Roy Keane's late arrival at the Irish training camp for the game against Portugal has been explained. Apparently, it wasn't because he remained at Old Trafford for treatment on his dead leg; it was because Fabien Barthez drove him to the airport.

Vinnie Jones admits that his appearance in the film *Gone in Sixty Seconds* brought back some poignant memories – namely the average length of time he stayed on the pitch while wearing a Wales shirt.

Middlesbrough have run into problems, following their decision to recall last season's video highlights due to the departure of Christian Ziege to Liverpool. They've managed to track down one copy, but admit they don't know the identity of the person who bought the other one.

Sp*rs boss George Graham was in court for speeding the other day. When asked about the case, he said he would appeal against the £100 fine but, as far as the three points were concerned, he was more than happy.

Posh Smiffy

Wisey Changes His Mind And Stays!

ISSUE 12 February 2001

Countdown to Chaos

I can't remember there ever being a season that I have been so let down and disappointed by Chelsea… which is quite a bold statement, I suppose, considering that I have been supporting (and more importantly, watching) them since 1967. Hey, hang on a moment, some may cry, what about those dark days of the 70s and 80s that you old gits are always going on about? Well, the fact is we just never had the dreams and ambitions of winning championships in those days like we had at the start of this season. We were sh*te and we knew it! But we did have great fun watching, travelling and making new friends! Come to think of it, every Saturday was like a holiday and, more importantly, the Club loved us and we were all one big happy family. However, those days are gone and now our club hates us, and it seems that we are only now welcome at the 'Village' – if you have more money than sense!

I think I am still very disappointed over Luca's outrageous dismissal. The man loved Chelsea and he led us to victory more than once. An unemployed unknown with no real track record has replaced him. His post match interviews are just an embarrassment and I for one just don't bother watching them any more. The real fans know that the Uniteds and Arsenals of this world are just laughing at us. At the end, Luca was obviously distressed and distraught, and some say this was because of the actions of Bates.

Bates is never going to leave our club and, let's face it, he will never change. Bates' quest to become the "Man United of the South" (hey, doesn't it just p*ss you off when he says that?) will destroy this club. He now really hates us grass roots die-hards, and has become obsessed with trying to buy success with some poor quality, 'get rich quick' foreign has-beens. Don't get me wrong, I don't hate Bates – I just don't like his arrogance and ignorance towards everyone, especially us!

My heart goes out to those poor souls who purchased the away season ticket in the summer. The thought of having to watch them home and away fills me with a sense of nausea. To be honest, I was quite happy when the West Ham game was called off. It's only the New Year and our season feels over already. My lifetime dream of seeing Chelsea walk out with the Premiership is fading by the week. This was going to be our season, but it's all fallen flat and if we don't get it sorted soon, then relegation could well be ours – and the unthinkable cheap day returns to the likes of Huddersfield and West Brom could once again be marked on our calendars.

Try to do something to save our season, Bates. We are still seeing players performing without heart and passion, and that really hurts. Get rid of anyone not ready to die in a blue shirt and get rid of that crap foreign management set-up. It's never going to work and we are becoming an embarrassment. At the moment, I for one won't be renewing my season ticket next season. Let's get sorted, Bates, before it's too late.

Bluebear

ISSUE 13 March 2001

Give Us a Song

You are a bunch of idiots! Call yourself an army? How can three people make an army? Anyway, the dribble you produce should be banned from Chelsea. I don't know why Ken Bates allows you to continue. The rubbish you try to peddle borders on both the libellous and obscene. Even though I admired Matthew Harding, I realise why Ken wanted to do things his way. I have read some of your scare stories and lies on both your web site and in this magazine.

The fact is Bates has been both the saviour of Chelsea and the force behind the success that we have achieved. If it had not been for his business sense and good prudence, we would not be in the position we are in today. Even though the share price is not as strong as it could be, the fact is that, longterm, they will both rise and serve to be the stabilising influence that the Chelsea Village scheme foresaw when they first laid their plans.

Why you try to undermine Ken's influence is beyond my comprehension. Call yourself supporters? You should go down to QPR and try to 'help' them! Failing that, you should crawl back into the cesspit that you came from.

Yours anonymously,

A real fan

Ah, another satisfied reader!

*****

No Silver Lining In This Claudio

When it comes down to it, we all like constants in our lives. We like to know that the four walls around us will still be there come the end of each day, that the woman (or man in some cases) we want to be with is by our side, and that the work we go to each day doesn't disappear overnight.

The same thing with our football. We, as Chelsea fans, have been used to a steady and gradual improvement from being sh*t (albeit with the capacity to beat all the bigger teams on our day) in the early Nineties to being brilliant in the late Nineties, and all of us expecting to win something come May.

The descent back to being sh*te isn't complete yet, but the speed of the descent from Vialli's glory days has been far too swift for most of us to take. It ain't right – it's too fast – and it's Bates inflicted. Given that all was not right – and I am not among a minority who believe that we weren't going in the right direction, having won five trophies in two and a half years – if you believe there was something fundamentally wrong then why did Vialli go (and not a player or two, and why did Ranieri come?).

If a player at Anfield in the late Sixties and Seventies had been p*ssed off at a certain Mr Shankly, do you think it would have been the player or the manager who would have been up the road? The row between Sexton and Hudson and Osgood at the Bridge in 72/73 left Chelsea minus two of its heroes.

The row between Vialli and his players, if it existed, was settled in the exact opposite manner. If Bates was determined to get us into the Champions League at all costs, because the financial rewards and the wage bills are such that Chelsea can no longer afford to play domestic football only, then why oh why did he get a manager who knew little of English football, could hardly speak to the squad and had left his previous club, Atletico Madrid, the third biggest club in Spain, on the point of relegation?

I personally don't agree that we should have dumped Vialli. I think we would be on the verge of further silverware now if he had been here. His record suggests that would be so. At an average of 2.5 trophies a season, it's difficult to imagine a better manager.

But he's gone. Like a woman walking away from you when you were convinced that together you were the best thing since sliced bread, it's no good looking backwards.

So look forward – what silverware do you see accelerating to Stamford Bridge now that Signor Ranieri has had the best part of a season to sort out a squad of multi-talented, multi-award winning millionaires? Not a whole lot. The Middlesex Cup, maybe. SEVEN MONTHS of almost constant football saw Ranieri steer our beloved Blues to their first away victory of the season. That's cr*p. That's pathetic. That is not the form we have had under previous managers for the past six years.

Give him time, give him space – that's been the mantra of people since Ranieri's arrival. To be fair, it's not his fault he's here. It's Bates and Hutchinson's fault. We've given him a chance, and by and large he hasn't looked close to taking it.

I was among the 'lucky' few who got tickets to Ipswich on Boxing Day. It got me away from the in-laws, and I saw CFC going 2-0 up, then, when all seemed right with the world, Claudio decided to make it work properly. He had Wise as left wing-back, and I wouldn't like to say where Leboeuf and Desailly were supposed to be. We went from being clearly on top to being clearly on bottom with a couple of swift, ill-considered decisions.

How many of you, when you heard that Gronkjaer wasn't injured, were absolutely stunned that he sat out the whole of the first half at Highbury in the FA Cup? I have seen many strange goings-on since Claudio took over and, come to think of it, since I started supporting the Blues in 1970, but few were so bad that Basil Fawlty's missus could have answered questions on them in an episode of Mastermind – specialist subject The Bleedin' Obvious! He's had his chance. He's cocked it up. He should go. Now.

I had to laugh the other day. Saucy Sandra – Blue and White Army's resident woman – was seriously going to the Ladies' Lunch at the Bridge, as advertised in Ken's column in the programme. Apparently her sole objective was to ask one of the guests of honour, a certain Ms Dwyer, what had made her fall for a hairy, old millionaire. I couldn't think of a printable reply.

Ipswich took some liberties at home a couple of months ago, didn't they? I remember when they would have got a slap for it – but this time we had a sweeter revenge as, having gone one down, and looking like we were suffering, we then responded fantastically to win 4-1. As the third and the fourth went in, I had the greatest pleasure of starting a song in the Matthew Harding: "*It's just like playing Norwich.*" They didn't like that one bit, and it's great fun hearing a song that you start spread throughout the entire Bridge. Try it out – you might discover some of the excitement that a certain Mr Greenaway felt when he led the hordes through the decades of conducting the 'Shed Orchestra'. Anyway, sod Ipswich – I hope they had a nice journey home after losing so heavily to that "*small club from London*".

I had an e-mail yesterday from a mate who had waited, with the rest of us, so long for an away win this season. It read: 'RON GREENWOOD, BILLY BONDS, JOHNNY LYALL, HARRY FUCKING REDKNAPP, WE BEAT YOUR BOYS, WE FUCKING WON AWAY!!!'.

It wasn't so long ago that, after beating Man Ure and Sunderland away in the Cup, some serious (too serious) respect was being paid to the Marshmen from Upton Park. Now that Chelsea have exposed them for the crap they are, perhaps some normality will return to the press, and we'll hear no more of Harry's Beautiful Face or Di Canio's silky skills. Har-har-de-har.

Did you see the chaos surrounding the Worthington Cup Final in Cardiff? What will it be like with a couple of well-supported teams in the FA Cup Final, especially after it was disclosed on the radio that the Severn Bridge and tunnels on the Paddington-Cardiff railway line are both due for serious repairs that weekend?

If it goes ahead, which is still doubtful with the current foot and mouth disease around the country, then it will go off in a big way in Cardiff that day. Apparently when some Brummies were making their way back to their West Midlands nirvana the other week, it took five hours to travel the 111 miles, and up to eight hours for the Scousers. If a team the Cardiff fans don't like gets to the Final, there will be three sets of mugs looking for the off before and after the game – and no escape route.

I struggled personally after the defeat at Highbury in the Cup. It was our Cup. It might be the same Cup that Colin Hutchinson said he'd rather lose and get selected to play in the Champions League, but for the fans it's not like that at all. To lose so badly, with no guts whatsoever, was distressing. It's been a long time now since we had nothing to look forward to for the rest of the season, from the end of February.

It got so bad that the perennial favourite, the trip to Three Point Lane in April, was left with hundreds of returns from the Chelsea fans who no longer cared. Why spend money following Chelsea; why drag yourself around the country on a wet and windy night if the players don't give a sh*t? Why indeed?

Well, it didn't help that Bates sent out his annual demand for money, by mid- April at the latest, to get another season ticket. I reckon that if the deadline had been a week after the performance at Highbury, where would have been a severe drop in sales. I was so pissed off with them – the team, Bates and Ranieri – that I was seriously considering not spending my hard-earned on them. Why spend such a large proportion of your income on a group of people who don't seem to care and who don't put in half as much effort as you have to get there (not just the travelling, but earning the money to get there)? I will be renewing my season ticket for next season, but it was by no means an automatic choice. Pull your collective fingers out, Chelsea.

Come on you Blues.

Slim Jim

*****

You Must Be Joking! – T*tt*nh*m Special

Q: Why can't you circumcise T*tt*nh*m fans? A: Because there is no end to those pr*cks.

Q: Why do pigeons fly upside down over Three Point Lane? A: Because there's nothing worth crapping on.

Q: Why does a T*tt*nh*m fan whistle while he is having a shit? A: So he knows which end to wipe.

Q: What's the difference between Three Point Lane and a cactus? A: On a cactus, all the pricks are on the outside. Q: What's the difference between a T*tt*nh*m fan and a trampoline? A: You take your shoes off to jump on a trampoline.

Q: What is the difference between a battery and a T*tt*nh*m fan? A: A battery has a positive side.

Q: What is the difference between T*tt*nh*m and a bucket of horse manure? A: Horse manure works wonders on grass.

Q: Which sexual position produces the ugliest children? A: Ask a T*tt*nh*m supporter.

Q: What is black and brown and looks good on a T*tt*nh*m fan? A: A Doberman.

Q: What have you got if you come across a T*tt*nh*m fan buried up to his neck in sand? A: Not enough sand.

Q: Why do T*tt*nh*m fans carry lighters around with them? A: Because they lose all their matches.

Q: What's the difference between a lift and T*tt*nh*m? A: A lift doesn't take nine months to go down.

Q: Why are T*tt*nh*m the strongest team in the Premier League? A: Because they have been propping up all the other teams all season.

Q: What is the difference between a T*tt*nh*m fan and a monkey? A: One's hairy, stupid and smells – the other one is a monkey.

Q: What's the difference between OJ Simpson and T*tt*nh*m? A: OJ Simpson had some sort of defence.

ISSUE 14 APRIL 2001

The Thoughts of Chels Guevara

Talk Bates was on again in March (03/04/01) with the current Village chairman pontificating on everything from football to Huntingdon Life Sciences (the animal cruelty experts). Brian Moore, surely one of the more gentlemanly of sports presenters, was hosting the show but, as usual, Bates started trying to run proceedings. Moore had warned listeners that they might not necessarily agree with Bates' views and told them not to be afraid to confront him with their views. The 'debate' started and the subject was the ongoing foot and mouth crisis. It was during this part of the broadcast that Bates mentioned the Maxwell Report taking ten years to reach its conclusion. Bates/Maxwell – Maxwell/Bates… birds of a feather?

After Bates had given the listeners a potted history on the disease, and after taking a couple of calls on the subject, Bates suggested that the discussion should turn to football. When Moore reminded Bates that it was he who wanted to talk about the subject, Bates simply said that he'd made his point. Ah, now I see – Talk Sport is merely a tool for Bates to spout his views on things and, when he had got HIS point across, that was as much as anyone else needed to know.

When a Chelsea supporter called Colin rang in to tell Bates that he would not be renewing his family season ticket, Bates proceeded to tell the caller that he would not be missed and that there was a waiting list of over one thousand. Whatever happened to listening to, and showing concern for, the customer's grievances or complaints? Anyway, the caller happened to call Chelsea's current manager, Ranieri, a clown. This brought an immediate retort from Bates, who said he would not sink to personal abuse and it was because of comments such as Colin's that people were turning off their radio sets.

It was here that Bates used a swear word for the first – but not the last – time in the broadcast. It might have been the Alzheimer's kicking in or, more likely, typical Bates rudeness and arrogance, but later in the broadcast, Bates accused Sports Minister Kate Hoey of having foot in mouth disease. In other words, it's not OK to have a go at someone that Bates likes, but when it's someone he doesn't like, all rules and etiquette go out the window.

As the show went on, Bates seemed to get increasingly frustrated at some of the callers, and it sounded as though he was trying to run the show himself. I suppose he's fishing for some kind of career when his days at the Village are over. I'll concede that Bates is indeed controversial and excellent listening (where would this column of the fanzine be without him?) but I'm sure that, after due consideration, those who run the station would not be able to handle him more than once a month.

When a Hull City supporter rang in to ask Bates what he thought about the larger, more successful clubs helping out the smaller ones, the current Village chairman made the point that losses of £1m that Hull had were a sign that the locals didn't want to support the team or that the finances had been managed badly. I wonder what the excuse would have been if someone had called in to ask why the Village had made losses that amounted to many times more than the sum lost by Hull.

Perhaps the worst part of the broadcast (for me anyway) was when Bates joked about setting a precedent for sacking a manager after he had successfully won a trophy. He was, of course, referring to the outrageous dismissal of Chelsea legend and Chelsea supporter, Gianluca Vialli. Luca, please don't take Bates' comments to heart. What you did for us here will always be remembered and there are still many of us here who long for you to return. Soon, when those currently running affairs at Stamford Bridge have been sent packing, the way may yet be open for you to return and finish the job you weren't allowed to.

Chelsea hero Gianfranco Zola spoke for many when he said that he didn't fancy the idea of the club entering the InterToto Cup. He said it would mean that the players would only get two weeks break during the summer. Following Franco's statement, Bates proceeded to tell those attending a function that any Chelsea player who didn't want to play in the summer tournament would not be wanted by the club.

Yet again, I find myself with an opposite opinion to that of Bates. My reasons? Well, just look at Aston Villa. They went as far as the semi-finals before crashing out to Spanish side Celta Vigo. That in front of a crowd of little over 11,000. There seems little doubt that Villa suffered as a result of their exertions.

Surely it would be better if the Chelsea players were fully rested for the summer and came back both mentally and physically fit for an all out assault on the Premiership.

While Bates boldly predicted that, should the club enter the competition, they would win it, there are issues other than the players' fitness and qualification for the UEFA Cup to consider. One has to wonder how many people would bother turning up to watch the games and what price they would be charged for admission.

The scenario would appear to leave the management in something of a quandary. Should admission be lower than usual, it might give fans the idea that a precedent for reduced prices for Cup games has been set. So, next season, should Chelsea draw a minor team in the League Cup, as we did against Huddersfield two years ago, would there be a reduced price policy to ensure a bigger attendance or would the club charge regular admission prices and risk the scenario that might see crowds as small as ten or twelve thousand attending the games at Stamford Bridge.

Whatever the club decide, the fact remains that should Chelsea fail to set Europe alight as they did this current season, the Village accounts will no doubt show yet another loss to match those of recent years.

Hopefully, by the time that this season ends, the records will show that Chelsea have qualified for a UEFA Cup place by virtue of a league placing (as opposed to winning England's only InterToto place) or, dare I say it, a place in the Champions League.

What will happen remains to be seen. For now, I'll wish you all the best for the summer and look forward to seeing you all again next season. Don't forget, keep the faith – things WILL get better.

Trust me … I'm a Chelsea supporter!
Chels Guevara

*****

El Presidente

He came to power by dubious means. He has kept power by dubious means, and it's also very dubious whether or not he knows what democracy means. Some very dark forces are at work behind him. Rumours abound of drug money, threats of drug-related violence. More rumours abound of false accounting and back-handers to government officials.

His arrogance towards those that have an interest in what he sees as his kingdom (and to everyone else for that matter) is legendary; his ignorance even more so.

His foreign policy has come under extreme criticism from all quarters, except his own supporters, and the way he's going he will start World War III, or die trying.

Always a supporter of capital punishment (that's death, by the way, not a season ticket to Highbury), he would not lose a wink of sleep if someone he has power over died. He has displayed this trait on TV documentaries before now.

People he doesn't agree with around the world are spoken of as part of 'an evil empire'.

Perhaps these are traits in all powerful men, but I rather think it's just the odd megalomaniac that has these 'I'm alright Jack, stuff everyone else' attitudes. Of course, there is a bad side to everyone, and powerful men especially have been known to let down those who trust them the most (their wives), but surely there have been few who have plumbed the depths that *El Presidente* has.

His right-hand man, 'General' Colin, has been involved in a few famous battles in the past, and this experience may be crucial if and/or when the real stories behind the drugs money, bribes and fraud come before a national enquiry.

As Hitler, Lenin, Mao, Sutcliffe and Maxwell all found out – your mistakes will come back to haunt you, and your only escape will be death itself. Just for the record, hands up how many people thought I was writing about one Kenneth Bates esquire?

Well, I wasn't talking about Bates – it was President George Dubya Bush that I was describing. Of course, old Ken, a legend in his own lunchtime, would never have let a passage such as that above to be used to describe him without bringing the full weight of his lawyers down on our heads.

So while I'm not rich, and while Bates is alive, I wouldn't dream of saying one bad word about our beloved leader.

Slim Jim

*****

The Manifesto

Smash down the hotels, flats and any remnants of the current incumbent chairman's reign.

Redevelop Stamford Bridge into a 55,000 all-seated stadium with provision for an experimental 10,000 capacity safe standing area. We've got the space – let's use it!

Equitable pricing structure, ensuring that the maximum amount of people are given the opportunity to attend matches live, irrespective of income. Return of the 1970s 'Matthew Lion'.

No shirt sponsorship.

Work within budgets generated from the football based economy.

Encourage a youth structure as well as a complimentary education programme for any associated youth players.

Supporter representation at board level.

A supporters' trust, ensuring both the stadium and football club's future. Do more to accommodate supporters' considerations when arranging kick-off times.

Work with football institutions such as BBC TV's *Match of the Day* etc (best coverage for the greatest number of people).

Encourage links within the local community, thus ensuring the club retains its affinity and identity with the local residents.

Work with the local council and residents to ensure the least amount of disruption to the local community.

The Politician

ISSUE 15 AUGUST 2001

Learning the Hard Way – Tales from an Adolescent Youth #1

When I was a lad, money was tight and I took great care of what little possessions I owned. We were forever moving house, desperate to avoid paying debts the family could ill afford. I'd like to recall one particular tale of woe, and how I quickly realised that life was about smart thinking.

It came soon after we had moved into a house on the estate that was commonly accepted to be the roughest in the area. The house was far from picturesque but it was functional, and we soon accepted that it was to be home.

I was allocated the back bedroom and took great pride in unpacking what meagre possessions I had managed to accumulate during my early years. Posters of Chelsea were lovingly unrolled and stuck to the wall adjacent to the bed. Imitation Chelsea kit that had seen better days was carefully folded and placed in a rickety chest of drawers that nestled against the far wall. Life was about to change and living here was going to be one almighty challenge. Looking out through the dirty window panes, I could see that the garden was a fair size. More importantly, it was long and flat and would be ideal to have a kickabout in. I rushed down the stairs and bust through at the back of the garage, football proudly tucked under my arm.

It was now the mid-70s – Chelsea had self-imploded again. The stars had been sold on and whilst the new players were still my heroes, I belonged to those supporters who had fond memories of that golden era. Their names had a better ring and were instantly more recognisable to innocent passers-by as they went about their normal daily business.

I imagined that I was Peter Osgood running out onto the lush Wembley turf. I kicked the ball towards the empty goal and gleefully milked the adulation of the Chelsea faithful. Suddenly, my daydreaming was shattered by the sound of the ball thudding against the flimsy panels that were all that remained of the once-solid fence. Mother raised her voice and bellowed out of the kitchen window: "Will you be quiet out there, we don't want to upset the neighbours on our first day!" Little did we know what lay ahead.

For the rest of the afternoon, I practiced improving my ball skills, dribbling around discarded pop bottles, proudly emulating Charlie Cooke. The sun was beating down and the air was thick with those awful flying ants. Any sudden movements had me retching, as one of those dreaded insects disappeared into a mouth gasping for air, desperately trying to refresh my adolescent lungs. It certainly was a hot, sultry summer's day.

I had yet to make any friends in my new environment. I secretly wondered if anyone on this fearsome estate would share my unwavering loyalty to all things Chelsea, or would they all be long-haired hippies, aligning themselves to that supposed darling of the North Bank, Charlie George? By now, I had single-handedly won the FA Cup for Chelsea. Ron Harris had held the defence together, while Ossie had destroyed the opposition with two superb diving headers.

Basking in the afternoon sun, I sat down and leant against the rickety fence, pondering exactly what to do next. I needed some companionship but felt alone in this desolate new neighbourhood. With the sweat pouring off my brow, I decided that it would be less tiring if I took over the role of Peter Bonetti. Casually I began throwing the ball against the walls of the house, ensuring I caught it cleanly and didn't offer the opposition's rampaging forwards any chance of netting a rebound. Time was passing, and I knew father would be home from work very shortly.

I always got on well with father. He used to come home from work, get changed and we'd have a kickabout in the back garden. Usually I would have to be content with being the goalkeeper, poised for action between two fir trees. However, that was in the old house. This house was different and I suspected we'd have to adopt the jumpers for goalposts philosophy. It might have been because I wasn't focused on what was happening in front of me that the inevitable happened. I misjudged the flight of the ball as it bounced off the brickwork, and instinctively pushed it high over the imaginary bar. I neglected to realise that as a consequence of this inept action, it was actually sailing high over next door's fence.

Instantly I was mortified. My ball, my best friend, was gone. I sat forlornly on the ground, pondering what to do next. I anxiously peered through a knothole in the fence and could see my ball nestling amongst the rubble strewn across the neighbour's garden. Against my better judgement, I dragged the dustbin over and positioned it against the fence. In one sharp movement, reminiscent of a hooded SAS soldier, I was over the fence and into enemy territory. I gathered my ball under my arm and furiously headed towards my friendly manor.

Suddenly I was aware of being lifted off my feet from behind. I had no comprehension of what was happening, only that I was in imminent danger of being strangled by my shirt collar. The next thing I can remember is being thrown onto my backside amongst the rubble in this not so salubrious garden. I struggled to my feet and confronted my assailant. Once I had wiped the summer dust out of my eyes, I could see that he was a good few years older than me, and he was wearing a red football shirt with a Man United badge badly sewn onto it. If I were not so shaken up, I'm sure I would have take the piss out of his needlework expertise.

He looked deep into my eyes and scowled menacingly at me. "New round here, aren't you?" he bawled. Too shaken to speak, I just nodded my head. "We don't like intruders in our gardens on this estate, and we have rules to abide by. What were you after?" I looked at my ball and just pointed. His face was now only inches from mine when he questioned which football team I supported. By now I was beginning to recover my senses. Foolishly refusing to back down, and showing no cowardice, I proudly proclaimed: "Chelsea".

This didn't appease him at all. If anything, it made him even angrier. Stepping back, he enquired whether I thought I was hard. Not looking to be viewed as a wimp, I nodded my head. What was I thinking of? This bloke must have been four stone heavier than me and ten inches taller! "Prove it", he shouted, "How?" I enquired in my most threatening voice. "Easy", he replied, "Around here we have an initiation ceremony. It's called the Three Kick Challenge". "What's that mean?" I hesitantly replied. "Well, first I kick you three times and then you kick me three times, and so on, back and forth until someone gives up", he explained. I immediately knew that it would be painful but I was determined to put up a brave front and hopefully make a new friend in the process.

Mr United decided that he would have the first three kicks. I didn't expect anything else – after all, he was bigger than me, older than me and held the upper hand. I hoped that I could withstand his three kicks without tears streaming down my face or, even worse, collapsing in a blubbering heap on the floor. I just hoped that I would get the chance to show that I had the balls to withstand his kicks and get some in myself. I hadn't even considered how long I could last.

As he prepared to take his first kick, I tensed every muscle in my body. In a flash, his right foot caught me flush in the stomach and I almost doubled up. I could feel tears welling up in my eyes but desperately held them back. The second kick caught me on the thigh and inside I was secretly grateful that he had obviously misjudged it. However, nothing prepared me for the third kick. His left boot caught me flush in the bollocks and immediately I went down like a sack of spuds. After a few moments, I struggled to my feet, tears streaming down my face, and I probably called for my mum. However, I was desperate to have my three kicks.

As I stood up, I couldn't see my foe. I screamed out that it was my turn, but there was no response. Suddenly I caught a glimpse of Mr United in his kitchen window. I bellowed out that it was my turn, but he just grinned and shouted out the window: "It's alright, mate, I give up. Take your ball and p*ss off over the fence!" For an instant, I was totally confused. Then it dawned on me: 'You take three kicks until someone gives up… ' I had been well and truly stitched up. Done up like a kipper.

I vowed revenge but never got the chance to take it. Weeks later, some older boys told me that Mr United ran with the Cockney Reds and was a known face. Fortunately, our paths rarely crossed and he never gave me any more aggro over the few months that we stayed in that house – but my hatred of Manchester United had been born. It is a hatred that has survived until this day and will probably stay with me forever. Thankfully, the full frontal kick in the nuts did not affect my chances of fathering children. I wouldn't want to miss out on another generation of D's carrying on my loathing of the red jersey and everything associated with it.

As for Mr United, we have never met since those days but, a few years later, when the hooligan scene was in full swing, I did catch a glimpse of him on a TV news report. I offered a wry smile to myself as I witnessed him suffering a merciless beating at the hands of the ICF. Revenge comes to those that wait!

Juvenile D

*****

The Woman's Own Pages – Lager

It was a typical Saturday morning and I had woken up feeling sick. Not because I had drunk too much the night before, nor because I was pregnant (which I wasn't by the way). I was feeling sick because it was football day and my boyfriend and I were off to watch the game with a few of his friends. It was not the ferocity of the opponent that I was dreading, nor was it the momentum of the occasion; it was just an ordinary Chelsea game. So what was it I was feeling sick about, I hear you ask. Well, I'll tell you in one word: lager. You know the stuff, comes in a can (or a bottle if you're posh), smells horrid and turns an ordinary, nice, decent sort of bloke into an all-singing, all-dancing, drunken idiot.

Now don't get me wrong, I am not a stick in the mud. I enjoy a drink as much as the next person and I have even been known to sink a few too many vodkas then pass out in bed. But where I differ from the average male football fan is here: I do all that in the comfort of my boyfriend's or my own home – not in public. I do not feel it necessary to down ten pints *before* every single football game and then another ten afterwards. My boyfriend, of course, has an excuse for every single pint that he guzzles down his greedy little throat. There's the "my mate bought it, it'd be rude not to drink it" excuse, or sometimes I hear "they'll think I'm a poof if I don't drink it". But the most frequent of all his self-justifications is "it's the law – you have to drink when you go to football". What rubbish. I can survive an entire football game, including the pre-match warm-up and the post-match celebrations /commiserations, on just a couple of glasses of Malibu and Pineapple, so why can't he?

It's not so much a case of what he drinks that bugs me, it's really the fact that he feels the need to drink as much as he does which really gets my goat. My biggest annoyance of all, though, is the time he starts drinking, ie on my way there, while on the Tube. I get so embarrassed when he insists on stuffing his pockets with cans of lager, then starts chucking it all down his neck as if his life depends on it. The last time he did that, I was so mortified I had to go and sit somewhere else. There was no way I was going to sit next to someone exhibiting all the class of a wino, even if he was my own boyfriend! So what is it about lager and football? Why do so many men think that it is impossible to enjoy a game of footy without getting drunk first? And why are my suggestions of slowing down and drinking halves, met with looks of sheer horror and comments along the lines of "poofs drink halves"? Is it a masculine thing?

So lads, don't be surprised when the next time you come over all amorous after a football game and you are pushed away. Women don't want a lager-smelling mouth slobbering all over them. So think before you lap up one more "swift drink", or that may be the only thing you will be lapping after a game.

You have been warned!

Hey Guys, Show Us Yer Legs!

'Female football fans' – I bet those three little words strike more fear into most of the men reading this, than those other three little words (Editor's note: I had to think for a minute then as well. Therefore, for those who've forgotten, the other three words are: I… Love… You).

I can imagine that upon hearing "female football fan", the vast majority of men folk begin to conjure up images of silly little screaming teeny boppers at a David Beckham-themed pyjama party. Or worse still, they visualise a lager-swilling, curry-scoffing and arm-wrestling Tattoo Annie.

Now, I am not saying that there is anything wrong with a woman who can hold her own during a hearty rendition of *"The referee's a wanker",* but I would like to make it clear to all the men reading this, that not all women who frequent football grounds are there with the sole purpose of obtaining David Beckham's autograph, nor are they there to prove a point, that they can beat a man at his own game.

Most of us do actually go because we enjoy the sport. We get the same rush out of smelling the air as it is filled with fried onions and horse manure as you men do. To me, there is nothing better than donning my woolly hat and scarf, and tripping off to the game with that knot of excitement in my stomach and an extra spring in my step as I anticipate the match ahead.

I'm sure many men reading this are sitting there now, declaring that women only go to football games to ogle footballers' legs. Those kinds of remarks are more off target than a Chris Waddle penalty. These days the shorts are so long and the socks so high that there is barely two inches of thigh to behold anyway. Perhaps the men that come out with those kind of ridiculous comments are the same men who are sitting there now, arms folded and cursing that women don't belong at a football ground anyway. Men who bare an uncanny similarity to the comedian (and I use the term loosely!) Frank Skinner, who is quoted as saying: "Posh people and women should be barred from football games". I can see the man's logic.

I suppose a woman who knows her stuff in regard to the beautiful game and has a fair pair of knockers is a bit much for the average man to handle. Which is probably why some bright spark, namely a bloke, invented the charming phrase, now a classic at most football grounds: "Get your tits out for the lads". Knock us down a peg or two, that'll teach us for having the audacity to cheer on our team. I don't think!

Let me reverse the tables for a minute. How would a man like it if a woman, in full earshot of a crowded pub, declared to her friend that she wasn't impressed with the size of his packet and that she reckoned she could cast her eyes over better tackle in a fishing shop? I doubt very much if those comments would be met with the same grin and girly blush that I am accustomed to dishing out every time my chest is compared to two puppies fighting in a sack.

Now, at the risk of sounding like Mary Whitehouse's primmer and sourer-faced sister, I would like to recount an incident that occurred during Chelsea's 4-1 stuffing of Ipswich last season. A very scary-looking skin-headed man, who had earlier mocked me by asking whether I had travelled down from Norwich on my tractor, was declaring his admiration for the classic flick Debbie Does Dallas. I turned to him and, in my firmest of tones, asked him if he had to discuss the merits of porn films during a football game I was trying to watch.

The man looked at me, bemused that I had actually dared to voice my opinion, and immediately retracted his previous comment by shouting to his friend: "Ere, mate. Do you mind not talking about porn, I'm trying to watch the fucking game here!" His friend looked stunned.

But his expression wasn't a patch on my boyfriend's face, now totally aghast at my cheek. That little moral victory set me up for the rest of the day. This man had incurred my wrath and learned from it! I had won. I had actually managed to convince a member of the opposite sex that I was a genuine football fan; not some lust-driven woman determined to catch a glimpse of well-toned thigh.

Well that just about brings me to the end of my little piece here, and I shall soon quietly climb back down off my soapbox. But before I go, can I politely ask all the men reading this to think before they are about to comment on the size a football fan's chest, during the forthcoming season.

I for one have heard every tit joke around, and find them all about as thrilling as the prospect of a date with that handsome chap Luke (been bobbing for apples in a deep fat fryer) Chadwick. But time is flying and I really must go and get the latest copy of Soccer Hunks from my newsagent before he sells out…

Natasha

*****

You Must Be Joking

Two Sp*rs fans, Vile and Scum, were sitting in their local pub. Two men walk in, both carrying a huge fish, and neither of them had fishing rods. Being nosey bastards, Vile and Scum asked the two men how they caught the fish without using fishing rods.

"Well, all you do is this. One of you grabs the other one by the ankles and lowers him from a bridge, and you hang on until your mate catches a fish." The two Sp*rs fans thought it was a great idea, and thought they would give it a go. They left the pub and went to the nearest bridge, Scum then grabbed both Vile's ankles and lowered him from the bridge.

Nothing happened for a few minutes, and Scum was starting to get really tired of holding on this mate's ankles, when he heard Vile scream.

"Pull me up, pull me up." "What is it? Did you catch something?" he asked. "No", Vile pleaded, "There's a train coming!"

A Sp*rs fan is driving happily along in his car with his girlfriend when he's pulled over by the police. The police officer approaches him and asks: "Have you been drinking, sir?"

"Why?" replies the man, "Was I all over the road?"

"No" says the officer, "You were driving splendidly – it was the ugly, fat bird in the passenger seat that made me suspicious."

ISSUE 16 SEPTEMBER 2001

Chelsea or England?

It's Saturday night, August 30 – an evening that goes down in football history (in England, at least), because the national team has just hammered Germany 5-1 in Munich. I, like many, many other supporters, am looking on, believing but euphoric.

I turn to Mrs EuroBlue, who, not being English, is not quite so euphoric. But she understands that this is a monumental occasion. And I ask her "Which would you prefer, your country to win the World Cup or your team to win the League?" She would prefer the World Cup. I plump for Chelsea winning the League. In fact, I would settle for a top three finish rather than England winning the World Cup. She doesn't agree.

It's not an original debate. In fact, the question has become something of a cliché, with polls held on websites and debates raging on message boards, including our own, as well as the issue mulled over sagely in pubs across the land.

Is this a Chelsea thing? Am I unpatriotic? After all, I support a club stuffed with foreigners – so much so that during many international games I find myself guiltily rooting for England's adversaries, as their squad usually contains more Chelsea players. The recent friendly against Holland, which saw three Chelsea regulars take on Frank Lampard for England, is a case in point.

Let's imagine a hypothetical England v Holland match. Jimmy Floyd Hasselbaink dances first around a frustrated Ashley Cole, then a clumsy Sol Campbell, before slotting the ball home past a wooden David Seaman. The colours on the shirts will mean little, and my reaction could well be the same as if it were a Chelsea v Arsenal match. Sorry.

Or maybe it's the fact that our club, for all its prestige and glory, is not used to winning titles. A few trophies in recent years, maybe, but not the League, not the heavy silverware. If, like Mrs EuroBlue, you support a team that has won everything and does so regularly, in her case Real Madrid, you can afford to be generous and occasionally bestow a title on the rest of your fellow countrymen.

Is the status of Chelsea what causes me to put club before country? I asked a completely unrepresentative group of friends what they thought. Those that supported the big clubs in their country – Bayern Munich, Manchester United, Real Madrid, Anderlecht or Galatasaray – could afford to be generous. Their club will win again. Those that supported small clubs also, they don't expect to win the title. In that case, you could well cover yourself with glory by associating yourself with the national team instead. But if you are a supporter of a club that doesn't take winning for granted, and has often come close against the odds only to lose out, you will be gunning for that club.

Chelsea, despite winning many cups and trophies, have come close to the Premiership, only to fall behind in the race. We are the runners up. Is it frustration that makes us all the more keen to win over all other considerations? A friend who supports Roma confirmed – but then again, having only just won the Scudetto, Roma fans are not yet used to that feeling of victory.

Both arguments are fair, but they maybe disguise the defining factor, which is that you support your club differently. I didn't choose to be an England supporter. By virtue of my parents and passport, it was handed down to me. I haven't done much to manifest that I'm an England supporter either. That would be a bit sad, as England play only a couple of times a year. A few more when it's a World Cup or European Cup Final year (conveniently, those finals take place after the Premiership season has ended, providing a football fix).

But Chelsea? To support your club, you have to work hard. In a given season, there could be over fifty games to follow, maybe even sixty. That makes for a regular cycle of expectation, followed by elation if Chelsea win; misery if they lose – every week, and often more frequently. Living that, you become Chelsea through and through, and their fortunes on the pitch will define your mood for the coming hours – or days – after the final whistle has blown. Chelsea becomes a fix and the link visceral, a sort of soccer biorhythm. We all know the quiet tedium of the close season, but even when the Premiership is suspended for international duty. I find that my interest in the national squad is only a palliative as I wait for the Boys in Blue to return.

You forge your allegiance to your club through years of abuse from other supporters. You temper it through confronting your support for that club with the intense sporting rivalry on the pitch, inevitably prolonged off it. And you realise that the other supporters feel just as passionately about their team as you do. Cut us open and we bleed blue: we have been marked and branded and our loyalties made ever stronger through following our club week in, week out. The support for Chelsea – shared with few and surrounded by many who don't – is much, much stronger than that for England. Millions upon millions support England, so that affiliation is diluted. We who support Chelsea are a select few who find ourselves huddling together for comfort. And by doing so, our support is boosted.

From the sample on the Blue And White Army message board, it would appear that I am far from being alone in putting club before country. A poll on the official Chelsea site suggests that a massive 75% have 'greater emotions' for Chelsea, and only 10% for England.

Don't get me wrong: I like this England team. It is young and dynamic, with a good mix of individual skills and team spirit. To see Frank Lampard and, later, John Terry don the England shirt is a source of pride for me. But one of the reasons that I like them is the fact that the old beer-soaked, jingoistic culture has been purged. This England team has a Swedish manager, and the individual players have honed their skills through playing against some of the finest players from around the world in the Premiership. Is there a parallel with Chelsea? A slim one, but I like to think so.

I want England to do well, and was overjoyed to see the nature of their victories. For England to win the World Cup would undoubtedly be a lift for me. Look at what happened in France when their squad won the World Cup and European Cup: the country felt good about itself.

With luck, this year will see both Chelsea and England covered in glory. Having a Premiership trophy in the cabinet, I might feel slightly more generous towards England next year.

Euro Blue

*****

Cosmopolitan Village Blues

There's scarcely a ground in the land whose interior hasn't been transformed beyond recognition over the last five years. Stringent new safety standards have resulted in the bulldozing of the much-loved terrace. Stamford Bridge, which for most of us has been our oasis in life's long journey for so long, has now changed beyond belief. The builders are finally moving out after the best part of thirty years!

Football at Chelsea is no longer a sport, it has become a very big business. Bates can now make money seven days a week rather than once a fortnight. We all know that this has always been his dream! Corporate hospitality, sponsors, advertising and megastores are now all part of our club's life. Merchandising is worth millions to Bates, and our club shop will now sell us anything we are gullible enough to buy – garden gnomes, cycle helmets, oven gloves and condoms to name just a few. Just where will it all end? Hotels, night clubs, shares, credit cards etc, at last the Bates Village is almost complete.

It's almost impossible to believe now, but there was a time when nobody wore replica team shirts. In the early 60s, football fans sported rosettes and rattles. Later in that decade and throughout the 70s, the fashion was for scarves, both silk and woollen. However, in the 80s, anonymity was the name of the game, as fans eschewed all tribal markings in favour of casual attire. Now, however, no self-respecting supporter is anything less than naked without their £40 worth of nylon.

One good thing about today's game is the fact that we have almost seen the death of the football hooligan inside all Premiership grounds. It's good to see kids and girlfriends etc enjoying the game and not afraid to show their colours. There was a time, especially in the 70s, when we would visit some grounds and we would fear for our lives. This was the decade when the hooligan was the 'King of the Castle' and violent disorder, assault, throwing missiles and causing criminal damage was the name of the game. Football related arrests have declined over the last ten years. Ticket touting and disorderly behaviour are very common round most Premiership grounds. However, drink related offences are still the biggest problem. Police forces normally say that rain is the best crowd controller, but most games nowadays pass without major incident.

I really do feel that the Bates cosmopolitan Village has been built on the backs of the Chelsea faithful, with a little help from Matthew Harding.

It doesn't seem that long ago that we had the Save the Bridge Fund and, before that, Cash for Chelsea, which needed millions but raised pennies.

Of course, nowadays you can tuck into a lobster and wash it down with a cheeky Chardonnay at the Chelsea Village as a pre-match warm-up meal. However, my own tastes are somewhat humbler. For those of us who were raised in The Shed, it's the aroma of fried onions and the sizzle of burger that gives us our erection!

As with any successful business, certain things become expendable because at the end of the day, loyalty doesn't count for a great deal. Loyal supporters and players have found this out in our recent history.

Bluebear

*****

Pat Nevin – Blue and White Army legend

Patrick Kevin Francis Nevin was born on 6 September 1963. He was from that dying breed of footballers: a winger. Pat was signed by John Neal from the Scottish club Clyde in May 1983, for the princely sum of £95,000. I dread to think what his market value would have been in these days of inflated transfer dealings.

Pat had sublime talent and was able to go by players almost at will. However, in his first season at Chelsea, he strangely didn't feature in the first game. Pat made his debut as a substitute in a Milk Cup tie against Gillingham in September 1983. He made such an impact that night that he didn't miss a game for the rest of the season. His breathtaking ball control and delightful audacity endeared him to the Chelsea faithful.

Although a winger, Pat didn't neglect his team duties. He was very rarely caught in possession, preferring instead to utilise his supreme skills to bamboozle defenders with slight of feet. Pat's role in the Second Division championship winning season cannot be underestimated. With an ability to seemingly hold the ball forever, and equally able to play wide on the right or wide on the left, Pat was the catalyst that provided a hatful of goals for his striking partners, Kerry Dixon and David Speedie. John Neal recognised his natural ability, and quite often his tactical ploy when things were not going well was to bark out the order, "Give it to Pat!"

In his first season with Chelsea, Pat scored 14 goals – a remarkable contribution from someone originally perceived as a fragile wide man. One of the highlights of his first season was a mazy 80-yard dribble against Newcastle when Pat appeared able to beat the opposition at will.

When Chelsea returned to the top division, Pat didn't let his standards drop. A continuing run of mazy dribbles and defence splitting passes created numerous chances for the rampaging front two of Dixon and Speedie. Pat had the unerring ability to be able to rescue the ball out of situations where everybody in the ground thought he had taken it too far, and deliver yet another curling, looping cross. He also possessed a remarkable awareness and, for someone so small and seemingly fragile, remarkable courage. Defenders who were constantly chasing his shadow were not averse to trying to kick him out of the game. But Pat was quite often too quick to be kicked and the defenders were left kicking shadows.

Unlike other footballers, Pat was a bit of a maverick away from the game. His outside interests included a devotion to obscure rock bands. Pat and the famous indie DJ, John Peel, were from vastly different backgrounds, but two of a kind when it came to obscure music. Pat's literary interests included a variety of subjects. He had a passion for Russian literature but wouldn't be averse to being spotted with a copy of the New Musical Express. During his time at Chelsea, he constantly suggested that he did not want to play football for a living past the age of thirty. Thankfully, that was something that didn't happen, although he was not to grace a Chelsea shirt in the era.

Pat's remarkable rise from Scottish football obscurity to potential international star became complete when he won his first international cap against Romania in March 1986. His skills were to see him gain a total of 28 caps during the period 1986-1996. A small number for someone blessed with such skill. Whilst the defenders in the English game resorted to kicking him as a last resort, those on the international scene didn't wait to be embarrassed by his wizard-like ball skills. Pat often suffered brutal retribution for leaving defenders chasing his tail.

Such was Pat's impact at Chelsea, that he was constantly likened to another Scottish wing wizard, Charlie Cooke. The crowd at Stamford Bridge took both men to their hearts and both were warmly acknowledged as being worth the admission money alone. Indeed, such was the stature of Pat that when he missed a penalty against Manchester City in a Milk Cup tie, with a shot that rolled not very gracefully along the floor, no verbal retribution was ever taken. I personally cannot recall the wee man ever being the subject of any sort of verbal retribution when he was at Chelsea.

However, Pat was destined never to be a one club man, and he was soon to move on.

It was during the 1987/88 season that the team lost its way. Previous seasons had seen Chelsea finish in the top regions of the table, but success was fast diminishing. This was reflected in Pat's on-field performances. Team-mates found it increasingly difficult to find Pat with the ball. When it did reach Pat, two or three men invariably marked him. Pat continued to work diligently for the team but often cut a forlorn figure, desperately hoping that he would receive the ball in an area of the pitch that favoured him.

Chelsea eventually lost over two legs to Middlesbrough in the play-offs, and were condemned to the Second Division. Pat exercised an option in his contract and was sold to Everton at the end of that season. The fee was fixed by a tribunal at £925,000, a bargain being the description offered by Chelsea supporters at the time. Strangely, Everton were hoping to get him for less than the tribunal fee. The following season, Chelsea added a hard edge to the team by signing Graham Roberts and Peter Nicholas, but the faithful still had aching hearts. Our Pat was gone, never to return in a shirt adorned by our club crest.

Pat Nevin's Chelsea career was over. He had made 237 appearances, plus five as a substitute, and had scored 45 goals. It was to be several years before we were to encounter somebody with as much skill as Pat Nevin in a Chelsea shirt. Indeed, I personally think that the arrival of Gianfranco Zola can be deemed as the time at which somebody arrived with a skill level to match Pat's.

Pat's career at Everton was a frustrating time. He was unable to fully recapture the magic he generated at Chelsea and was in and out of the team. One particular moment I recall is his return to Stamford Bridge in an Everton shirt. Pat was given a rapturous reception befitting the return of a legend. Indeed, I don't think there was a person in the ground who didn't issue a wry smile when Pat scored, even if the great man looked suitably embarrassed about his goal and jogged solemnly back to the half way line.

In his time at Everton, Pat made a Cup Final appearance but, unfortunately, ended up on the losing side. Significantly, it was the all-Merseyside final that was a fitting tribute to those that lost their lives in the Hillsborough disaster. Pat drifted out of automatic selection for the first team at Everton and moved across the Mersey to Tranmere. Pat left Everton during the 1991/92 season. His record with the Toffees was 109 appearances and 16 goals scored. This meant that Pat dropped down into a division that was not respectful of his ability, and where football was played that did not fit his style. Despite this, Pat had an enjoyable period at Tranmere, making 193 appearances and, coincidentally, again scoring 16 goals. It was during this time that, if I'm not mistaken, Pat served time as Chairman of the Professional Footballers' Association. Only those with the highest regard from their fellow professionals find themselves bestowed with this honour. In the season 1996/97, Pat returned to his native Scotland, firstly with Kilmarnock and then onto Motherwell.

At Motherwell he has occupied several roles, most notably those of player and Director of Football. Gone are the fresh-faced looks of the young man what arrived at Chelsea. They have now been replaced by an ageing face with a receding hairline. But if you close your eyes, you can still see Wee Pat flying down the wing at Stamford Bridge, with defenders trailing in his wake, looking up to provide one of those pinpoint crosses or doubling back to beat the same defender again. That was what made Pat one of our legends: the ability to beat somebody for fun, and with ease.

My favourite memory of him relates to a midweek game at Goodison Park. At the time, Pat was playing for Mersey neighbours Tranmere Rovers. As kickoff approached, this small figure could be seen hurrying to his seat in the away end. To my delight, I realised it was Pat, and he came and sat next to me. This showed where his heart still lay. The away support chanted his name, while the home fans looked on in bemusement. Unfortunately, I was too awestruck to strike up a conversation with this God-like figure, but it certainly made my night.

Pat Nevin – please take your place in the Blue and White Army Hall of Legends.

Juvenile D

MATTHEW HARDING'S
BLUE AND WHITE ARMY
ISSUE 17
www.BlueAndWhiteArmy.net
£1
NOV 2001

Who's The
Daddy
Now!!

Bosnich Gets His Chance

ISSUE 17 November 2001

Deb' Arkles – Tales From Another Seedy Night

I couldn't let an issue of MBHAWA hit the streets without giving you a further insight into life behind the bar at Deb' Arkles, your favourite watering hole. Although it has been a monumental couple of weeks with England qualifying for the World Cup and all that, this friendly hostelry still found time to hold it's annual 'Mock the North' night.

As usual, a top class comedian was hired – well, top class for the money we could scrape together on such a meagre, midweek client base, and the venue subsequently rocked to the sound of laughter. Obviously, most of the jokes were too blue to even appear on the pages of such a publication as this, but some have satisfied the sensor and have thankfully been reproduced for all to enjoy.

If anybody feels slightly offended then, in the words of a top comedian: "tough shite". In times when nobody knows what is around the corner, and the western world is fighting to maintain its right to free speech, I'm going to make sure that, in the words of the late Frankie Howerd, I am at least going to raise a titter or two.

As the ales were sunk and the inhibitions started to lift, the comedian took to the stage. First topic of ridicule was our dear friends from Urinal. Apparently, news was just filtering through that there had been a tragic accident. On returning from a night out, the vehicle carrying the Urinal squad had crashed, unfortunately killing several players.

On arriving at the Pearly Gates, the players were told by St Peter that they would have to confess their sins before they would be allowed into Heaven. Roy Keane was first in the queue and St Peter asked him: "Have you ever touched Sir Alex Ferguson's penis?" Keane replied: "I did once brush it with the tip of my finger". "Dip the tip of your finger into the bowl of holy water over there and pass on through the gates", replied St Peter.

Paul Scholes was next in the queue. "Have you ever touched Sir Alex Ferguson's penis?" asked St Peter. "I did once toss him off", replied Scholes. "Wash your hand in that holy water over there and pass on through the gates", said St Peter.

All of a sudden there was a scuffling in the queue and Andy Cole pushed to the front ahead of David Beckham. "What's going on there?" asked St Peter. "Well", said Cole, "If I'm going to stick my tongue in that bowl of holy water, I want to get there before Beckham dunks his arse in it!"

Unfortunately, that particular joke rather set the mood for the evening, as those privileged enough to have purchased tickets roared with laughter. As the evening progressed, the topic of discussion moved on to that of the Olympics. Much mirth was generated by the announcement that the next Olympics were to be held in Liverpool.

In best Scouse tradition the events will be somewhat unusual. I'd like to recall the full repertoire of events, but such was the intensity of the occasion, combined with the quantity of ale drunk, that a lot were lost amidst the sound of laughter. However, please feel free to enjoy those that I can still recall: Hammer – Competitors in this event may choose the type of hammer they wish to use: claw, sledge etc. The winner will be the one who can cause the most grievous bodily harm to members of the public.

Shooting – A strong challenge is expected from the local competitors in this event. The first target will be a moving police van. In the second round, competitors will aim at a Post Office clerk, a Bank Teller or Securicor wages deliveryman.

Cycling Time Trials – Competitors will be asked to break into the University bike shed and take an expensive mountain bike owned by some mummy's boy from the country on his first trip away from home. All these events will be timed against the clock.

Swimming – Competitors will be thrown off the bridge into the Mersey. The first three survivors back will decide the medals.

Men's 50km Walk – Unfortunately this will have to be cancelled, as police cannot guarantee the safety of anyone walking the streets of Liverpool.

Closing Ceremony – Entertainment will include formation rave dancing by members of the Liverpool Health in the Community Anti-Drug campaigners, synchronised rock throwing and music by the Toxteth Boys Band. The Olympic flame will then be extinguished by someone dropping an old washing machine onto it from the top floor of the block of flats next to the stadium. The stadium will then be boarded up before the local athletes break into it and remove all the copper piping and the central heating boiler. At this point the evening drew to a swift close. Apparently the comedian declined the offer of an encore. He stated that he was bloody starving and was heading off up Fulham Broadway for a late night scoff. His parting words were:

"I can't afford to eat in this place, it's too bloody expensive"

The Bar Steward

*****

Matthew Harding RIP

In a tribute that we hope is befitting of the great man, we have decided to concentrate on the man's love of Chelsea and recall particular incidents that will give you a greater insight into the life of Matthew Harding.

In order to do this, I personally must first offer my thanks to Alyson Rudd, author of Matthew Harding – Pursuing the Dream, for providing most of the material that once again provided me with the inspiration to sit down and take time out to honour someone who helped define our club's future. It will also hopefully confirm the belief that despite all his wealth, Matthew was a genuine Chelsea supporter and a true football fan.

Matthew, the football club director, took great delight in shattering the belief that directors should strictly adhere to a code of etiquette. An etiquette that implored that they should refrain from offering biased verbal opinions and should strut around dressed like city gents, having previously arrived in a plush chauffeur driven car.

The fans' director took extreme delight in travelling by train to Stamford Bridge wearing jeans and a replica Chelsea shirt. Before venturing into the grounds of the football club, Matthew regularly succumbed to the obvious temptation of a few pints of Guinness at the Imperial Arms. Only

101

then would he make his way towards the East Stand, pausing to change into a shirt and tie in Ken's office, then resuming his role in the Directors' Box.

Matthew first watched Chelsea play on 3rd November 1962, the opponents were Newcastle and Chelsea ran out worthy 4-2 winners, a fact that Matthew could readily recall.

Although extremely wealthy, Matthew preferred to avoid the trappings of the rich on matchdays. Realising that the day itself was an event to be savoured, he adhered to the grass roots sentiment of the game he loved so much. Obviously, there were occasions when his wealth became very beneficial, allowing him to charter planes and helicopters to games. However, it must be remembered that this was not done as some grandiose gesture, but as a means of sticking to business appointments and ensuring he watched his beloved Chelsea.

On these occasions, Matthew's personality ensured that he didn't hide the fact that he was wealthy and had to travel posh, quite often he would ask associates and friends if they would like to accompany him on these journeys. On other instances, Matthew would take great delight in travelling hidden amongst the masses of the working class Chelsea support.

One such occasion is majestically recalled in the book by David Gilbertson, who mistakenly believed he would be travelling to Anfield with Matthew in opulent style:

"Not thinking about it, and as I'm going with this multi-millionaire who is going to put me up in the Adelphi Hotel, I bought myself a first-class ticket for the train. I'm sat in the first-class compartment, waiting for him to arrive and there's no sign of him. The train pulls out of the station and I thought he'd been held up at work or something, and I'm just wondering what I'm going to do as I have no ticket or anything and I can only get into the ground with him. The train had been going for about five minutes when all of a sudden he steams in in his shirt sleeves and says: "What are you doing? You'll never get rich like me if you pay first-class. I'm in second-class." Once again, this reiterates just how at home Matthew felt with the army of travelling Chelsea fans.

As a supporter before a fortune was made in the business world, Matthew had very similar idols to the rest of us: Bobby Tambling, Terry Venables and Peter Osgood to name but a few. Osgood, however, was Matthew's personal favourite, described so eloquently in Matthew's own words as: "The one who got my heartstrings. Still has. He kept me alive as an adolescent."

In later life, Matthew was to share many a Guinness with the great man himself before home games at Stamford Bridge. Drinking in the Imperial Arms, Osgood would be greeted by Harding with the words: "Here comes the King." It was an obvious indication that memories of an adolescent worship still held a place in his adult heart.

Perhaps another indication that, despite his obvious wealth, Matthew still behaved as a true supporter came soon after Ruud Gullit signed for Chelsea. Matthew proudly paraded around wearing a Gullit shirt, signed by the man himself. He resembled a supporter proud to have acquired his hero's signature, never once believing that wealth elevated him to a similar status as his blue shirted heroes.

Matthew also showed another trait that emphasised his standing as a true supporter. Often, those with wealth are strict to condemn those that do not perform to the best of their abilities. Like so many Chelsea supporters, Matthew refused to knock anyone wearing a blue shirt. Instead, he preferred to see all things blue through those familiar rose-tinted spectacles that many a Chelsea supporter has been known to view proceedings through. This is borne out in Alyson Rudd's book by the words of Ross Fraser, who said: "He didn't like criticism of players. As soon as they put on a Chelsea shirt, that was good enough for him."

However, on more than one occasion his wealth and love of football combined to cause misunderstandings in the media. It was well known that Matthew admired the mercurial talents of Matthew Le Tissier, and would have loved to have seen him sign for Chelsea. At a lunch sponsored by the Sunday Express, Matthew found himself in the same room as Lawrie McMenemy. Showing his wicked sense of humour, Matthew pulled his cheque book from his pocket and made a cheque out to McMenemy for £7million. At the foot of the cheque he put 'For Matthew Le Tissier'.

The cheque was promptly passed across to Lawrie's table via a waiter. Lawrie roared with laughter and despatched a note back, saying: 'You'll never get Le Tissier playing for a London club. He'll only play where there are seagulls and sandy shore.' Undeterred, Matthew wrote another cheque for £7million and scribbled on the bottom: 'From Chelsea-on-Sea Football Club'. Again McMenemy saw the funny side and roared with laughter. However, reporters witnessing the exchange totally misread the situation and subsequently reported that Chelsea had officially made a £7million bid for Le Tissier. Incidentally, Le Tissier was another autograph that Matthew successfully obtained, thereby increasing his collection.

If any of you still have any doubt that Matthew was a true fan, then you might recall with surprise when I tell you that Matthew joined the Chelsea Independent Supporters Association (CISA) in the late 1980s, before any Chelsea fan had heard of him. His loyalty to CISA probably helped them gain an exclusive interview with the great man in 1994.

The subsequent article helped Matthew to impose his thoughts and beliefs to supporters who had grown tired of watching Chelsea underachieve and a time when Chelsea, led by Hoddle, were on the verge of an FA Cup Final appearance against Manchester United. The piece also gave an insight into how Matthew became financially involved with the club via a quarter-page advertisement in the Financial Times. The interview gave no indication of Bates' forthcoming indifferences to his financial contribution that were to surface over the coming months and years.

Such was Matthew's love of football that quite often his business meetings would only last ten minutes, to be followed by a 25-minute chat about the previous evening's game.

Other insights into Matthew's love of the game and his acceptance as a genuine fan came from Tom Watt. Tom is known to many as Lofty from EastEnders, but, since leaving the soap, he has developed a critically acclaimed writing career. Tom and Matthew met on several occasions and always exchanged jovial banter surrounding all things football.

Tom recalls one particular occasion when himself and Matthew discussed a Chelsea v Arsenal match. It was the game in which Nigel Spackman lost his cool and punched Martin Keown on the back of his head. Spackman was subsequently sent off.

"I spoke to him to have an argument about him applauding Nigel Spackman off the pitch. I asked was giving Spackman a standing ovation really setting an example?"

It might not have been Lofty's, but Matthew's reaction was no different to that of 20,000 other loyal supporters that day who live and breathe Chelsea. In the same moving extract, Tom again offers a further insight into the characteristics of Matthew Harding the real supporter:

"As a football fan, you really do think this bloke is one of us. He was just the sort of person you would choose to go to a football match with. He was opinionated but massively well informed. There are people who know a lot about the game but don't have the passion, and there are people at football matches who go completely bonkers without understanding what's going on in front of them. But he had both, he was very well informed, had strong opinions and jumped up and down. He had nothing at all to do with that kind of executive box mentality which says I wonder if Ryan Giggs is going to play well today. All he wanted was for Frank Sinclair to kick him up in the air. He didn't really talk 'football speak', although he could appreciate the other teams' players and would say 'I wish we could sign him.'

Personally, I think that single paragraph would adequately sum up exactly how you and I would like to be described in the event of our demise. It eloquently sums up exactly what supporting Chelsea is all about. In this article, I hope I have given you a greater insight into the life of Matthew Harding. I apologise to Alyson Rudd for relying so heavily on her excellent book, but it really is the most complete and moving description of the life of Matthew Harding that I could find. If you haven't yet purchased it, I urge you to go out and buy it. You will not be disappointed.

I'll leave you with one final extract from Alyson's book. Once again it comes from Tom Watt. The first 50% of the extract confirms what the majority of Chelsea supporters already knew if Matthew had lived long enough to have been given the chance; the final words, unfortunately, confirm that you should never believe everything a Gooner tells you:

"He would have been a hugely popular chairman of Chelsea. He would have either gone down in history as someone who completely revolutionised the role, someone who was amazing, or he would have been a complete disaster."

Juvenile D

ISSUE 18 December 2001

Application for a New Post

Well, it appears that what was common knowledge on the rumour mill was true. Colin Hutchinson, our Managing Director, is to retire at the end of the season. It's not for me to speculate or confirm that any rumours of a fall out with Ken Bates are true or not – my finances are particularly stretched at this time of the year without getting drawn into any libel action. However, I do feel that we should offer our thanks to Colin for the fine work he has done. I can remember when news of his appointment first filtered through. I couldn't believe that a club of our supposed class had the gall to try and improve itself by pretending that employing someone from Wimbledon would be a step in the right direction. How wrong I was.

If it hadn't been for Colin's vision and dedication, we would probably never have enjoyed the success we have done over the previous years. His persuasive tongue has seen a multitude of foreign stars sign on the dotted line for Chelsea. In some cases, this feat has left us licking our lips in anticipation. I don't know what you said to those players across the negotiating table but I'd hate to cross swords with you across the poker table – you sure seem to play a convincing hand. Colin's departure will unfortunately leave a void to be filled. I mean, where do you find someone who is capable of matching his achievements?

I've only ever met Colin once, and he probably wouldn't recall it. It was a cold day behind the East Stand and he was hurrying to get into the stand. I approached him with apparent nerves of steel and politely asked him to sign a football I was getting autographed for a friend of mine. Almost without looking up he replied "certainly", and without breaking stride put his signature firmly in a space left on the ball. He had accomplished the task with minimum effort and without any disruption to his intended plan, a sign of someone with class.

So where should we look for his replacement? How about me? I'd just love to do that job. I can see myself now, relaxing in an oak panelled office, sitting in a reclining chair, discussing business over the phone with a multitude of players' agents. But do I have the qualifications to fill the role? I believe so. I'm now approaching my best years and can call on vast experience in an industry where customer satisfaction and safety is paramount. I've supported Chelsea for longer than the current chairman, so that must stand me in good stead. I also come from a stable, flawless background and have recently completed a year-long course in management. I can see you are warming to me already, aren't you? Just imagine it, Juvenile D in a place of power within the confines of Chelsea Village. What fun we'd all have.

Unfortunately I'd have to seriously ask myself if I could work with the current chairman, Ken Bates. On the surface we appear to be vastly different characters and it may not be a match made in heaven. I'm not sure if he'd ever leave me to get on with the job or whether he would be constantly looking over my shoulder. Surely he wouldn't argue if I managed to persuade a few stars to join his beloved football club? I've already worked out that the back five of Cudicini, Babayaro, Terry, Gallas and Melchiot could be the backbone of the team for the next decade. It's just other areas that need strengthening.

How could he possibly offer any argument against me spending £70-80m to secure the services of Rivaldo, Figo and Beckham to supplement the emerging talents of Sam Dalla Bona? After all, what is another £80m on a debt that is already colossal? Chill out, Ken, we know you have access to this publication so just take a deep breath and think about remortgaging again. I'm sure it will be OK – trust me, I've done a management course. Just think of the service that midfield would provide the front two of Hasselbaink and Gudj*hn*en. I'm sure the domestic glory would soon be followed by European glory, and everybody knows that this would generate huge funds to chip away at our enormous debt. I can see you are really warming to me now, Ken, aren't you?

With reference to my salary, I realise that it is current business etiquette not to disclose the current incumbent's salary. Therefore, I can only speculate as to what Colin received each year. Consequently, I would be happy to do the job for in the region of £50,000 per year. I know that this would represent a considerable saving for you but there is method in my madness. You see, this wouldn't be what I consider a real job, more of a love affair. Financial reimbursement is only required to feed Doris and the urchins. Myself, I'd just be happy with being around Chelsea Village all day and playing my part in ensuring my beloved team dominate football for years to come.

I can almost feel that you are sorely tempted to give me a ring, aren't you, Ken? Let me offer you further persuasion. I can join the Village staff at a moment's notice. Well, 28 days actually, but that is a mere grain of sand in life's hourglass, and I can be in position to sit on Colin's shoulder for the final few months of the season. This would enable me to pick up the tricks of the trade, learn the little secrets that you don't get fed on a management course and generally get to know how the world of Chelsea Village operates.

I realise that competition for the post will be fierce, so I don't expect an answer in the next few days. Be careful, Ken, this is a very important decision you have to make, so please be sure you make the right choice. However, don't take too long. Another employer may well snap my services up. Just think Cudicini, Melchiot, Gallas, Terry, Babayaro, Dalla Bona, Beckham, Figo, Rivaldo, Hasselbaink and G*djoh*sen – that should whet your appetite. Ken – I can be contacted at all the usual places listed in this fanzine if you decide to take me up on this offer.

Juvenile D

*****

You Must Be Joking

An Arsenal fan, a Sp*rs fan and a Chelsea fan were all in Saudi Arabia, sharing a crate of smuggled booze. All of a sudden, the police rushed in and arrested them. After a long trial, during which their lawyer pleaded for clemency, they were sentenced to life imprisonment. By a stroke of luck, however, it was a Saudi national holiday the day after their trial finished, and the extremely benevolent Sheikh decided they could be released after receiving just twenty lashes each of the whip.

As they were preparing for their punishment, the Sheikh suddenly said "It's my wife's birthday today, and she has asked me to allow each of you one wish before your whipping."

The Arsenal fan was first in line. He thought for a while and then said: "Please tie a pillow to my back."

This was done, but the pillow only lasted ten lashes before the whip went through, and the Arse fan had to be carried away, bleeding and crying with pain when the punishment was done.

The Sp*rs fan was up next, and after watching the scene, said: "Please fix two pillows on my back." But even with two pillows, the whip went through after 15 lashes.

The Chelsea supporter was the last up, but before he could say anything the Sheikh turned to him and said: "You are from by far the best part of London – Chelsea has some of the finest restaurants, nightclubs and hotels in the whole of the Capital, and your football team is surely the finest in the world. In recognition of this, you may have two wishes… "

The Chelsea fan replied: "Cheers mate, your most royal and merciful highness, and for your kind sentiments may I request for my first wish that you give me not twenty but one hundred lashes?"

The Sheikh was astounded and said: "You are indeed a very brave man, and if one hundred lashes is what you desire, then so be it. And your second wish?"

"Tie the Sp*rs fan to my back!"

Chelsea Sven

Thanks For Everything Roberto - We'll Miss You!

ISSUE 19 March 2002

Chelsea/Rangers

Recently on our website's message board, there has been a little discussion about the Chelsea/Rangers connection. Regular contributor Chelsea Chris was, for me, correct in stating that it started after a friendly match in aid of the Bradford Fire Disaster Appeal.

I remember the match well. Going back a bit further, I remember the days when the Shed used to chant for either Rangers or Celtic until it reached a crescendo, always ending with a chorus of Chelsea. Chelsea in the Sixties, Seventies and Eighties always attracted a Scottish support, probably because of the many Scots who played for us.

Back to 1985: Chelsea hastily arranged a match with Glasgow Rangers the Friday after the Bradford fire, to raise funds for the victims' families. Over three thousand Rangers fans travelled down to London for the friendly and mixed in the pubs of Chelsea. At that time, it was fairly rare to see so many away fans in the home pubs at Chelsea; even rarer, so many in full colour and singing.

The Rangers fans, however, came with a hand of friendship, not trouble, and after some initial looks and stand-offs in some pubs, were welcomed. The friendship and camaraderie continued during the match, with Chelsea taking a 3-1 lead, the Shed sang "Let them score", as we dominated. Rangers did get another goal back!

The Shed, towards the end and as an act of friendship, sang "We hate Celtic", to which the Rangers fans reciprocated with "We hate T*ttenham"! The singing and drinking continued after the match into the late hours, and many new friends were made.

The following February, Chelsea played a return friendly at Ibrox. Nearly two thousand Chelsea went up for the midweek fixture and, like our Rangers counterparts, we sang in the Rangers pubs and the streets of Glasgow, and were warmly welcomed. Like the first game, the result was 3-2, but this time in Rangers' favour.

The following March, I went to Ibrox to see my one and only Old Firm match. It ended in a 4-4 draw. Travelling back on the overnight train, I got back to London to watch Chelsea beat Man City 5-4 in the Full Members Cup Final. Seventeen goals in two days! What surprised me at Ibrox was the selling of Chelsea flags. What I did enjoy was the warm friendship given by the home fans.

Over the next few years, Rangers fans made regular trips to watch Chelsea in English league matches, and a few Chels made reciprocal journeys to Ibrox. Chelsea/Rangers bobble hats appeared and the friendship was healthy. What became disturbing for some, were the political elements linking up with each other and turning the friendship into a political one. For most Chelsea fans, their team is their religion, and the same could be said about Rangers fans and their side.

For Celtic-supporting Chelsea fans, of which there are many, and other Chelsea fans who had no affiliation to Rangers, the link became strained. Likewise up in Glasgow, not every Rangers fan supports Chelsea. Many of them like T*ttenham (spit) and various other English sides.

The friendship amongst supporters still exists, but not quite the same as its peaks in the late-80s and early-90s. In the late-80s, some sections of the Chelsea support blamed the Rangers fans for crowd trouble at Chelsea matches, whiles some sections of the Rangers fans used to blame Chelsea fans for crowd trouble at Rangers matches.

The T-shirt sellers outside both grounds keep the links up, with various Chelsea/Rangers T-shirts. The recent incident at Aberdeen was blamed by some Rangers fans on the Chelsea Headhunters – eyewitnesses saw them wearing the shirts! Such T-shirts are, of course, on sale outside Ibrox as well as Stamford Bridge.

I see nothing wrong with friendships between clubs of two different countries. Since the 90s, Chelsea have competed in European football and many new friends have been made abroad. For me, and from a footballing perspective, such relationships can only be good for the game.

The Independent

*****

D-I-MATT-E-O, singing D-I-MATT-E-O

I was going to write about other team's players. I was going to write about, amongst others, Nigel Winterburn's last ever FA Cup match, and how he got stuck in the toilet at half-time and how no-one told him the second-half was about to start, and how everyone was on the pitch waiting for him while he was wiping his a*se. Great team-mates and manager, eh Nige? I was going to write how he was always horrible to Chelsea – because you always were horrible, Nigel.

But now his FA Cup history is just that. Chelsea have knocked West Ham out of the FA Cup and because he's such an old git, that's the end of Winterburn's FA Cup contributions. Old Nige's something like 38 now, and it's OK if he retires from football. Time doesn't stand still. What should Glenn Roeder do with horrible, ex-FA Cup man, Winterburn? During the TV interviews with grinning Chelsea players, I think we got the answer. Drifting from the un'appy 'Ammers' dressing room came the strains of an old song. From Chelsea's ecstasy to West Ham's XTC – *"We're only making plans for Nigel"*!

However, something struck me hard in the pit of my stomach when I happened to have a look at the sports news on the internet on 19th February. It said a 31-year-old had to retire from football. A 31-year-old who played for Chelsea. A 31-year-old who had scored an absolutely brilliant goal inside 42 seconds on his first appearance at Wembley with the mighty Blues.

I, and a few others, had waited for 26 years for Chelsea to win a proper trophy. Robeto Di Matteo walked onto the lush, green Wembley turf, jinked one way then another, before unleashing an unstoppable shot. The ball rocketed into the roof of the net, the Chelsea roar lifted what passed for a roof over Wembley's Olympic Gallery, and Robbie's dad described to Robbie's blind sister how her brother had got the ball in his own half, dribbled past two Middlesbrough midfielders and from 35 yards out, had shot… and scored! For that, Robbie, if for nothing else, you will be welcome in my house until the day you die. I will never forget what you've done for us. Chelsea salutes you. Then, of course, he does the same again three years later, in the 2000 FA Cup Final. Brilliant. If ever you want a player in your side, it's one that consistently scores the winning goal in a Cup Final.

Well now, Robbie, you're 31, a multi-millionaire, own a restaurant in Fulham, got a young daughter with a pretty wife (despite rumours of nine-bob notes being straighter), time on your hands and hundreds of thousands of Chelsea fans who will put you up in their house and wine and dine you, and ask what was going through your head when you got the ball in your own half, dribbled past two Middlesbrough midfielders and, from 35 yards, you'd shot… and scored!

So, all in all, Robbie, although it's very sad that you broke your leg so painfully in three places, and we missed out on another four or five years of your particular brand of Italian skills, you've already done enough to live forever in our hearts, which is more than 99.99% of the world's population can claim. Ta. Ta very much. Grazie (that's "Ta very much" in Italian to those that don't speak the lingo like what I do!).

Slim Jim

*****

Got a Spare Ticket?

Just before Christmas, an exiled Chelsea supporting friend of mine rang me from Guernsey to ask whether I'd be able to get him and his girlfriend a couple of tickets for the Liverpool game. "No problem", I told him, as I'd heard someone else might have a couple going begging.

After making sure that the spare tickets were still available, I called my friend in the Channel Islands and told him to book his flight to London. I arranged to meet them prior to the game on the Fulham Road, where I would give them their tickets.

Now, my friend who had the spare tickets was, when hearing that the people flying over for the game were a couple, kind enough to sort out two seats together for them. This involved him asking two season ticket holders to swap their usual seats for those for which he has spare tickets. The season ticket holders duly obliged and everything was set in place.

My friend who had the spare tickets was selling them on behalf of a couple of people who were unable to make the game themselves. This was because the fixture – originally scheduled for Saturday 15th December – had been put back a day to the Sunday for the benefit of the armchair viewers and Sky TV. The tickets in the West Stand Lower Tier had cost £35 each.

The people who originally purchased these tickets obviously wanted their money back and the couple from Guernsey were more than grateful for the chance to watch the game; and paying face value for them was the least they would do.

The day of the game arrived and at 3.45pm outside Fulham Town Hall, the couple from Guernsey, my friend with the season tickets and myself met up, and all parties were introduced. My friend produced the season tickets and the couple handed him the £70 for the West Stand tickets.

Suddenly, eight policemen surrounded us and accused my friend of being a tout. He was asked to step aside and explain his actions, while the recipients of the season tickets were asked to step the other way and explain theirs. I was stuck in the middle and was worried that it had all gone horribly wrong, as I watched my friends being systematically asked for identity and to empty their pockets. To cap it all, they were also videoed by another police officer. One officer, a sergeant, was told that season tickets were, according to the rules, fully transferable but, despite being given this information, he was unsure that he was being told the truth and demanded to see proof that this was the case.

By this time, it was 3.55pm and kick off was only minutes away. My friend who had provided the season tickets told me to go, and that he would sort things out. I left, but for the remainder of the game and until I saw him afterwards, I was worried that both him and the couple might have missed the game. Thankfully they didn't, but not before they'd been delayed until 4pm and made to miss the kick off.

While understanding that the police have a job to do as far as the touts are concerned, their manner was somewhat intimidating and they seemed totally unsympathetic when the story of why the tickets were being exchanged was explained. Although they didn't bother to arrest anyone or confiscate any tickets – after all, they had no grounds – the fact that they took serious convincing leaves questions about the job the police do regarding touts.

To most Chelsea supporters attending matches at Stamford Bridge who arrive via Fulham Broadway Tube, the usual touts are there regularly. When plying their trade, they seem to make their actions blindingly obvious and you don't need to have gone through a police training course at Hendon to be able to spot them.

It is common knowledge that the police have an arrest quota to fulfil, but surely trying to make up the numbers by collaring people who are innocently exchanging tickets between genuine supporters is an over exertion of police power. Perhaps the police would consider a 'safe area' where genuine supporters might be able to meet and exchange any spare tickets they might have without fear of being arrested for touting.

Those who are seeking tickets or, indeed, those who might find themselves with one or two too many, could do worse than contact www.ticketexchange.freeuk.com, which is a service that has been set up by Stingray, one of the Chelsea Official Website's most respected chatters.

By using this free service, those without a ticket are put in touch with those who might have some spare. All tickets are sold and exchanged for face value and, to date, there have been hundreds of satisfied customers.

Tommy Ticket

*****

Matthew Aston

On Wednesday 16th January 2002, in a 3rd Round FA Cup replay against Norwich at Stamford Bridge, Gianfranco Zola scored a goal that for many will be one of the finest they have seen. It will, no doubt, be a leading contender in BBC TV's Match of the Day goal of the season competition for this year's FA Cup campaign.

The goal by Zola was a breathtaking strike and, in years to come, will surely rank alongside Peter Osgood's goal at Old Trafford in the 1970 FA Cup Final, and Robbie Di Matteo's at Wembley in the FA Cup Final of 1997. However, it was not just pure brilliance that made the goal so special.

When interviewed after the game, Franco let it be known that he was dedicating the goal to the memory of Matthew Aston, a young boy who had died days earlier from a form of brain cancer. Zola made no fuss about what he's done. He simply told the story of a boy for whom he was a hero, and for whom he kept his word.

Matthew had, as a dying wish, asked to meet Gianfranco. Through Chelsea's Gary Staker, the player responded immediately. The last time

Gianfranco visited Matthew was on the Thursday before Chelsea's FA Cup 3rd Round tie at Norwich.

When it was time to leave, Matthew, who had been holding Gianfranco's hand throughout the meeting, would not let it go. All in the room knew that Matthew would live for only a few more hours. Gianfranco promised to dedicate the next goal he scored to Matthew.

Matthew Aston, aged eight, died on Saturday 5th January. As we are all aware, the next goal that Gianfranco Zola scored was the one that captivated the football world. The goal was one of sublime brilliance; a goal that only a magician such as Zola could conjure. It was a goal that will live long in the minds of those who witnessed it. Those fortunate will be able to say in years to come: "I was there".

In Chelsea history, the goal will be ranked amongst the finest ever seen at Stamford Bridge. Franco's act in dedicating it to Matthew Aston made the strike greater still.

The dignity and sincerity with which Gianfranco told the story of Matthew, gave proof to the fact that the Sardinian is a giant of a person, despite his diminutive appearance. Both his goal and his magnanimous gesture are confirmation that he is probably the greatest footballer Chelsea were fortunate to have ever had.

Chels Guevara

*****

You Must Be Joking

The CIA had a vacancy for a hitman. The final three candidates for the job were whittled down to a West Ham fan, an Arsenal fan and a Chelsea supporter.

The hopefuls' last assessment was a test of their nerve and involved the CIA instructor taking the candidates one by one to a door and, after giving them a gun, telling them: "We must make sure that you're able to follow our instructions to the letter. Inside the room, you'll find a Sp*rs fan sitting on a chair. Whatever happens, you must shoot him dead. If you can't do it, you haven't got what it takes."

Before the door to the room had even opened, the West Ham fan lost his bottle and said: "I can't do it. Even though I'm from the hardest part of

London, I haven't got the heart to take a life in cold blood." "Hard luck", said the CIA man, "You've failed the test."

The same instructions were given to the Arsenal fan, but unlike the Hammer, he went in. However, after a minute there was a loud knock on the door, and when the instructor opened it, the Gooner came out. With tears in his eyes because he knew he had failed, he said: "Even though I hate Sp*rs, I haven't got the heart to kill an innocent victim."

"Unlucky", the CIA instructor told him, "If you can't do that, there's no way you can work for us. Sorry, but haven't passed the test."

Finally it was the Chelsea supporter's turn. In an instant, he went into the room and within seconds shots rang out, followed by screaming and sound of crashing and banging on the walls.

After a couple of minutes the Chelsea supporter emerged. He wiped the sweat from his brow and said to the CIA instructor: "I don't know what went wrong there but the gun was loaded with blanks. I ended up having to batter the Sp*rs fan to death with the chair. Can I have the job?"

The Joker

ISSUE 20 April 2002

That's Football

Anyone who has ever tried to organise an event will know that nothing ever goes quite to plan. For months it was mooted that a group of us would go to Watford to pay homage to the most successful manager in our glorious club's history. When the trip was first publicised, the response was fantastic.

However, finding a suitable date became almost impossible. Coupled with the fact that, despite what Ken Bates may think, we don't have the vast funds to purchase tickets up front, we found that we had a real dilemma on our hands. Just as we thought the trip would not happen, and we were feeling somewhat disillusioned, assistance came from an unexpected source. A Chelsea supporter, who I'll only identify as D to preserve his anonymity, approached us on the fanzine stall and gave us a contact number of someone who would be able to help. Once again to preserve anonymity, I will only refer to this second person as G.

G was contacted and, much to our delight, smoothed the path for a party of Chelsea supporters to visit Vicarage Road. All that remained now was to once again publicise the event and determine the precise number of people who wanted to pay homage.

Ten decided to make the trip. When we originally put the idea of a visit to the readers of this fanzine and those who read our website, we had more than fifty responses. Due to necessity (and, of course, the last minute nature of the arrangements) the Good Friday date was the most convenient for all parties. We apologise to all those for whom the Bank Holiday date made the visit impossible.

After exchanging numerous e-mails and phone calls, it was agreed that our party of ten would meet up outside Watford's souvenir shop at a predetermined time. With the tickets safely collected on the morning of the match, Doris, Urchin D and myself waited outside the shop for the others to arrive. Weather-wise, we couldn't have selected a better day. The sun was shining and there wasn't a cloud in the sky.

Soon, the others began to arrive. I hadn't formally met any of them before, but I felt as I if didn't need to. After all, they had all formed part of the Chelsea family we were all so familiar with and proud of. With tickets safely despatched to all relevant parties, it was agreed that we would meet up again once in the ground. Doris and myself decided to hang around outside the ground as one of our party had yet to arrive.

Outside the ground, there wasn't the intense activity that seems to envelop Stamford Bridge on match days, but there was still a certain amount of hustle and bustle. A camera crew from BBC TV's Football Focus were busy interviewing supporters about the recent ITV Digital fiasco and the effects they thought it would have on their club. With approximately two hours still to kickoff, I decided to venture off in search of a film for my camera that I hoped would capture some pictures later in the day.

Casually I walked down the road and found a newsagent. Once inside, two females adorned in official Watford uniforms immediately accosted me. Blocking my way, they asked if I was one of the many Chelsea supporters who were coming to Vicarage Road today. A little bemused, I wondered just exactly what G had informed those employed by Watford Football Club. I didn't need to know how they knew I was a Chelsea supporter – the CFC jacket obviously gave the game away. After a polite conversation, we wished each other well and I returned to the ground to rejoin Doris.

Sitting on a wall whiling away time, I looked up to see three vanloads of Police park about ten yards down the road. The officers immediately started to disembark and head in our general direction. Thoughts of Chelsea in the 1980s flashed through my mind, and any apprehensions I had about this trip not being a good idea immediately surfaced. However, I couldn't have been more wrong. The officers merely glanced at us and then dispersed to go about their general match day duties.

By now the sun was beating down and it was very untypical Bank Holiday weather. It's not often you can get a tan in March. Suddenly, the stewards sprang into action and started to move the barricades that were blocking the road down to the East Stand. Not sure of what exactly was happening we moved closer to observe proceedings. Peering down the road, I could see a coach emerging through the traffic. As it got closer, it became obvious that it was the Watford team coach.

Having an inquisitive nature, I tried to see who exactly was on the coach. I could see a bald head, but I wasn't sure if it was Luca or not. By now, the coach was right next to us. The figure I'd spotted wasn't Luca but turned out to be Ray Wilkins.

What happened next was quite amusing. I looked at Ray and smiled. Ray looked at me, glanced away and then looked back in disbelief, looked away again and then looked back with a broad smile on his face. It was almost as if Ray was taken aback at seeing several people resplendent in Chelsea colours.

Finally, the one remaining member of our party turned up. Kick off was only 15 minutes away, so we entered the ground. Upon taking our seats, it was immediately noticeable how different it was to Stamford Bridge. Children were openly encouraged to attend and were allowed to congregate at the front of the stand to watch the players warm up. Stewards were almost nonexistent and the atmosphere seemed so friendly.

Kevin Hitchcock was immediately in front of us, helping with the pre-match preparation. Seizing our opportunity, we bellowed his name. Kevin turned around and, seeing the Chelsea regalia, gave us a beaming smile. He walked over and willingly posed for a picture; and he almost looked pleased to see us. More importantly, Kevin was to play a major role in realising our predetermined objective later in the day.

As promised by G, our seats were adjacent to the Watford dugout. The game itself was almost immaterial. It's hard to get emotive about a game when you don't really care who wins. Nevertheless, it was entertaining at times and Watford, under the influence of Luca and his coaching team, played some nice football. However, watching Watford wasn't the real reason for our visit. It was to pay homage to Luca.

From our seats we were able to watch the great man in action. It was almost like being back at Stamford Bridge a couple of years ago. Luca was almost manic in his desire to see his team win. Every good pass was met with encouragement, whilst every misdemeanour was greeted with that look of anguish we all recognised as coming from the heart. The game eventually ended in a 0-0 stalemate and the supporters began to file out of the stadium. After the game, we remained in our seats until the stadium was empty, save for the players warming down. It was now some twenty minutes since the game had ended, and we spent our time talking to a guy from Look at the Stars, a Watford fanzine.

Kevin Hitchcock was milling about on the pitch and, once he'd finished talking with his opposite number from Bradford, he sauntered over and had a chat with us. Seconds later, Luca strode purposefully down the tunnel and emerged from its darkness into the by now dwindling sunlight to greet us. After overcoming the initial shock that it was actually happening, and that it was the man himself in front of us, the atmosphere became very relaxed. Realising that time was at a premium, it was impossible to ask Luca all those questions everyone had taken hours thinking of. Thankfully, we were able to get our one real message across:

It was explained to Luca that, although there were only a small number of us present, we represented thousands of Chelsea supporters who appreciated and, indeed, were very grateful for everything he'd done for Chelsea Football Club.

Luca seemed genuinely touched by our message and proceeded to shake us all by the hand. He then gave up more of his valuable time posing for a multitude of pictures, answering questions, holding conversations and signing various pieces of memorabilia.

Often when you get the chance to meet someone you idolise, you end up disappointed. However, Luca was different. He made time for us and genuinely seemed to be touched by our presence. When offered our condolences for the shabby way that he was treated by Chelsea Football Club officials, he retained his dignity and, without a hint of reticence, simply said: "That's football."

Sadly, our time with Luca soon came to an end and he strode over to attend the press conference. Our little party took time out to bask in what had just happened, and suddenly all the heartache associated with planning the trip seemed irrelevant. As they say: Mission Accomplished. Finally, before I close this article I must once again offer thanks to G and D. Without their help, I doubt whether this particular adventure would ever have got off the ground.

Also, I must thank everyone we met from Watford Football Club, including Terry Byrne and Ray Lewington, who were good enough to have a quick chat with us during the game. Thanks also to Kevin Hitchcock for the "Good luck to Chelsea" message that he gave us.

Juvenile D

*****

You Must Be Joking

If you're Chelsea, you can beat Sp*rs, you can beat Man United, but you can't beat sex.

On the other hand, if you're Spurs, you can beat a carpet, you can beat a rug, but you'll never beat the Chelsea!

Deep down, though, Sp*rs fans are OK … about six foot under is deep enough!

Why did Bates take a pencil with him when he went to see the accountant? Because he wanted to draw a line under the Chelsea Village debts!

What will be going up and never coming down? The price of watching Chelsea!

What do you call a man with no ears? Ken Bates!

Ken Bates died and a few days later, the devil dragged him by the hair to the Pearly Gates. St Peter asked him: "What do you think you're doing? I don't want him."

"Oh come on, do me a favour", replied the devil, "I've only had him three days and he's converted the furnace into a hotel!

Emile Heskey's wife wanted him locked up – she had had enough of him so she went to the police and told them, "Please help, my husband has been hitting me." The police gave the following advice … "Don't worry. Just carry a goal post in each hand and he'll never hit you!"

The Joker

ISSUE 21 August 2002

Neil Smith - Chelsea Supporter

When I was a kid in the mid-Sixties, I was intrigued by the regular graffiti which seemed to manifest itself overnight on the bus shelter, local village hall or on the Scout hut nearby to where I lived. What did it all mean? Who did it? Commonly, there were statements such as 'Ban The Bomb', 'Make Love - Not War!', 'Mods Rule!', 'Elvis Is King' and 'I Love Paul McCartney'.

As I neared 10 years of age, I was tipped off as to who the perpetrators of the slogans were. As they were in their teens, they were able to stay out later (after sundown) and partake in this unsociable pastime.

Despite my good upbringing, I longed to be able to add my own contribution. As it was, I managed to 'bribe' a schoolmate's older brother to do it for me. It was a bit like paying for an ad in the local paper and being charged per letter. What is required needs to effective, but short and to the point. I managed to get my options down to a short list of three. They were …

Chelsea For The Cup; Osgood Is God; Osgood For England

A few days after my request, the following appeared daubed on the wall of the "Garibaldi" pub …

OSGOOD CHELSEA

Not really what was required, but a start nonetheless. It provoked interest from others for a time until it disappeared, covered by an entry that stated that the landlord was watering down the beer.

I digress from the main event. As I became more 'worldly-wise' and began to venture beyond the borders of Suburbia, I managed to view other artists' offerings and the words 'Osgood' and 'Chelsea' became inseparable.

When the man finally left the Bridge, I remember a tearful young lady ringing a radio station and proclaiming that Chelsea without Os was like chips with no fish. A fellow Shedite called me to say that he was checking out Southampton's fixture list as he would need an 'Ossie fix' as soon as possible as he feared watching Chelsea would no longer give him a buzz.

Several weeks later, he and my brother came to blows outside the Bridge when he suggested that the 'Number 9 shirt' be retired and that Chris Garland, the then incumbent, was a ... well, not up to standard! Sad ... but understandable.

The hairs on the back of my neck still stand up whenever I watch the re-run of the 1970 FA Cup Final replay and Ossie's moment. For years afterwards, whenever the boys appeared in the change golden yellow stockings, my Chelsea clique would glance at each other and reminisce with a nod and a wink, even if we were playing QPR or Palace.

However, some of my favourite Osgood memories saw him wearing the 'Hungarian' colours of red shirts, white shorts and green socks.

One day at Loftus Rd, at least three Rangers players were bearing down when, with one pirouette, they all fell in Osgood's wake in a scene that might have come from the "Keystone Cops". The late Brian Moore delighted in showing the clip of film again and again on his "Big Match" programme that used to be broadcast on Sundays. ITV even set *it* to music; "Something" (in the way be moves) by Shirley Bassey.

Always the showman, there was that time at the Goldstone Ground when the Brighton crowd were baying for his dismissal whilst being lectured by the ref. There were no red or yellow cards in these days and, as Ossie trotted towards the tunnel, the home support erupted in joy. Not for long though as, after crossing the touchline, he turned and ran back onto the pitch, much to the dismay of the previously rejoicing Brighton fans.

I could go on and on, but I think Tommy Docherty still says it all for us on the 'Chelsea History Video'. He says, "A great right foot, a great left foot, brilliant in the air, a big heart ... what more could you ask for?"

Only last season, when making my way home from an evening fixture, I stopped off in an Earls Court watering hole and caught sight of Angus, one of the original Shed Boys.

As we were talking, I asked him how long he'd been following Chelsea? "Well", he said, "Put it this way ... I was at Burnley the day that

" … I immediately interjected with, "The day that Ossie scored the best goal you'd ever seen?"

"Yes, indeed", came the reply. How does the song go?

"We've got some memories, albeit from the 70's, when Ossie and Co restored our pride..."

Thanks Peter, for all those memories.

Neil Smith

*****

Build A New Ground? This Is How I'd Do It ...

With Chelsea Village plc in an obvious financial crisis, MHBAWA makes no apologies for reprinting a slightly reworked version of an article that first appeared in issue 14. With the collapse of the ITV Digital deal and the general concern about football's viability, the Financier considers what he'd do if he had the money to pay off Chelsea's debts and rebuild Stamford Bridge. His plans are for a stadium with a 55,000 capacity.

One of the most common 'objections' to the original article was that Chelsea would never attract 55,000 regular supporters. In my opinion, attendances of that figure would be easily achievable if the admission prices for games were cheaper.

Those currently in charge of Chelsea Village have planned for an approximate 42,000 all-seated stadium and expect the demand for tickets to match the capacity. Last season, most of the Chelsea homes games sold out with the current and, in our opinion, extortionate pricing structure.

To fill an imaginary 55,000 capacity ground would mean that the club would have to attract 13,000 'new' supporters. That is discounting either a 1500, 3000 or 5,000 away following. With a sensible policy that came within most people's budgets, finding extra supporters, especially in a city the size of London, should not pose too big a problem. Here are some figures for the income that Chelsea might expect – should both a new stadium be built and the following pricing structure implemented: Standard seating

17,000 seats at £14 x 19 games = £4,522,000

18,000 seats at £22 x 19 games = £7,524,000
Away section 5,000 seats at £18 x 19 games = £1,710,000
Family section 3,000
Children £8 x 19 games = £456,000
2,000 Adults £14 x 19 games = £532,000
'5 star' class seating 7,000 seats at £50 x 19 games = £6,650,000
Executive boxes, seating 30 people 10 boxes at £3k x 19 games = £570,000

The above revised figures give a total of £21,964,000. Admittedly, it is probably less than the figure that Chelsea will earn from just season ticket sales alone in this, the 2002/2003 season, but all in all, I think it is a sound base from which to develop our financial strategy.

The prices for the family section would mean that an adult with two juniors, aged up to 16 years, would be able to attend a game for a total sum of £40. A 19 League and all domestic cup games season ticket for an adult and two minors would cost £760. That is not only £40 cheaper than the present comparable price, but would allow for 5,000 patrons as opposed to the 2,199 that the present Shed End Family Centre currently allows for. Ken Bates once stated during a "TalkSport" radio appearance that at the time, there was a waiting list of over 1000 for a family section season ticket. How many more would there be with a larger and cheaper section?

The price of £14 for admission per head for the 'cheaper' of the standard class seating, would work out at £266 for a 19 game season ticket, while a similar arrangement for a £22 seat would cost £4l8. These two prices are in contrast to the present 'renewal before April' prices of around £485 for the Lower Matthew Harding Stand and those in the Upper Tier would, had they applied in time, have paid £635,

Of course, those in the Upper Tier automatically get domestic cup games included in the price of their tickets. However, even if Chelsea managed to get eight home ties in both the FA and League Cups, at £22 per game, the total cost is £631, £4 pounds cheaper than the renewal price.

Not so at the moment, where present holders of 'all game' season tickets receive no discount or money back if Chelsea don't have any home draws. Season 00/01 for example, saw only one Cup game at Stamford Bridge. We would therefore, with our scheme, allocate all season ticket holders their own seats in the event of a home draw in either of the Cups and offer them first chance to purchase them. Using this current season as an example, an Upper Tier season ticket, with seats costing £22 on a match by match basis, would have cost a mere £440 - a saving of £195.

In issue 13, I estimated that if one programme was sold per person (using an imaginary attendance of 55,000), a profit of £2,090,000 could be achieved. I'll keep that total, and add it to the £21,964,000 I estimate that could be earned from my model of a fair pricing structure. The two figures give a total of £24,054,000, This is, of course, before any 'extra' income that home ties in the domestic competitions would bring.

During the BBC TV series entitled "'The Men Who Made Football", Ipswich Town chairman David Sheepshanks revealed that, in a season or two, even the bottom placed Premiership side would receive a figure in the region of £12m. It is difficult to foresee a scenario where Chelsea finish bottom of the table but, even if they did, adding the £12m that Sheepshanks mentioned working total gained from admission and programmes, will now give an imaginary running total of £36,054,000. This total would be boosted if Chelsea were drawn at home for any Cup games.

Then there is the merchandise. At present, Chelsea have a kit sponsored by Emirates Airlines. As a consequence, fans that purchase replica shirts now advertise an Arab airline as opposed to a car window company. I accept that the sponsorship money is important but, as a Chelsea football supporter, I would rather wear a team shirt that has no advertising on it whatsoever. Of course, if my plan were to be put into action, I'd also reinstate the 1970's Matthew Lion crest.

Should this badge return, together with an abandonment of any sponsors name, I would predict a massive sale of Chelsea shirts to those who feel aggrieved at not only having to advertise a product, but also feel a certain affiliation to the club crest that was dispensed with by Bates. As for advertising, we would, unlike Bates, make use of the fact that Stamford Bridge is directly under the flight path for aircraft landing at Heathrow airport. A few years ago, Richard Branson wanted to advertise his "Virgin" logo on the roof of one of Chelsea's stands. I'm not sure what price was offered by Branson when he made his approach but, speaking as a layman, I'd say that it would have to be worth at least a couple of million to someone or other – if only for the prestige.

Using the famous figures quoted by the disgraced Newcastle directors, it seems that a shirt costs as little as £5 to produce. Allowing for a figure of £10 for manufacture, a fair retail price for the product would be in the region of £20. Working on a conservative figure, and using basic figures to illustrate the point, sales of 100,000 shirts alone would, if there was a £10 profit margin on every item, bring in an imaginary £1m income. My figure of £20 per item is cheaper than the £30/£40 that people are asked to pay at present.

Rounding down the figures, but adding our imaginary £2m from 'roof advertising' and the imaginary £1m in from shirt sales alone, that gives us a running total of £39m income in any one financial year.

Arsenal will soon have a new stadium that will see them able to hold the biggest crowd in London. What price Mr Bates' claims now that Chelsea has one of the 'finest grounds in the country? Some time ago, Sunderland's chairman announced that there would be a reduction of prices at the Stadium Of Light. This policy was announced to avoid less than capacity attendances when, for example, a Cup clash is shown live on television.

Unlike our own current chairman, the board at Sunderland think it more important to have people in the ground as opposed to 'fans' watching the game on the box. Bates was, at the time the original of this article was written, pushing his idea of pay-per-view football matches to enable those who don't go to Stamford Bridge, the chance to see Chelsea live.

All well and good if one can't attend matches, but the priority should be to encourage as many people as possible to go and see the games live. After all, 100,000 people watching Chelsea from their sitting rooms does little to enhance the atmosphere at Stamford Bridge, Surely the best solution would be to have a ground full to capacity with adoring supporters, holding on to every Chelsea pass of the ball like their life depended upon it, AND have 100,000 pay-per-view fans.

What price pay-per-view? Using another conservative estimate, and using a an imaginary £10 price for viewing, 100,000 x 10 home games would, in theory, bring in a further £10m. Add that to our running total, and we have got an impressive imaginary total of £49m.

In the initial pail of this thesis in issue 13, my plans would be dependent upon having our debts cleared and having finance in place to rebuild the ground. Assuming this had been carried out, our £49 million would give a solid base from which we would devise our strategy for paying staff.

Not being an accountant, I have no knowledge of the workings of the Inland Revenue or, come to that, the amount of tax due on our £49m. However, I'd back a plan that would see a sum of money to be held against a tax bill, say £10m. That sum, accruing interest at a rate of 4%, would gain £400,000 per year.

That could equate to five staff members on £40,000 per year, and 10 staff members on £20,000 per year. Not much you might say, but enough to pay for 15 potentially key members of staff. We would, of course, also have our remaining £39m working total remaining with which to pay the staff and the players.

With the remaining £39m figure, we could afford to pay 50 players and associated staff £200,000 per year at a cost of £10m and still have £29m left on our imaginary running total. Allowing for a tax bill of £4m per annum, our working total still leaves us with £15m. Allowing a further £5m for other various expenses, we still have a figure of £10m left,

With the recent debate about players' wages, it has become clearer by the minute that football's 'bubble' is deflating at an ever-increasing pace. Whether the professional game will implode completely is in question, but it is now clear that the majority of future top-flight players will certainly not see the same mega wage packets that many Premiership stars can command today. Those fortunate enough to be picked for Chelsea would be given lessons on economics in the real world. Players will be expected to play for more a more realistic wage. Just exactly how some of the current Premiership breed can justify earning £25,000 / £30,000 per week, when a sizable proportion of those on the terraces would be lucky to be making that sum in a year, is a question I suspect that many supporters would like to put to at least one or two.

While everyone appreciates his goals, Jimmy Floyd Hasselbaink's wage demands are truly obscene. Even at a reported £27,000 per week, it became obvious that E*dur Gudjoh*sen's agent didn't think his player was earning enough. Whether you rate him or not, Sam Dalla Bona wanted to stay at Chelsea and, had they offered him somewhere in the region of £10k per week, I think he would have. Even though I think that even £l0k per week is extravagant, I could see Sam's point of view when other players such as Slavisa Jokanovic were earning somewhere in excess of £25,000 for the same seven days work.

Chelsea Football Club has in the past few years, without doubt, produced the finest crop of youngsters that the club has seen. Recently at least three or four prominent names are usually available for first team selection and another handful are away on loan gaining valuable league experience. Add to them the players who Chelsea have sold, sometimes without giving them a first team chance, and already one has got a potential team to play the best in the Premier League

A future Chelsea FC should aim to have the nucleus of their side from those that have come through the youth ranks. Bates, referring to his Chelsea Village plans, once spoke of a "dash for growth" policy. With the recent financial problems having made much of the news in the past couple of months, it is clear that Chelsea's 'dash for success' worked in the short-tem but the policy is now failing due to a shortfall of cash.

Working with the figures used in this article, there is still £10m,'in the kitty'. This money could be used in part to fund joint ventures with Hammersmith and Fulham Council. A £5m committment from Chelsea to both the Borough and the local amenities for the local residents, would, in effect, help Chelsea strive to be a club that really did try to get the local community involved.

That done, we'd still have £5m left. Not much but, in this imaginary potential prospectus for Chelsea Football Club, I have been using basic figures and conservative estimates of profitability. Judging from the current climate in the 'real football' world, I estimate that my figures are, and would prove to be, somewhat short of an actual realistic realisation of profit.

When Bates falls, Chelsea supporters will have to act quickly to save the club they love. It must be hoped that someone somewhere, some Blue Angel, will be on hand to lead us out of the mire and on to a brighter vision for both Chelsea and football in general.

In an article elsewhere in this edition of MHBAWA, the author wonders how anyone could afford to undertake the job of rebuilding a Stamford Bridge capable of facilitating the arrangements I have outlined above. Personally, I haven't yet given up on the hope of meeting a Chelsea supporter with the odd half billion pounds to spare – failing that, I'd like to meet 50 Blues fans with £10m or even 100 Chelsea supporters with £5m etc, etc. By the time that the figure is broken down to 30,000 Chelsea supporters, the sum each would have to invest to find the £500,000,000 I'd like to find, would be in the region of £16,000.

Some leading banking institutions now give clubs a 'mortgage' facility to enable them to purchase players. Could there ever be a possibility that the same arrangements might be given to supporters to help them gain a genuine stake in their club? £16,000, albeit at an interest-free rate, would, over a 20-year period, cost a little over £66 per month to repay.

True, the burden for supporters paying another £66 per month on top of the money they spend attending matches would not come lightly and the prospects of enough supporters actually agteeing to invest such a sum is very unlikely. That said, the club already tries to attract extra income by way of their hotel facilities, restaurants, nightclubs and museums / 'World's of Sport'. Many supporters genuinely feel they are contributing to Chelsea's long-term future by spending money in these Village inspired schemes. However, a venture with clear goals as far as the future of a business run for the benefit of a Chelsea FOOTBALL Club might inspire some to drink a few less pints each game in favour of putting a few pounds towards the cause.

As mentioned earlier, the sums used in the model to illustrate what might be done at Chelsea are somewhat conservative. If correct, the potential realisation of profit might be somewhat greater than the figures produced above. With a sensibly managed approach, the actual 'cost' to supporters of purchasing Chelsea might, with funds being directed straight to Chelsea's future by the club itself, be less than the £16,000 quoted above.

More realistically however, organisations such as "Supporters Direct" are working with supporters of many professional and amateur football clubs the length and breadth of the United Kingdom with the aim of helping them become stakeholder owners of the teams they support.

Ken Bates' vision of Chelsea is somewhat different to the one described above. Hopefully, this article might lead to some debate. However, I'll leave you, the reader, with a question … Of the two schemes - Bates' or ours' - whose do you prefer?

If after having read this you assume I'm dreaming, you'd be right - I'm dreaming "Matthew's Dream"

The Financier

ISSUE 22 October 2002

Truth Or Fiction - You Decide

A Chelsea supporting friend of mine was having a holiday, by way of a tour of the USA. One of the many places he visited was a remote bar in the hills of Nevada. He was chatting to the bartender when he spied an old Native American sitting in the comer. He had tribal gear on, long white plaits and a wrinkled, well worn face.

"Who's he?" asked the Chelsea supporter. "That's the Memory Man," said the bartender, "he knows everything. He can remember any fact. Go and try him out."

My friend went over, introduced himself, and asked whether it would be okay to put his memory to the test. As the Red Indian agreed, my friend was thinking, 'He won't know about English football.'

The memory man nodded to him and said, "Ask me anything!"

"Who won the 1970 FA Cup Final?" "Chelsea." replied the Memory Man. "Who did they beat?" "Leeds." was the reply. "And the score?" "2-1 " "Who scored Chelsea's first goal?" "Peter Osgood." was the old man's reply

My friend was 'knocked out' by this and, when he returned home, he told everyone about the Memory Man. A few years later he went back to the USA and decided to try to find the impressive Memory Man. Eventually, he arrived at the same bar and, sitting in the same seat, was the old Native American. It appeared that he had, over the years since my friend first met him, aged considerably. Showing off somewhat, my friend decided to greet the Indian in his native tongue. He approached him with the greeting,

"How." The Memory Man replied, "Diving header in the six yard box!"

Urchin D

*****

Question: Which player scored in a FA Cup final, a European Cup-Winners Cup final, a League Cup final, was in the initial squad for the 1966 World Cup, played in the 1970 World Cup, won the FA Cup with two different sides, stole the FA Cup, was a father at 17, broke a leg, had a number-one hit with one group and a number-five hit with another, necked Raquel Welch, married three times, has been banned from football and driving, was acquitted by a jury, went bankrupt, took a millionaire club chairman to court and won, bounced back to become an accomplished after-dinner speaker and TV pundit, and in the age of Gullit, Vialli, Zola and Hasselbaink was still voted Chelsea Football Club's all-time greatest player?

Answer: Peter Osgood

*****

The wisdom of Alan Corfield

Although the rest of the MHBAWA staff think that he's 'mad', Alan Corfield again appears on a couple of these pages, After all, he's young, keen, a good chap and, in time, we think he'll see sense.

*****

Obscured amid the spectrum of broad opinion, eventually some semblance of truth must become apparent. I cannot see how people not involved in the day to day running of a business can possibly know its financial strategy, or the means by which that company operates.

So many people seem to have a definitive panacea to altering Chelsea's pricing policy whilst simultaneously deriding the tenure of the up to date administration, The last issue had more than one offering on this subject, complete with bold statements ... of fact?

One writer stated that Chelsea, "Had made no provision to pay this off". How does he know? Is this a common knowledge thing that slipped by me? Maybe he believes the Press Reportage and its anti stance. Did Ken Bates tell him personally? I doubt it!

As a commercial concern, Chelsea Village seems to have sounder independent prospects than, say, British Nuclear Fuels or British Airways. The inevitable period of consolidation is upon us, superseding the quick fix years is the key to any success and I firmly believe that is how Chelsea Football Club perceives the future.

The prophets of doom among you could always support those doyens of excellence ... T*ttenham! In a relatively short space of time they have transformed from being a bigger and infinitely more successful club than ours, to becoming no more than a gnat sized problem in one League Cup match spread over a decade or more. Can you see the progression?

The gloom that is forecast for Chelsea's catastrophic downfall has absolutely no foundation. I merely see commonsense prevailing as predictions of less TV money and the subsequent climate on players' wages takes on a reality check,

Put the situation in context. Chelsea have no money? We missed signing loan target Di Baggio by a very small margin in the closing transfer window. Can't afford the wages? Of course Chelsea can afford it. The truth is clear: Chelsea have money, they will merely spend it more wisely in future.

Surely no one imagines the financial arm at Stamford Bridge hasn't carried out studies for maximising profit? Why should a business cut prices just to satisfy a handful of romantic dreamers still stuck in 1978? The past was good times, but it was a transition to ... progression! Today is better times. Alter your horizons and see the success in front of you. Stop bloody whinging about it and harking back to the good old days of crumbling stadia and crap football. The whiners should be lauding the new dawn we find ourselves in and see for the first time in years, the true potential of the club and the team. At the beating heart of the optimism and the spirit that envelops it is ... Chelsea Village!

I am proud of it. You should be too!

*****

Ian Hutchinson

Many Blues Fans would have shared the immense sadness I felt at hearing of the passing of 'Ian Hutchinson'. An era of 'might versus talent' was graced by a forward whose selfless courage paved the way through fortressed defences. Chelsea fans adore a trier and Hutch always gave more than 100%. That, more than his outrageously huge throw in, was the reason why we loved him so much. To those of us over the age of forty, Ian has more than a special place in our hearts. The everlasting cameo in our minds eye of the lanky, all elbows battler who was so awkward to defend against, is imprinted on the memory forever. For many, the most enduring of those memories was the windmill arms after launching one of those famous 100' plus throw-ins.

Whenever the Blues won a throw near the combat zone, the chant of *"EEE-AN, EEE-AN HUTCH-IN-SON"* would automatically waft across the ground. This was a plea to summon our mighty weapon to take his station. Opposition defenders would actively seek to concede a corner rather than face one of Hutch's bombs hanging tantalisingly over the danger area. Hutch supplied Peter Osgood with many of his goals during his relatively short career. Taking the brunt of opposing defenders' aggression, he often provided Ossie with the space to create openings. It was a prolific partnership that will eternally remain a part of Chelsea folklore. Hutch himself averaged better than a goal every three games and his tally of some 58 goals was an amazing return considering the amount of appearances he managed before injury cut his Chelsea career agonisingly short.

Ian was, of course, up against such genial and friendly characters as Billy Bremner, Norman Hunter, Tommy Smith, Nobby Stiles, Dave Mackay and refereeing that was less protective than today's rules would allow, which is putting it mildly. Little wonder the punishment took its toll on his knees. Premature retirement ensued after four or five seasons of being hammered as he shielded, protected, and fought for Chelsea's cause. He was never found wanting. He never flinched or shirked his role.

It was only last May, at Peter Osgood's testimonial at Carshalton Athletic, that I finally met and shook hands with my two boyhood heroes. Ian looked painfully ill, but I didn't realise how briefly his tenure would be. 54 is so tragically, cruelly young.

On behalf of all Chelsea fans, I wish to extend our deepest condolences to his family and friends. His loss weighs heavily on all of us who saw him play regularly. He had fire in his soul. He had guts. He had BLUE BLOOD pulsing through his veins.

He is an all time Chelsea great. Rest in Peace great man, you will be missed!

Alan Corfield

ISSUE 23 November 2002

Penguins' Blues

In those black and white days in the late sixties and early seventies when I became an incorrigible Chelsea fan, all the English matches televised in Iceland came from the Midlands two weeks after they were played and cut down to forty-five minutes. They were played at such places like Derby, Coventry, Wolverhampton, Leicester and the second biggest city in England, Birmingham.

Names like Kevin Hector, Alan Hinton, Derek Dougan, Keith Weller (the one and only) and Tony Brown were household names amongst those unfortunate souls who had been hooked on the drug called football. I even had a soft spot for Tony Brown and The Baggies at that time.

But there was another team in Birmingham coming into prominence in the 1972-73 season - The Penguins. Yes, I seem to remember that Birmingham City were called the Penguins in those days. They wore white-breasted shirts with dark sides, back and sleeves, probably some shade of blue (TV was black and white back then, remember).

If this is total bollocks, I can always hide behind a deteriorating memory caused by old age and less than healthy lifestyle for the last three decades and a half. Anyway, Birmingham City have always been The Penguins to me. And after they won promotion to the First Division in 1972, I recall being subjected to more Penguins' matches than I care to remember. In fact, it is nothing short of a miracle that I didn't become a supporter of one of those dull Midlands clubs with all this coverage. In fact, I had a hunch that some of the visiting clubs who ventured into those gloomy areas played a more exciting type of football. That's how I fell in love with Chelsea, even if I had to be content with seeing them only two or three times on the telly during each season.

Because of this scant TV coverage of my favourite club, I have seen Chelsea play The Penguins only once, in the 1973-1974 season if my memory isn't playing tricks on me. As all the games on Icelandic television came from the Midlands, it was our away game, Although Chelsea at that time weren't enjoying anything like the success of the golden era a couple of years earlier, they won the match, and in fact I think they won both their matches against the Penguins this season.

My fading memory tells me that there were quite a few goals scored, The (real) Blues netting four times with two answers from the flatfooted Penguins. Osgood scored one and Tommy Baldwin probably got a brace. Who scored the fourth I couldn't possibly recall even if my life depended on it. I'm pretty sure, though, that it wasn't my favourite player, Ian Hutchinson, may he rest in peace.

Who of those Penguins scored, I can't remember. Every other player in their team seemed to have the surname Latchford and a few of the players were called Bob, so it only stands to reason that one of them fitted both criteria. Probably Bob Latchford scored for them, possibly Bob Hatton - unless it was that wonder kid later to become the first million pound English player, Trevor Francis. Who cares anyway?

The next season Chelsea were relegated but climbed up to the first division again a couple of seasons later, only to be relegated again in 1979 for a five year exile from the top flight. Guess who got relegated too. Yes, The Penguins!

During those two seasons, 1977-1978 and 1978-1979, The Blues managed to beat the Penguins three times, one of the games being a nine goal thriller played on New Years Eve 1977. Unfortunately I didn't see that particular game - it most certainly wasn't shown on Icelandic TV. But a yellowish copy of an Icelandic newspaper from that time tells me that Chelsea won 5-4 and Tommy Langley enjoyed a hat-trick. That's it. Not who scored the other two and not a word about the goal-scoring Penguins. I'll bet Francis was on the score-sheet. It was his second-last season before he joined Nottingham Forest for a cool million when the Penguins went down with Chelsea.

Both Clubs had mixed fortunes in the eighties, but the nineties have seen Chelsea rise to power again while the Penguins have been languishing in the nether regions. Now they are back to the top flight after a long absence but I wouldn't mind if they were sent straight back to obscurity. Even if they pretend to be The Blues, they will always be the same old Penguins.

Cool Blue

"Booty ahoy me hearties...hoist the Jolly Roger!"

ISSUE 24 December 2002

John King

MHBAWA is proud to publish the following article in which our own Billy Bookworm interviews a top Chelsea supporter and the cult fiction writer responsible for The Football Factory, Headhunters, England Away, Human Punk and White Trash.

What inspired you to write The Football Factory? I thought about the all the things that happened in the late 1970s and 1980s, and then the 90s came and there weren't any books that dealt with the things I was interested in. You know, the music, the football, the fashion. I wrote The Football Factory because it's the kind of book I'd have liked to have read myself. I sat down, started to write, and the book just evolved. There was no great plan to it. Football and the culture around it is a big part of my life. I suppose I did it because I wanted to write about the things that were such a big influence on me. I wanted to try to get across some of the thoughts that I was having.

Had you written anything before? The Football Factory was the first book I wrote but I did a couple of issues of a fanzine (Verbal). It was fiction based, London's small answer to Rebel Inc which was going in Scotland and published my first short story, a short version of Millwall Away. They were also publishing Irvine Welsh and Alan Warner, so I got to know them. I was asked by Mark Wyeth of Club Ska to get involved with an evening to celebrate the music of the Ruts and I produced a special edition called 'the Human Punk issue'. Human Punk is the title of a Ruts track and I named my book after it. The Ruts night edition had guest writers and contributors. I also did a few things for The Chelsea

Independent in the very early days when Nick Brown was editor. It was a good fanzine then and I liked the way Nick let people write in and hold their own debates. Funnily enough, I saw him the other day and we were talking about that. People should be allowed to say what they think.

When did you realise that you could write? I hated school and the only books I used to read then were things like Skinhead, Skinhead Returns, Suedehead, Boot Boys, Chopper, plus the Confessions Of A Window Cleaner etc … series, but literally anyone can write. If you can talk you can write and, if you've got a story to tell, the chances are that there's a book inside you. It's not going to come straight away and it will take some hard work. Writing doesn't have to be an elitist thing and, over the course of the last four or five years, there have been some great books coming out from modem fiction authors such as Irvine Welsh, Alan Warner and Ben Richards.

What are your influences? Music more than books really. I went to see a lot of bands and, before Punk, I was into David Bowie, Slade, Sweet, that kind of stuff. Then I started watching and listening to bands like the Ruts, the Clash, the Pistols, Penetration. I loved the Jam. They were a fantastic band. Again, their lyrics were great. Paul Weller was a Punk, I don't care what anybody says about the way he dressed or anything like that, for me he was fantastic. I didn't like The Style Council though! I was never demonstrative enough to appear on stage with a band myself and I suppose that writing books is my way of expressing myself in the same way as a singer or a band put across what they want to say in their songs. I always try to write about something.

The Football Factory isn't just about football, it's about Britain, everything really. White Trash is about the National Health Service and the way that people are looked down on by the authorities, while Human Punk is a story about the music and culture that I was into, but also about a friendship. Book wise, I'd say that my main influences from England have been people like Alan Sillitoe, Aldous Huxley, George Orwell, but I really like American writers, the likes of Charles Bukowski, Hubert Selby Jr, John Fante, his son Dan Fante, Woody Guthrie. Many English writers come from an Oxbridge background and are very constrained, whereas American writers seem to be more free moving.

How do mean 'free moving'? There are fewer rules. Because of their backgrounds English writers are more precise, stick to the rules and lack imagination. Many American writers don't seem to bother about the boundaries and just write exactly what they feel. All the ideas are in my head and I think that the faster I get them out, the better. I wouldn't even know how to construct a sentence properly, Those things don't really bother me. As I said, a lot of my ideas come from the music I listen to and the type of music that I really like - Punk - blew away all the rules and people just did what they wanted. That's what I try to do in what I write. It's a case of me trying get down all the thoughts in my head as fast as I can. I don't try to plan what I write. I try to keep up with the rhythm of the thoughts as they come to me.

Am I right in assuming that Alan Sillitoe has read The Football Factory? He's read them all. He did the cover lines for the Vintage edition *of* White Trash, which was a real honour for me. Martin Knight and myself got to know him about four years ago and he's our mate now. He's a really great bloke and it's amazing to think that I know him. With his books, even though many were written years back, you can easily identify with the situations. The things that he writes about are universal. His latest, Birthday, is well worth a read.

How much of yourself have you put into the characters in the books? Most of the situations and characters have been conceived as a result of my experiences. The good thing about writing fiction is that there are no limits, you can write what you want. People often ask me if a certain character is based upon anyone in particular but I've never done that. One of the strange parts of writing Human Punk was that it was hard to remember exactly what records were out at the time that I was writing about. A couple of times, I'd get to a scene where I thought, 'I'll mention that track here' but when I checked out exactly when it had been released, I realised that I was writing about a time before the song would have even been recorded. Even looking back and thinking about the slang we were using made me think. A lot of the terms in use now were used back in the 70s and 80s, they've come back, some with different meanings, Then there was the 70s gear we used to wear - flares, DMs, shoulder length hair.

How angry are you? Yeah, I've got things to say, I don't think I'd be a writer if I didn't. Why write something that doesn't challenge anything? There is a lot of stuff going on but we're always being told we've never had it so good. We're being sold out to the European Union and most people can't be bothered to think about what's going on around them. What's all that about? Money and big business is muscling in and eradicating British culture, taking away our democracy

Have you got anything new coming out? I'm working on a book called The Prison House. The story centres on someone who gets imprisoned in a foreign jail, He is housed in a prison called Seven Towers and I'm thinking of tying it in with the Seven Deadly Sins. I've only just started it so I don't want to say too much about it yet because I don't know what it will end up like.

Have you done much travelling? Yes, I've done some travelling. I went to Europe when I was younger and I used to follow England abroad - Spain, Denmark, places like that. You know, the usual stuff, inter-rail passes and sleeping on the trains. I went away for a year once, and went to Sri Lanka, India, Nepal, Thailand and Burma. Another time I drove across America and down into Central America, went to Hong Kong, through to China and got the Trans-Siberian railway back, I wrote a little bit about the railway journey across China and the Soviet Union in Human Punk.

If I can pin you down, who would have been your favourite band between the Clash and the Ruts? I like them both. They were different in that they lasted different amounts of time. Obviously, because of Malcolm Owen's death, the Ruts only lasted a short time. Most people believe they would have reformed if he had lived. I used to go to see the Ruts and the Clash a lot. Human Punk is the name of a Ruts song. The Crack is one of those LPs on which every track is saying something - a real down-to-earth social commentary. The Clash seemed to go on and on and produced tons of material. White Man In Hammersmith Palais is one of my all-time favourite singles.

How did you meet Martin Knight and Martin King? I met Martin Knight when Alan Hudson's book The Working Man's Ballet came out. He'd read The Football Factory and we just got friendly. When he was writing

Hoolifan I got to know Martin King. Along with Alan Sillitoe, Martin [Knight] and I formed The Flag Club, basically where some of the new authors meet up and have intellectual conversation - well, we get p*ssed really, It's a social thing, though obviously we talk about books a bit.

Have you read many of the books detailing the tribal aspect of supporting a football club? I loved "Hoolifan" and "The Naughty Nineties". They are the top books in my opinion. I enjoyed Colin Ward's Steaming In, that came out in the 80's, and also thought Armed For The Match, Icky's story, was very good. It challenges the whole legal aspect of making football hooliganism such a major crime. If I was the Chelsea chairman I'd make Icky the head of security! I enjoyed "Guvnors", the Mickey Francis book about Manchester City. Although it wasn't as cultural as Hoolifan, it was in a way the north's version of that book. Fair play to him for putting that bit in about that night Chelsea went up there and took over Manchester! That was a good day out, wasn't it? I hate that book by Bill Buford, Among The Thugs, and don't think much of Dougie Brimson's stuff either. The worst books are by those people who write as outsiders looking in, while the books that have been written from the inside out are the ones that stand up. They're more true to life and reflect a lot more of the humour of the situations rather than just concentrating on the violence. Most of the people who start out trying to condemn the violence just end up focusing on it and making it a whole lot bigger than it actually was.

If you could change your life, would you rather have been in a band than been a writer? I'd rather have been a Chelsea footballer before anything else. Every Chelsea supporter of my age wanted to be Peter Osgood or Alan Hudson - I still do! When I was a kid, I used to have number 8 - Alan Hudson's number - on the back of my Chelsea shirt and when I was playing football, I WAS Alan Hudson! After that, I would've loved to be in a band but I'm too shy for that. I've never done a reading. I couldn't get up on a stage, it's just not me. I like being an author. I'm very lucky.

What was your first Chelsea game? Chelsea 2 Southampton 2 in 1970. John Hollins scored in off the post, Mick Channon scored twice for them - broke the net with one of them - and David Webb scored our second, There were more than 44,000 there and I went with my Dad. In those days, Chelsea was a magical club and, if you came from West or South London, from their suburbs and satellite towns, they were the only team to support.

Often, in the Shed, there must have been at least 10,000 kids in there. It was great to be a part of that. Nowadays, Chelsea have got a great team, but I can't help thinking about all those people who used to go but who now can't afford it anymore. It's a shame for them, a shame for their kids and a shame for Chelsea. If the team we've got today had the support we used to have we'd be Champions by now. It's true what they say about good support being worth an extra point.

Do you still go to watch Chelsea? I don't go as much as I used to and sometimes I'm happy just going along to have a drink. I had a season ticket up until a couple of seasons ago, I was at the 2000 Cup Final and too many people there weren't real Chelsea, even though they might have been wearing club colours. It was more fun for those watching it the pubs around Wembley.

Getting to the 94 Cup Final was, for me, one of my most exciting times following Chelsea. It was great just getting to the Cup Final after all those years of heartache. Everybody there was proper Chelsea, though obviously the day ended in tears. In some ways it was better than actually being there when we won it in 1997. The Cup Winners Cup Final in Stockholm was best of all though. We stayed five days, got pissed every night, I shook the hands of Peter Osgood and Ron Harris after the game, and it all worked out cheaper than one of the official fly-in/fly-out excursions.

Do you like the new Stamford Bridge? I think that they should bring back terraces. Football is about having two terraces at either end of the ground, isn't it? There should be a massive terrace where the hotel is now. Even with the seats, in the old days at Chelsea, you could go into Gate 13 and sit with your friends, sit anywhere. All-seater stadiums didn't change anything with regards football hooliganism. All the boys were going in the seats anyway. CCTV has changed the way that people support their teams. Nowadays, you can't even have a bit of banter with the opposing supporters without the risk of being thrown out or arrested.

What about Claudio Ranieri? I don't suppose he would have been most people's choice and I don't suppose he has the same charisma as Gullit and Vialli, but I'm pleased with what he's done. He's brought the age of the team down and they are playing well. Gallas has been brilliant and we've got John Terry, Jody Morris and Carlton Cole doing well now too. You've got to try and have five or six local lads in the team. Look at Man Utd. Their success came on the back of them having five or six local lads and youth team players who had come up through the ranks. As far as Chelsea is concerned, fair play to Ranieri - he's playing two wingers and, as a side, they're starting to play really well together.

Favourite all-time Chelsea player? Alan Hudson. But I loved Peter Osgood, Charlie Cooke, Pat Nevin, and from the modern era Ruud Gullit, Gianluca Vialli, Gianfranco Zola - there are loads of favourites. People like Garry Stanley and Steve Finnieston, Clive Walker and Joey Jones. Micky Droy and Ron Harris. Eddie McCreadie's Blue And White Army was a more or less totally home grown side and they really belonged to us! We've had some great players over the years, and I've had some great times supporting them. Come back another time and I'll tell you a few stories just about Chelsea!

Billy Bookworm

*****

CONVERSION ON THE ROAD TO EUROPE

Hello. My name is Norvern Muppet and I am a Clownio hater. Hate, perhaps, is too strong a word, but when the man says, 'Together with all our hearts', I find therein lays the problem. Then you look at Chelsea of recent times, we. weren't together, at all, in any way.

We found your substitutions puzzling, your impassive arm-fold peculiar and your tactics downright perplexing. There are too many times when it was not only us, the fans, but also, so we read and heard, that the players themselves were as untogether and bewildered with Mr Clownio's antics as the rest of us. But then came Goodison, December 2002, and I have seen the light. I am a changed man, and as any good, fresh convert will attempt to do, I want to share my new inner peace. It has taken a long, long time. Claudio, the man has been in charge of my beloved

Blues for well over two years. But it was only on Saturday that I finally witnessed what he was all about. And I love you Claudio, with all my heart.

The day in Liverpool began auspiciously. As far as I am aware, for the first time since the regular 1970's name call from the Shed, as soon as the players ran onto the Goodison pitch, the Chelsea choir only sang a roll call. Now it might have happened since, but I don't know when.

I asked Mr. Chelsea Up Norf, who has missed only one Chelsea game, home and away, Europe included, in the last goodness-knows-how-many years (and that was a rearranged fixture, when he'd already booked to join Rangers on one of their European tours). He said Chelsea had sung a pre-match roll call in Betis, but he hadn't heard one in England since ....

It started with *"C*rlo, Ca*lo ..."* No surprise, that man has been a star lately, hope all the rumours of Italian interest are just that.

Next up, to my surprise, *"Super, Super Frank..."* I haven't been to that many games lately (two new sprogs and less than half a life...) and hadn't realised how popular he has become. I know the £11 million price tag was nothing to do with him, but it is a heavy weight to bear. He has the makings of a Chelsea legend.

"Marcel, Marcel Desailly ..." I was pleased to hear this, I don't think the Stamford Bridge faithful have paid him enough respect during his time here. The man is a legend.

"Oh, Jimmy, Jimmy ..." What else can be said about this infuriatingly lazy, wildly prolific, second best centre forward that Chelsea have ever had. (Osgood is still, officially, God).

"La, La, La La Zola.." This man deserves a statue outside the Bridge. I hope we can keep him for ever, as coach, as chairman, as Presidente. The respect he gets at every ground I go to, shows just what a super star our little Sardinian is.

"We've got two Marios ..." Not quite sure if these two deserve the same respect (but I did like Melchiot coming over at the end of the game and throwing his shirt into the crowd) but it is a nice line nevertheless.

And then it was kick off. And after such a fun build up, bringing back for me all the memories of the name call from the Shed and that long wait for the chant to travel over the running track to the player, until he raised his arm in appreciation and we clapped him in return, the game was even better. It was at Everton that I saw just how good we have become. It has taken a long time for Claudio to build what he wanted, but we can see its impact now. They say he made Valencia great, but left before be could be a part of their success. I think he will be here long enough to be part of some trophies here. Soon.

There was a determination about Chelsea I haven't seen for a long, long time. A togetherness, yes. With all our hearts. They fought for us, for each other. They are so solid it is awesome. And they are so confident that it was no great surprise that one of the Mario's got the first goal in five minutes. We all have that belief now, and when Jimmy added the second, there was a certain inevitability about it. It may not be the sexy football of yesteryear, but it has an undoubted appeal.

Chelsea not only played well, we sang well too. It was one of the best away supports I have been part of in recent years. I loved it. Despite this, after one of the songs, someone behind me said about how brilliant Ranieri had done. "I wouldn't go that far", I called back. A few laughed. I mean, it was Clownio after all.

The man behind got quite heated in his defence of Claudio and I backed down. I couldn't be bothered to argue. I just told him, "yeah okay, you say this, you say that, but when was the last time you heard us sing a song for Ranieri?" I mean, two years in, and we just don't.

The only time I have ever heard a song for him was at Liverpool, last season, at the first of our two 1 - 0 defeats in the last minute. Then a rather muted *'Ranieri's Blue and White army'* came and went. I was sitting next to Old Man, who you all know, if you go away. I told him that made a change. The only other song I had heard that mentioned his name, had been lead by Old Man, *"He came from Italy, to fuck up Chelsea, Ranieri, Wooaa..hoo ... Ranieri..."*

For a long time I have been one of Runny Nose's greatest critics. I have ceaselessly ridiculed him, both in print and in the pub. At the start of last season, I said that that was enough, it was clear he was going to stay, I had to start supporting him. He was a Blue. But I knew I didn't really mean it. And after one more of his bizarre tactical aberrations, I began to abuse him again. But here I was at Everton. And the tactics of this supposed European Master were plain to see and working. It was there on the pitch. The system worked, the players were working their socks off.

Ranieri deserved his break. And after the players' first roll call since the 1970's, Claudio deserved his song. Thinking about what I had just told the Claudio supporter behind me, I started the chant for him. Now, as many of the people who know me will testify, I am a noisy bar steward. Not a few will move to another seat rather than sit and listen to me. But I do get things going, and I enjoy myself, so fuck 'em.

I put my head back, *"RAN-E-AIR-EE'S BLUE AND WHITE ARMY ... RAN-E-AIR-EE'S BLUE AND WHITE ARMY ... RAN-E-AIR-REE'S BLUE AND WHITE ARMY..."* And it worked. It really took off, round and around again. I persisted throughout the game and other chants for him went round too.

I hope he heard it. Claudio deserves the break. And I am a believer. A convert on our march to the Champions League.

Together with all out hearts.

The Norvern Muppet

*****

So You Think You Know Hasselbaink …

Our No. 9 is a misunderstood man. Most fans think that the three times winner of the golden boot is a miserable son-of-a-B who can't stand his team-mates and is waiting in the wings for a long rumoured move to Barcelona (once the transfer window opens) in January.

Fact: His real name isn't Jimmy His actual name is Jerrel but he only likes being called this by his close friends and family. He only became known as Jimmy in 1995 in Portugal when the Campomairense chairman announced him to the press as 'Jimmy'. The name stuck ever since, which is probably lucky for us as Jerrel is harder to build into a chant.

Fact: His mother sold bread rolls on the streets of Surinam for a living. Jimmy was bom in Paramaribo, the capital of Surinam, on 27 March 1972. As the youngest of six children he was looked after for by his sisters (his father had walked out before he was three) while his mother earned a living selling rolls.

Fact: Only seven years ago Jimmy didn't have a job or his own roof to live under. In 1995 Jimmy was living in the Dutch town of Zaandam with his mother, who by then had emigrated to Holland, where he played for a non-league team made up of Moroccan immigrants in Amsterdam called Neerlandia,

Fiction: He has been a prolific goal scorer all his life. His first contract came in 1990 with a minor professional club called Telstar. His attendance at training was said to be irregular but he succeeded in making four appearances - not scoring in any of them. He then got another chance at AZ Alkmaar, in the Dutch First Division (which like here is one below the Dutch Premier League), and managed just three goals in 35 matches. League Goals Season Club Games Goals 1990-91 Telstar (Holland – semi-pro) 4 0 1991-92 AZ Alkmaar (Holland) 26 2 1992-93 AZ Alkmaar (Holland) 9 1 1993-94 Unemployed 1994-95 Neerlandia (Holland – amateur) 16 22 1995-96 Campomaiorense (Portugal) 31 12 1996-97 Boavista (Portugal – cost £150,000) 29 20 1997-98 Leeds United (Yorkshire – cost £2m) 33 16 1998-99 Leeds United 36 18 1999-00 Athletico Madrid (Spain) 34 24 2000-01 Chelsea (cost £15m) 35 23 2002-02 Chelsea 35 23

Fact: He has a, shall we say, 'Commercial' outlook on life. In 1993 he joined FC Zwolle and despite appearing in their official team photo never actually ran out for the club. He walked out over a reputed £70 a month difference and didn't play at all that season. His departure from Leeds was an acrimonious one, when O'Leary's parting shot was to publicly slate him 'greedy' for reportedly asking for wages that would have made him the highest paid player in the league. Off the pitch, Jimmy likes a good deal too - he buys his clothes when he is in Holland or Italy because he thinks London is too expensive.

Fiction: He asked to leave Chelsea. It was Chelsea who considered selling him. According to Trevor Birch, Barcelona made an offer for the Dutch striker, but it did not match up to Chelsea's valuation at that particular time. Birch said, "There were discussions with Barcelona about Jimmy - but it quickly became apparent their valuation and ours wouldn't meet. So we quickly closed those discussions."

According to the sports news network Teamtalk, Chelsea are keen to do business with Barcelona because they are looking to reduce the remaining £5m they still owe them from the purchases of Zenden and

Petit. Barcelona saw this as bargaining tool to offer them a lot less than Chelsea's valuation. Jimmy, caught in the middle of this, has more than once declared that "everybody knows football is a business" and having witnessed first hand the bankruptcy of Atletico Madrid, he is well aware that his employer as well as he can choose his destiny.

When asked about being linked with Barcelona, Jimmy told reporters, "I said, like a normal professional, that I would listen to what they had to say. It's not that I wanted to go, but if a club the size of Barcelona comes in, you have to always listen."

The added appeal of Barcelona to him must be the opportunity to link up with one of his best friends in football, Patrick Kluivert.

Fiction: He is frustrated with life at Chelsea Jimmy is a very emotional person and on the pitch wants to win more than anything. We may laugh when ten players are celebrating a great goal and he is sulking because they didn't pass to him but that, my friends, is the sign of a single minded winner. He may shout at his team-mates but he claims that half the time this is borne out of frustration with himself rather than his team-mates.

At 30 he feels he has only four years left at the top flight and, considering he is generally ignored by the Dutch management (because he doesn't play "pretty football"), he sees the Champions League as the most important competition he can really compete in. For a player of his stature he has won very little and would love to achieve something great. If Chelsea can provide him with a platform to perform on in the Champions League, I am sure he would be more than happy to stay. He could have joined Valencia or Lazio but chose Chelsea because he thinks the English League is "fun" and the best in the world.

Fact: He is Chelsea's second ever best striker of all time. While Greaves has a better goals per game ratio, is Chelsea's record scorer in a season with 41 in 1960-61, and the first player to score 100 goals in league football before the age of 21, it is difficult to say how Greaves would have fared in the modern day and his reputation has been tarnished by his later association with T*ttenham.

I predict Hasselbaink will still be at Chelsea at the end of this season. With the start he has made, he is not going to win the Golden Boot this year, but by the time you read this he will no doubt be hitting them in left, right and centre again. A life-long favourite like Osgood & Dixon he will

Player	games	goals	average
Greaves	169	132	1.28
Hasselbaink	89	54	1.65
Tambling	298	164	1.82
Dixon	331	147	2.25
Osgood	379	150	2.53

never be, but I suggest we accept and love him for who he is - a highly competitive and mean goal machine - the best striker that we have ever seen gracing the turf of Stamford Bridge (at least for all of us under 40).

Technical Terry

ISSUE 25 January 2003

A Visit From The King

Producing a fanzine and running our matchday stall has to be described as something of a labour of love. Reward can come from many differing sources. A simple sale often renews a faith that is occasionally dented by a snide remark from a passing disbeliever. However, on the 30th November 2002, our humble little paste table was to witness a significant event.

It was to be a day like no other, a day when the very passers-by who pour scorn on our beliefs were to stop and stare in amazement. For several weeks, those that regularly visit our stall had been told that a Chelsea hero would be present to sign copies of his book; several believed us while others just assumed it was the talk of desperate salesmen trying to entice additional customers to sample their wares.

Fortunately, due to our connections, we knew it was no idle boast. Behind the scenes, negotiations had been ongoing for several weeks and they had been successfully completed. Chelsea legend Peter Osgood had agreed to bless our particular piece of Fulham Road with his presence. Significantly, his appearance was to be supplemented by an appearance of the co-authors of his book, namely Martin King and Martin Knight.

Osgood was expected to grace the stall at approximately 13:30 hours. Beforehand, he would be undertaking a lengthy signing session as well as conducting an auction for charity at the Goose public house in the North End Road. With the fanzine stall having been set up, as usual, at noon, we knew the wait for his arrival would be an agonisingly long one.

As time slowly passed, Martin King was the first to arrive, fresh from the auction at the Goose. Eager for the operation to run smoothly, Martin remained in contact with Peter and his entourage via his mobile phone. As is often the case with such events, the schedule began to slip. Slightly bemused punters, eager to catch a few minutes with a legend, seemed a little worried that perhaps he wasn't going to make it after all.

Thankfully, we knew better. Martin Knight had by now also arrived and informed us that Osgood had left the Goose and was on his way. Apparently, Osgood's signing session at the pub had gone better than expected and, due to demand, delay was now the order of the day.

Eager to catch a first glimpse of the great man, several pairs of eyes peered towards Fulham Broadway station, desperate to see Chelsea's greatest centre forward ambling around the corner.

Unfortunately, time dragged on, increasing the anticipation levels to an unprecedented high. Martin King made further frantic calls to the entourage before politely informing us that, "Osgood is only minutes away!"

Still we peered through the crowds, unable to glimpse his familiar face. By now a significant number of people had gathered around our stall and we were in danger of becoming submerged under a sea of expectant faces. Sinking beneath this unexpected deluge, we looked up to find that the great man had materialised. In a manner reminiscent of his playing days, Peter had slipped almost unnoticed through the defensive lines we had erected.

Trying desperately to clear sufficient space for him to comfortably perform his signing duties was the first major obstacle to be conquered. With expectant arms thrusting towards Peter from all directions, maintaining some sort of order was proving difficult. Thankfully, Martin King used his physical presence to create adequate space to allow Peter to get to the seat we had thoughtfully provided. After all, we couldn't expect a legend to be left standing, could we?

The next thirty minutes were hectic to say the least. The entire occupants of the Fulham Road seemed to congregate around our paste table. The stack of books disappeared in minutes, all I could see was a flurry of hands offering crisp bank notes for copies of the book whilst we frantically tried to give the customers their change. Buried beneath this frantic scene, Osgood remained unflappable - nothing seemed too much trouble for the great man.

Dedications were painstakingly written, hands were shaken and photographs were posed for with a genuine smile. Fathers watched in admiration whilst their young children stood either side of the Chelsea legend having their photograph taken, a lasting memento to treasure forever. But like all good things, it was soon to come to an end.

With the supply of books now gone and other duties to perform, Osgood was soon away and walking down the Fulham Road. Exhausted, we slumped against the wall and tried to reflect on what we had just witnessed. Our stall looked as if it had been hit by a tornado. The paste table was bowed in the centre and we were swimming in the cardboard packaging the books had been supplied in.

Giggling like two adolescent schoolboys, my accomplice and me tried desperately to return the stall to a status more becoming of a match day. It was whilst repositioning the wares on the table that a discovery was made that probably summed up just how hectic the thirty minutes had been. Buried beneath a pile of fanzines we discovered a solitary copy of Osgood's book. Opening the cover, we noticed that Ossie had dedicated it to two separate people. Inside the cover is a dedication to Neil and upon turning the next page there is a dedication to Tony. Now we were able to work out who Neil was but Tony still remains a mystery. The book is still in our possession and in its current state is highly unlikely to be bought by a punter.

However, if you know a Tony who has a brother called Neil, and who would like this remarkable memento, then drop us a line or see us on the stall - perhaps we can come to some sort of arrangement.

Those thirty minutes might well have been hectic, but they are thirty minutes I'll probably remember for the rest of my life. Often, when you meet your heroes, you end up disappointed … Peter Osgood was different though. In the chaos around him, he maintained a dignified, gracious presence and treated everybody with equal importance. Perhaps that's what separates those who consider themselves to be legends from those who are legends.

Our thanks go to all those who made the event happen, especially to Martin King and Martin Knight, fine writers and diamond geezers, and to Peter Osgood himself for taking the time out to make the dream come true.

Bacchanalian Blue

ISSUE 26 March 2003

Oi Nutter!!!

A recent debutant on the BAWA.net website, MHBAWA is pleased to publish the following article penned by, as his name suggests, an obvious fan of at least one of our two Marios …

I think its fairly safe to say that all football fans, whatever their team, love a nutter in the side. They not only help to amuse us when the team is doing badly, but their apparent grit and determination makes us feel like they're one of us.

We at Chelsea have certainly had more than our fair share over the years, and most can remember (or will know about) the notable examples such as Ron 'Chopper' Harris, Petar 'art thief' Borota, Mickey Thomas, Joe Allon, Vinny Jones and .... Mario Stanic?

'Chopper' Harris was (as the nickname tells us) a bit of a hatchet man, even in a period when thuggery was all too common in football (on and off the pitch). However, he was also (until recently) our most successful captain, and thus deserves all our respect (which he already has anyway) – Nutter!

Petar Borota wasn't as good as 'The Cat', but nevertheless was a decent goalie, who famously used to turn around to the Shed and celebrate whenever we scored. Not only that, but it seemed he used to fancy a Sunday walk during matches, calmly strolling to the halfway line as 6,000 Sheddites would shout "Get back in goal." These days, of course, he is more famous for being sent to prison for stealing works of art – Nutter!

Mickey Thomas was a decent player, whose finest hour must have been scoring a scorcher against Sheffield Wednesday when we were 3 - 0 down at half time (4-3 up, then Doug Rougvie f*cked it up). However, he also ended up in jail once his playing days finished, and always put himself about well on the pitch - Nutter!

Those of you seeing us in the early 90s will remember Joe Allon, the Geordie super-sub. He had the amazing ability of scoring practically every time he came on ... then steaming over to the Shed to celebrate with the fans - Nutter! Next up is Vinny Jones, Pretty much every football fan in the land has heard about his on the field misdemeanours. However, I've chosen a different reason for adding him to my list of nufters. When Vinny played for the Blues, he would come up to the Shed before every home game, and start a rendition of "One man went to mow". For this, Vinny – Nutter!

Finally, I wanted to point out one person in our current squad who is more than worthy of having the 'Nutter!' title inserted before his name. I'm talking about none other than Mario Stanic.

Most of us thought he should have gone in the summer, making way for a better player, or simply because the spare cash would be handy. How wrong I was! And let me explain what makes Mario worthy of the 'Nutter!'.

1. Let's start with that haircut – anyone looking like a girl, while so obviously being a bit of a hardman, deserves all our respect and admiration. Who else could have pulled that off? – Nutter!

2. He plays better out of position than in his chosen one – we know he's decent on the left wing, but even when he was left back he looked better than when he's on the right! – Nutter!

3. He has the uncanny ability to get booked in every game – no matter how strong or, as in the game against Blackburn, soft the challenge is, he always gets booked! – Nutter!

4. He is the only player in the side who genuinely performs his defensive responsibilities (however zealously) in addition to his attacking ones – Nutter!

5. His theatrical dives, even when nobody is within a five-mile radius, and just to annoy the opposition players/fans, provides light hearted entertainment to all – Nutter!

6. Finally, and perhaps the clincher, he has the silliest song of any of the players in the side - can anyone please explain the rendition of "Da da da da da da da da, Stanic, Stanic!" From the boys in the MH Upper, in the east corner No, neither can I! – Nutter!

Mario Stanic – we salute you, and hope you keep contributing your crazy ways to our club!

Stanic Worship

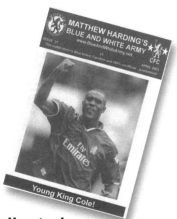

Young King Cole!

ISSUE 27 APRIL 2003

This edition of MHBAWA is dedicated to the memory of Matthew Harding

The Sheditorial

Welcome to this, issue 27. We here at MHBAWA are pleased to say that this is the first season that we have managed to produce seven issues of this publication. I'd like to take this opportunity to thank all involved in MHBAWA whether they be contributors, supporters, subscribers and the regular or occasional purchasers. Without you, MHBAWA would not exist.

Unlike the current fortunes of both Chelsea Village and, it seems, Chelsea Football Club, the future for this fanzine has been assured for the next season at least. Subscribers and regulars will, when they see the first of next season's issues, notice more changes that follow those which took place in the last issue. However, I'm sure that once they see what we've done, they will like what they see and we here hope that they will continue to support us by their patronage to these humble pages.

Next season, we will deliver some exclusive interviews with top Chelsea supporting celebrities, book reviews (including 'Human Punk" and "White Trash' by John King), your letters and articles, topical gossip and our views on how the future course of Chelsea FC should, in our opinion, be plotted. As it stands, it is only certain individuals from this fanzine, our website - www.blueandwhitearmy.net - and those from Chelsea Action Group who seem to be carrying the torch for those who'd like to see the end of both Ken Bates' time in charge and his Village dream. Whatever you think, his time at Chelsea will, we're sure, be ending soon!

Remaining with that theme, I'm sorry to have to report that progress at starting a Supporters Trust for our club has been slow, but it is going forward and those currently involved will be seeking to further the cause over the summer and into next season.

All individuals concerned will continue to strive for a more 'equitable' Chelsea Football Club, as well as continuing to campaign on other issues, including the reinstatement of the 1970's badge.

While Ken Bates continues to try to take the plaudits for what he thinks he's achieved, we will continue to remind him that, for all his bluster and for all he says he's done, it is us, the supporters, who are the Chelsea. Never try to forget it Batesy – 'cos we won't let you.

Finally, as this is the last issue for the current campaign, I'll leave you by saying that we here hope you all a have a good summer and come back refreshed and ready for next season, with your love of Chelsea as strong as ever!

The Guy Who Blagged Me

ISSUE 28 August 2003

The Fundamentals Of Chelsea Fundamentalism

The ideals and aims below are those upon which every Chelsea Fundamentalist places his or her faith. They are easy principles to follow and we here at cfcuk encourage all Chelsea supporters to place their trust and whole-hearted belief in them.

Think clearly - think BLUE!

The restoration of, and belief in, the '70's' crest.

The demolition of the Village hotels/apartments and a rebuilding of a stadium at Stamford Bridge that would allow a sixty, possibly seventy thousand capacity.

An equitable pricing structure.

A supporter representative on the Board of Directors.

No shirt sponsorship.

That the club should stress to those concerned, the importance of supporters being able to travel to and from games at reasonable times as opposed to having to cater for the mass ranks of the armchair spectator via live televised broadcasts.

A recognition that the club's 'bread and butter' is earned within the structure of the English leagues and FA, and as great a prominence as possible should be placed upon Chelsea's responsibilities, as part of the English league system, to the other 91 League clubs.

Chelsea Football Club is a worthy and up-standing concern that will not only put something back into the local community, but will also give that community a sense of pride in the club

It's YOUR club - keep the faith! Chelsea Fundamentalism is the ONLY answer!

The Visionary

*****

22/05/03 – Chelsea Millwall Riot!

Riot police were called to Bermondsey, as about 40 of Chelsea's top boys took on around 80 of Millwall's elite front-line troops. The fight, close to The New Den, was eventually broken up by police, but not before a member of one of Chelsea's younger firms was seriously injured.

While the Millwall crew had their young spotters out searching for the main Chelsea mob, a select few from West London's finest had slipped into the heart of enemy territory unnoticed, after travelling to South East London in small groups before eventually joining forces close to the ground.

After several hours of 'cat and mouse' with both their opponents and the local police, the two firms met on a small piece of waste ground between the myriad of railway arches that surround the Millwall stadium.

After the briefest of standoffs, the two sides began fighting, with neither wishing to concede any ground. While some individuals fought toe to toe, some of the combatants found themselves overwhelmed and were taking heavy beatings.

As the battle intensified, a Millwall 'snatch squad' picked out one particular Chelsea supporter who'd bravely steamed in single handed and managed to separate him from the rest of his comrades. As the fighting raged, the unlucky Blue was dragged away to behind the Millwall front line and was severely beaten before losing consciousness after receiving serious head injuries. As the rest of the Chelsea gallantly held their line, the police arrived to try to restore order. Protected by their riot helmets and wielding their batons, they got straight in amongst it as they tried to separate the two sides. Realising that the police had turned up, most of the fighting began to stop as people turned their attention to escaping from the long arm.

As both sets of supporters began to withdraw, the police suddenly found their resources stretched and those at the edge of their own lines began to come under pressure from both sets of supporters as some of the retreating foot soldiers began to skirmish with them. Eventually, however, the police were the eventual winners, as order - to that particular little part of London at least - was eventually restored.

As if you hadn't already guessed, the above 'battle' was a scene from a film that is being made of the cult classic book 'Football Factory' that was written by Chelsea supporter John King. Filmed within a Hasselbaink blast over the bar's distance away from the New Den (nah - it was closer than that!), the two firms were comprised of both genuine Chelsea and Millwall supporters (with a few other odds and sods thrown in) who'd sportingly agreed to turn up to take part in the day's events.

After at least 11 hours filming and many attempts to get the action looking right, there were the inevitable minor injuries to some. However, although at times some of the acting looked like it might turn into the real thing, as soon as the order "Cut!" was shouted, all involved just stood up, laughed about it and shook hands with their opposite numbers and prepared to do it all again. At he end of the day's filming, all those who took part then went back to the location base to find iced bottles and cans of lager waiting for them. As the now weary actors enjoyed their drink, all were agreed that it had been a brilliant day.

As the 'main actors', those who had the leading roles in the film were privileged enough to be allowed to see some of the footage that had been shot and, by all accounts, what they saw looked very real. Perhaps that is little wonder considering that most of those who took part had some experience or other of what might commonly be described as 'terrace culture'.

As I said previously, it was a top day and all involved are walking at least two inches off the ground, safe in the knowledge that they will have played their part in what will surely become the movie about football culture that will set the standard.

Those 'in the know' say that, while the filming is nearly complete, the long task of cutting and editing has still to come and the producers hope that it will be ready for release in the late summer of 2004. Stay tuned to this channel for more news on "Football Factory".

This story was first published on the BlueAndWhiteArmy.net website. What was said at the time still applies now - please, 'keep it here' for exclusive news on the film version of John King's classic novel "The Football Factory".

The Reporter

*****

An Open Letter

Dear Roman Abramovich,

My name is Blueberry and I am a Chelsea supporter and a Chelsea fundamentalist. For the last 4 or so years, I have been actively involved with this fanzine and it's associated website. Those who both contribute to and read what we print are amongst the most loyal and passionate supporters at Chelsea. For the last four or so years, some fellow supporters have placed their trust in this fanzine to represent them as best it can to voice their concerns and opinions about various issues concerning Chelsea Football Club and it has been the privilege of all concerned with this publication to have been able, in some small way, to serve them.

It is therefore, by the nature of the position this fanzine and website holds, that I write to in order that, on behalf of those supporters, I can express our thanks to you for saving our club from bankruptcy and possible oblivion. Never before, in all its 98-year history, has Chelsea needed a person like you. Without your financial input, it is doubtful whether the club would have been able to compete in the forthcoming 03/04 Premiership and domestic Cup competitions, let alone the Champions League. We, the Chelsea supporters, owe you a lot.

To own a club like Chelsea is a great honour. However, the title of owner brings with it the burden of responsibility for carrying the hopes and aspirations of the Chelsea supporters and it is with that thought in mind that I would like to inform you of some of the ideals that this fanzine, our website and other Chelsea fundamentalists hold dear.

One of our aims has been to create the conditions whereby a dialogue between the club and the supporters can be set up but, under the previous regime of Ken Bates, this has been difficult.

Although Ken Bates was *of* the opinion that we were just a 'trouble-making' publication, out to 'do him down', it is in fact, a body that has striven to preserve the very vestiges of the club's history and traditions.

While we hope that you, like us, live and breathe Chelsea Football Club, I feel it is my duty to inform you, as (if you'll forgive me) somewhat of a newcomer, about several issues that all Chelsea fundamentalists, those who are patrons to our publication and a great percentage *of* Chelsea supporters hold dear. I hope that you have been fortunate enough to have seen the club crest that was used before Ken Bates decided to abandon it in favour of the current design.

This is commonly known as the 70's crest by virtue of the fact that it was in use when Chelsea first won the FA and European Cup Winners Cups. Despite its popularity, Ken Bates decided to disregard it and, ignoring protests, refused to reinstate it. Subsequently, and for far too long, the Chelsea badge has been a somewhat poor imitation of what is a fearsome and glorious looking crest. It is the hope of many Chelsea supporters that you, once you have time to learn a little of Chelsea's history, will restore the 70's crest and give the players and supporters the chance to wear their Chelsea shirts with the same pride that the crest embodies.

Although some might regard this as a somewhat minor issue, it is of earnest importance to many. While Ken Bates undoubtedly had, in the face of property speculators, some part in ensuring that Chelsea Football Club remained at Stamford Bridge, many Chelsea supporters feel that his vision of how the club should be run was completely wrong and our fears were proved when, in the face of severe financial difficulty, he was forced to sell the Chelsea Village business.

Instead of building the loss making hotels and associated concerns, we feel that Bates should have concentrated on building a stadium. After all, there is enough space at Stamford Bridge for a stadium that could be the best in England, possibly in Europe. Since your arrival, amidst all the speculation, some have mentioned the possibility of Chelsea leaving Stamford Bridge and moving to a new purpose built stadium, possibly within the western boundaries of the M25 road system.

It is our hope that, while you look to invest in the greatest players that the world has to offer, you also consider redeveloping the stadium at Stamford Bridge and building a ground that would befit the best. After all, you have been quoted as telling the players that they are employed by the greatest club in Europe and it follows that the best players want to play in the best stadiums in front of the best supporters. If your plans for a successful team come to fruition, I'm sure you'll come to realise the potential to house more supporters than the current 42,000 capacity allows. It is our hope that, with the might that your finances bring, you can find a way to tear down the Village Hotel and the adjoining development and instead build a stand that would have a fifteen or twenty thousand capacity as part of a greater plan that would eventually encompass a 70,000 seater stadium.

A major concern that Chelsea supporters have had is the cost of admission to attend games. Football is the game of the people but unfortunately, under Ken Bates, Chelsea's prices have been somewhat extortionate and many passionate supporters have been unable to afford the price of attending matches. While we understand that you will seek some return for your investment in Chelsea, we hope that you will consider an equitable pricing structure that allows a greater number of lower income earners to go to watch Chelsea.

Without wishing at all to sound pretentious, the lifeblood of any professional football club is its supporters and, in your case, without us, the club, even with the world's best eleven players, would be nothing.

Chelsea supporters are proud to say that we are the best, the loudest and the most loyal that you will ever meet. Supporting our club is not just a past-time, it is a way of life. We hope that you will, while wanting the club to be the best, look upon us as somewhat of a twelfth member of the team and rank our faithfulness and loyalty as important to the success of Chelsea as the club purchasing the best players.

The help you have given to Chelsea is immeasurable and I can only thank you yet again. It is in you that I, on behalf of everybody that I represent and every other Chelsea supporter who thinks like us, place our trust and faith. In closing this letter, I must reiterate that it is sent with all our best wishes, highest hopes and deepest gratitude.

Welcome to the brave Blue world of Chelsea

Blueberry

*****

Over The Cold Turkey

As the tedium of summer fades and a new season kicks off, one could easily be sceptical about why we have missed football so much. Indeed, every pre-season seems to arrive quicker and quicker as the years go on, now it's a case where the end of a previous season and the start of the next seem to merge.

England friendly's, Confederations Cup, pre-season tours and tournaments, and then the customary games against lower opposition before the Community Shield and the opening weekend the following week. But despite all of the games over the summer 'break', it's just not the same! There's nothing quite like boarding the packed tube buzzing with optimism, then a pre-game shandy or two before stepping into the Bridge for a further pint (if you can stomach the overpriced concoction of froth, urine and H20 passed off as lager). And for the first game, the sun is always out and there is an even sweeter feel about the fortnightly pilgrimage to the Bridge.

Of course, this pre-season has not been without its excitement. There are some who are pining for the new season just to take a breather from this summer's off-field activites! All of a sudden we can buy anyone, and have been linked with pretty much everyone who can kick a football (so no Sp*ds players or Emile Heskey then). Rumours have varied from the sublime to the ridiculous, but there is no doubt that this has been the most fun pre-season I can recall!

There is no substitute for the Premiership and the basic question of will we come away with three points come 16:45. After the Abramovich takeover, inevitably the pressure on our boys from the media will be more immense than ever. Every dropped point or slip-up will be highlighted and celebrated by our many rivals (isn't it strange how we've become a lot more disliked since early July - odd that.) But we, the fans, are realistic as well as optimistic. It's been hard to take it all in and it won't be until Anfield on 17"' August when we see our team out there in a competitive game that it'll really hit home how much things have changed.

Despite the many unfortunate departures over the summer, we are fortunate enough to be able to look forward to many new talents lighting up the Premiership as well as being able to reflect on past players' excellence. This really is the start of a new era and I for one am excited by it. The old 'foreign mercenaries' tag cannot be thrown at us any more by our many critics, although it still probably will! With a healthy combination of young British internationals and hopefuls, as well as top class imports with their best years ahead of them, we have just the right mix to seriously challenge that seemingly unbreakable duopoly of ManUre and Arsenal.

Our appetites have been severely whetted for the new season and we have all enjoyed the signings and general good vibes surrounding the club now. With a (hopefully) long and exciting Champions League campaign to look forward to, as well as a real hope of being competitors in the three domestic competitions, this could well be the most interesting season in our history for many a year. There will be highs and unfortunately some lows, though here's hoping for many more of the former!

It's been a very long time coming - way too long. But at long last we can wave goodbye to the tedium of DIY, Saturday shopping, and the wearing out of End of Season DVDs and Videos from years gone by. So put them on the shelf you may or may not have put up for the missus on one of those long boring weekends, and look forward to the real thing at last! Good luck Chels - let's hope for a good opening to the season and starting the year as we mean to go on.

Carefree!

Famous CFC

ISSUE 29 October 2003

David Blaine - Got No Brain!

World famous illusionist/nitwit David Blaine is already planning a new mindboggling act of endurance, cfcuk can reveal.

The 'street magician' – currently suspended in a glass box over London's glamorous River Thames – is planning to obtain a T*ttenham FC season ticket and watch every home match for the rest of the season.

'There's no trickery involved and no way of escape,' said Blaine, speaking exclusively to cfcuk. 'For me, it's all about pushing the envelope of human endurance – stretching my tolerance to the limit.

'I'm not worried about the first few games, I'm worried about what happens later, when I'm tired and disorientated and just about to lose my mind.' Blaine claims to have rigorously prepared for this challenge by undergoing an intensive 30 year programme of not watching Sp*rs, however, some experts believe Blaine's latest attempt to shock the public is a step too far.

'There are limits to what a man can put himself through,' said official cfcfuk doctor Hertz van Rental. 'If he does attempt to go a whole season, watching Sp*rs could induce serious side-effects such as dementia and hallucinations – one particularly deluded individual once told me he thought he had seen B*bby Z*mora score a goal. It's not big, and it's not clever,' and I don't think we should be encouraging Mr Blaine.'

An angry T*ttenham fan growled, 'he doesn't fancy a game for us, does he?'

Hocus McPocus

King John - Turkish Delight!

ISSUE 30 November 2003

Besiktas At Home - A Very Tiring Trip

This time we tried a different arrangement for a Chelsea trip to London. Fly over, no accommodation, and then fly back home again. We have figured out by doing it this way we can see more matches, plus we don't have to take more than a day off work. In the end it turned out to be a very tiring trip. I guess the fact that we lost made it even worse - that plus the fact that I travelled despite having pneumonia. First time on English soil with penicillin treatment. Only death can stop me from watching Chelsea.

Anyway, Martin (who lives in Stockholm), my girlfriend Fluffo and myself left Stockholm West (Vasteras) airport early Wednesday morning. Ryanair took us over to Stansted. During the two-hour flight Martin and I talked about old Chelsea memories, while Fluffo took a nap. It was admirable hearing about Martin's ambition this season, as he plans to see 40 Chelsea matches live. So far this season he hasn't missed any, and he lives in Sweden. He has even booked Notts County at home in the Carling Cup! Have to admit, I am jealous. At Stansted we decided to have a few beers in the new O'Neill's pub, A few pints won't do the pneumonia any harm. As a matter of fact, it might even cure the thing. It really was a great way to travel, no bags, nothing at all to carry. A few drinks later, and we were on the train to Liverpool Street.

Got to SW6 some four hours before kick off. Saw a few mates, bought the new away shirt and had a bit of a singsong in the SO Bar. Had our seats in the Matthew Harding Lower, Gate 16, Row GG.

The result was a disappointment, and so was the attendance. It really should be more than just the 33 000 who were there that night. After all, it is the Champions League, and not just an ordinary Premier League match. Above all, it is CHELSEA.

After the match we had a good few hours to spend. We did that in a restaurant at North End Road, eating and drinking, and discussing Chelsea matters with our good friend Malcolm Carle (Chelsea Up Norf). The staff wanted to go home at half one, so we said goodbye to Malcolm and headed off towards Victoria.

Took the night bus just after two, and got to the airport at four. Checked in, got some duty free, and took off at 06.30 in the morning. Knackered!!! Got home, had a shower and straight off to work.

When I finally got my much-deserved sleep late Thursday evening, I had been up 40 hours. Well, what are you not prepared to do to see your beloved Chelsea (even if they lose occasionally)? At least we managed to do it, and we will do the same thing again, v Lazio and Sparta Prague. Same flights, same arrangements, but different score hopefully. It will be a whole lot easier if we win those matches ...

Harri Hemmi (Chelsea Supporters Sweden)

Gianfranco Zola - Still The Hero!

ISSUE 31 December 2003

Magic Box

Like most Chelsea supporters I became a gibbering news junkie during the summer, but in my case the cravings weren't only for details of the Roman Empire's latest confirmed signings and speculation over who'd be next, but also to get a definitive list of Italian Serie B fixtures. Why? Because a group of us had decided that we were going to go to Sardinia to see our sadly missed genius Franco Zola play live one more, maybe last, time.

When to go? Obviously the optimum time would be one of the weekends left blank of premiership fixtures for internationals to be played. The second weekend in October when Turkey and England were due to meet seemed best for us. In due course the Serie B fixture list for the 2003/4 season was released and, hooray, Cagliari would be at home on our chosen weekend. So, the not especially cunning plan was to get a cheap off-season flight deal to Alghero, find the way down south to Cagliari and the rest should be child's play. Or so you'd think.

We were just about to book the flights when a tale began to develop, a tale of self-interest, short sightedness and greed that wouldn't have looked out of place in our own beloved Premiership. The trouble started when the Sicilian team Catania launched a legal action against their relegation from Serie B last season. Catania went down fourth from bottom but, crucially, just a single point behind Napoli. During the season, Catania had drawn with Siena and in that match an ineligible player had played against them so, Catania argued, they should be awarded the game and the points. Catania initially lost their case but won on appeal. The second version of the fixture list was released, and again, Cagliari would be at home. Fantastic! But before we'd even had time to log on to

Ryanair.com, Napoli, the club who would now be relegated instead, bitched like mad and launched their own legal action.

The Italian FA, wanting to avoid any more expensive court cases, decided to let Napoli stay up but also to re-admit Catania. And then it just got silly. They also decided to allow two of the other three relegated teams, Genoa and Salernitana, to stay up and also to admit Florentine to the division from Serie C. A third version of the fixture list was released and again, Cagliari would be at home on our preferred weekend. While our fingers were poised over the "Send" button to book the flight deal, the rest of Serie B decided they didn't like the idea of expanding to 22 teams because then they'd have to share the TV money out in smaller portions. They decided to go on strike.

This sorry saga was taking more twists and turns than West Ham's team bus looking for Wigan, and on top of all that an Italian friend had warned me that Cagliari might not even play their games in Cagliari, they may play in the north of the island in a town called Tempio Pausania. We decided, sod it, we'll book the flights anyway, and if any games at all are played we'd have a 50/50 chance of Cagliari being at home. If they're away or on strike, well worse things can happen than having to spend a long weekend on a beach or in a bar. So five of us met up early on Friday morning at Stansted. Steve and Bella Spiller, Alf, Trotter and me, Dicko. Almost immediately, there was a good omen - Alf made an absolutely top drawer Z list celeb spot. In the queue to board our flight was none other than Michael Barrett from the terrible 70's BBC TV news/magazine show Nationwide. No sign of his half witted sidekick Bob Wellings, though. Surely a trip that gets off to such a quality start is going to be a cracker.

While the others dealt with the paperwork for the hire car in Alghero airport, I went to Tourist Information to try to find out where the game was going to be played. In the time between booking up and actually travelling, some of the Serie B teams carried out their threat to strike, then after further intervention by the courts, the Italian FA and the totally impartial and disinterested Italian prime minister Silvio Beriusconi (also president of AC Milan and chief executive of a certain TV Sports channel) Serie B was going ahead and Cagliari, lying in 5th place, were be at home to table topping Ternana on Sunday. The question now was - where?

An incredibly helpful guy in the Tourist Information Office made about ten phone calls on my behalf, and as the ever decreasing patience of the ever increasing queue behind me threatened to become a riot, he announced that the game was indeed going to be played in Tempio Pausania, not in Cagliari, and that tickets would be on sale on the day. He really was a very nice bloke and I felt positively guilty about having no intention at all of following his hotel recommendations.

Here's a handy tip for fellow travellers - always get a bigger car than you think you need. Alf, a seasoned hand at this, knew what of sort of tricks holiday car hire firms can get up to and had arranged for a 7 seater. What we got might just have seated 7 provided nobody had any luggage and two were circus midgets who'd each lost both their legs in some horrible, big top tragedy. As it was, the five of us were just about able to get our bags in and sit comfortably. Trotter took the wheel and we headed into Alghero town.

As it turned out, perhaps we should have listened to the Tourist Office man, although the weather was fabulous, about 70 degrees and a cloudless beautiful blue sky, it was the close season. A lot of the hotels had shut down for the winter and others were fully booked.

After being turned away a couple of times we were starting to worry but finally we got the last three rooms in a place built into a hillside overlooking the sea. After a fine (and cheap!) lunch in town and an afternoon spent relaxing by the pool and watching the sun set from the terrace bar, any perceived resemblances to Margate in winter started to fade.

Saturday dawned and on the way to breakfast we passed a few people who appeared to be elderly Germans, but on reaching reception we saw a huge, Alp like pile of Swiss passports. This was to be a recurring theme, all the hotels in Sardinia seemed to be either shut or full of Swiss crinklies. We never did figure out why. Anyway, they effectively made our decision about what to do: they'd booked out the whole place and we'd have to move.

When planning the trip at home we'd idly discussed some saddo plans for doing the nearest thing any of us would ever come to a pilgrimage by going to Zola's home town, seeing where He first kicked a ball etc (there was a vague recollection from an old English newspaper article that his earthly father ran a bar in wherever it was).

Well I thought it was an idle discussion but, once again, Alf had done some research and he said 'Zola comes from Oliena, it's near Nouro, I've found it on the map – let's go". So we set off on what proved to be a spectacular drive, first south down the winding coast road for about an hour, looking at stunning views of the sea and coastline. Then inland and up into the central mountainous region. In an ancient village looking like something out of the Godfather (alright, that was Sicily - but you know what I mean) we sped through a funeral procession, scattering mourners like sheep. How the friendly locals waved their guns and cheered us on our way. The 4000 Sardinian long homed cattle we ran into later were made of sterner stuff and we did have to slow down a bit for them.

After about 4 hours we rolled into Ofiena, and had a fantastic lunch in a real Sardinian restaurant. The proprietor, having identified us as English, immediately deduced that we were in town on a Zola related mission and, in the international language of pointing and grunting, managed to pass on some broadly coherent directions to 'Il Bar di Papa di Zola'. Oliena's up in the mountains but still gets pretty hot in October. And it's hilly. Very hilly. All right for the superfit like Trotter, who'd had to be persuaded not to stay in Alghero and run a half marathon he'd seen advertised, but not so clever for the more stereotypical fuller figured Chelsea fans such as Steve and myself. We walked what seemed like hours and miles, up and down and up again in nearly vertical streets until finally, in the Viale Italia, there was the Holy Grail, the Folk Bar. Ooh and look 50 yards up there - there's our car and the restaurant – what's Italian for "left" again?

A couple of life saving beers later and we were poring over the pictures and articles on the walls. One was a yellowing copy of the same Daily Express article from 1997 about this very bar and Zola's upbringing that we'd half remembered, The regulars seemed to have seen this sort or behaviour before - are we behind the times - has most of the Matthew Harding stand done this already? Just as we left, one of the blokes in the bar came out and called to us - he was holding an Italy shirt with 'Zola" on the back. Of course, we all wanted our photo taken with it. I like to think it's the one he wore at Wembley when he nipped in front of Sol Campbell and left Walker on his backside. Probably wasn't.

This was the only time Bella even came close to losing patience – so far she'd put up with all our middle aged adolescent nonsense with amazing good humour. 'You lot are sad, you're like big kids' she whispered to herself. Can't say she's wrong.

We left Oliena and kept heading east towards the coast. We managed to find an open hotel in a place called San Teodor, virtually deserted except for us and, inevitably, a Swiss couple. That night was Turkey v

England, but also Italy were playing and as you can imagine, a search for a bar showing the England game drew a total blank, so we watched the rather dull Italy match and went off to eat. Another great meal in another amazingly inexpensive restaurant, and a restaurant owner who, on finding out our nationality, claimed personal friendship with the island's most famous son. 'Yeah yeah', we thought to ourselves, maintaining a show of politeness. "Yes", said the owner, "Gianfranco - he eat often in my restaurant. When he come play golf with Ichi, You know Ichi? ' Steve pondered for a while "Ichi? You don't think he means Hitchy.' 'Si si, Ichi … Portiere di Chelsea no.' And it was true! Zola and Kevin Hitchcock were regulars. So we stayed for a few more "digestivos", oh my aching head.

And so Sunday, match day. We drove north up the Costa Smerelda and then turned inland following the signs to Tempio, the most notable event being a miserable failure to fill up at an automated petrol station - in our defence some local people couldn't make it work either. And.the first thing we saw on entering Tempio was a set of floodlights. Immediate investigation revealed that this was indeed the ground where the match was to be played.

It's quite a small ground, with a running track, a roofed main stand for about 3,000 fans and 3 open stands, one clearly temporary. No tickets about, but the deeply suspicious groundsman managed to communicate that maybe they could be bought in town. Well, we needed to find a hotel anyway so after a brief photo opportunity we went uptown. Tempio is not New York. We only saw one hotel and on enquiry we were able to get rooms, so we booked in, dumped the bags and met back down in the lobby.

Then came one of those moments in life you'd give anything to have over again, the door to the hotel conference room opened and out came the Cagliari team, track suited and fresh from their tactics meeting. And Zola was standing there a yard away! Too thunderstruck to say anything at all, at least I didn't say anything stupid. Trotter, who's the sort who'd have got us invited onto the team bus and round for dinner after the game, was already outside, and the moment was gone. When I gestured him in and told him, he just said 'Dicko you tosser - why didn't you speak to him?" I had no answer.

We went into town to look for tickets. Seeing a lot of people with Cagliari shirts and, by now more or less fluent in shoulder shrugging, eye rolling and pointing, we felt confident enough to stop one and ask where we might get tickets, It's amazing what detail simple hand gestures can convey, the guy clearly intimated 'Tickets? Buggered if I know, mate. I'm from Cagliari and I've never been here before.' We stopped at a bar where we were the youngest customers by about 50 years, then decided to go back to the stadium, where at last we got seats for the main covered stand and finally could relax a bit. The game itself was not close. Ternana looked anything but table toppers and Cagliari had the edge from the start. Zola was pulling the strings, Operating in a free role but mostly choosing the left wing, he was able to go past the right full back at will and eventually after beating his man yet again on the outside, put over a great left foot cross for a finish at the far post.

About 50 Ternana fans were sitting close to us on our left in the comer between the main stand and the end where the Cagliari ultras had taken up residence. We noticed a guy in a Chelsea shirt - number 25 Zola on the back of course - leaning over the edge of the stand behind the goal, taunting them loudly and with much gesturing. Eventually he made his way back to his seat and it turned out that he was the man in charge of the big drum that you always seem to get at Italian matches.

Ternana gave away free kicks regularly and, inevitably, one of them was on the edge of the box. Zola stepped up and curled a classic over the wall and away from the keeper but onto the underside of the bar. In the following scramble, the loose ball went out for a goal kick. None of the Cagliari players protested much, but that night on TV we saw that the ball had bounced comfortably over the goal line and a goal should have been given. I got a photo that shows why it wasn't; the linesman was level with the penalty spot looking for offsides, not level with the goal line.

The Ternana fans were, given their small number and the poor performance of their players, making an admirable job of getting behind the team, but when a chorus of *'Zola Zola vafanculo'* broke out I lost my rag. Leaping up, I improvised a quasi Italian 'fisting" gesture, much to the amusement of the nearby Cagliari fans.

Before half time Cagliari scored another, again Zola was instrumental in the move. Then a comedy moment. You're probably aware that Gianiuca Festa, the ex Middlesboro, player is also at Cagliari this year. In typical fashion he ran, or more like lumbered, 50 yards to get involved in a row that had nothing to do with him and got himself booked.

The second-half followed the same pattern and Cagliari stretched their lead to 3-0 with another tidily finished move. A Ternana player was sent off for a second yellow and Zola was subbed after about 75 mins, to a standing ovation, especially from the practically weeping English confingent (us). Cagliari seemed content to play out time but there was one more twist: with three minutes left, leading 3-0 and nothing much happening, Festa again got needlessly involved in a 'handbags' incident, the inevitable second yellow came and off he went. Zola looked just furious with him.

We left the ground and made a lot of new friends among the Cagliari fans who recognised the various Chelsea paraphernalia we had. They kept saying "Magic box" to us. 'Magic box', 'Magic box', and patting us on the back. We got back to the hotel and there were match programs on the front desk (well they didn't stay there for long) Later, reading one, we figured it out – 'Magic box' - that's what they call him in Sardinia.

Monday morning and back to Alghero for a leisurely morning drinking coffee, sightseeing and shopping. Then home - and wondering what Rome will be like.

Dicko

*****

Dear Deidre

The following letter and reply appeared in The Sun newspaper on Saturday 8th November this year. It was on the problem page and, while not admitting to looking at that particular section of the paper ourselves (the letter was cut out by a reader of cfcuk and sent in to us), we asked our very own agony uncle, Don Dilemma, to comment upon the advice given by Deidre, described in The Sun as 'THE WORLD'S No 1 AGONY AUNT', as we feel that hers was not the right solution.

DEAR DEIDRE,
My wife knew when we met that I watch Chelsea play football every Saturday, yet suddenly she expects me to give up my passion for the beautiful game. I am 26, she is 23, and we have been married for six months. Ironically we met at the train station where she works when I was on my way to watch a match. Our sex life is great and she's a lovely woman but this problem is causing us a lot of grief. She is threatening to

leave despite my efforts to compromise by only going to games once a month.

DEIDRE SAYS: If you have to cut down on going to matches your wife is being unreasonable. Making soccer a rival suggests she is insecure and it will always cause problems unless she is willing to change. Reassure her you love her but go to a match a month.

My free e-mail leaflet on jealousy explains self-help.

DON SAYS: In my opinion, Deidre is totally wrong, as missing Chelsea games will probably cause grief and upset domestically. What you should do is get your wife to save up and buy herself a season ticket of her own. Once she has been to Stamford Bridge and seen the wonderful Chelsea team play football, she will understand your passion for the game. The result will almost certainly lead to an improvement in your sex life, even though you claim it is already 'great'. The common interest you will then have in Chelsea will be a sound base upon which the long-term future of your relationship can grow. If she cannot attend every game because of work commitments, you can always lend her season ticket to a friend, thereby increasing your popularity with the chaps down at your local.

Don Dilemma

ISSUE 32 January 2004

Madrid Running Scared

On October 28th, the Spanish (and pro-Real Madrid) daily newspaper 'Marca' published a rumour that Chelsea (or, more specifically Abramovich personally) wanted to sign, as a new coach for Chelsea, the Spanish national team manager, Iñaki Saez. The article was filled with details: Saez would be given the run of one of Abramovich's houses outside London, he would also be given as a present a Rolls Royce Silver Seriph, Roman would provide Saez with Russian wood for the Spaniard's other business – furniture. And, so keen was Abramovich on this coach who had barely managed to classify Spain for the Euro-2004 championships in Portugal that, stated 'Marca', Roman was prepared to sack Claudio Ranieri that very day (when Chelsea beat Portsmouth 3-0).

The article was a bombshell – the 'Marca' switchboard was inundated by other news sources wanting to know more, and several British papers took the rumour seriously. It was, however, a hoax: December 28th is the Spanish equivalent of April Fools' day. Ha, and indeed, ha.

The fact that 'Marca' chose a rumour involving Chelsea taking away a key figure in Spanish football is symptomatic: the Spanish, and Real Madrid in particular, are obsessed with Chelsea. The Blues represent an unknown quantity that could, possibly, hurt their pride very badly. The Spanish sports newspapers are filled with rumours about Abramovich wanting to take away such-and-such a figure from Spain – whether it's Real Madrid's star players (apparently it is Luis Figo who is interesting Chelsea at the moment), whether it's the very real interest in Valencia's Roberto Ayala, whether it's the €30 million bid that Chelsea are said to be putting together for Sevilla's winger Jose Reyes, or whether it's a €3 million bid that the Blues were said to have made for an obscure member of Madrid's B team (who had never once played for the first team) by the name of JuanFran. And these were only the rumours noted in the last week of December.

Let us not develop ideas above our station: Chelsea are not Real Madrid. With their 28 League titles and 9 European trophies, Real Madrid are possibly the best team in the world. Chelsea are nowhere near that standing. Real Madrid are also one of the biggest 'brands' in football – second only to Manchester United. And that kind of success deserves all our respect. However, Chelsea have begun to learn from the big teams too, and particularly from Madrid, in that success is based upon money. And in the money stakes, Chelsea are currently the biggest team in the world. Sooner or later, that financial power will translate into results on the pitch and in the trophy cabinet.

Chelsea have already seriously rattled Madrid. When Chelsea purchased Geremi from the Spanish giants, the transaction was friendly, and mutually beneficial – alleviating Madrid of a player who had become peripheral. But then, Chelsea began to deviate from the gentlemanly norms of obsequy that Madrid expect - apparently Chelsea made a bid of €100 million for star striker and Madrid idol Raul, expressed serious interest in Ronaldo, and were said to have spoken to the recently-signed David Beckham, not to mention Roberto Carlos. Worse, Chelsea caused serious trouble by making a concerted effort to draw away Claude Makelele – Madrid's unsung hero but so effective as a defensive midfielder. Chelsea's success in bringing Makelele to London has left Madrid a much weaker team defensively. Players and coach recognise this continuously, even if the club's President, Florentino Perez (with his habitual bad grace) was scathing about the quality of a player who was recognised by UEFA as one of the best in last season's Champions' League campaign. Madrid really didn't want to sell him. But they had to in the end, as a result of Chelsea's determination.

If that loss was a body blow for Madrid (and which forced them to promote rapidly a number of youth squad players to the first team), Chelsea then seriously came in for right-back Michel Salgado. Chelsea were very close to signing him; indeed Madrid almost gave up on the player. At the very last minute, the defender chose to stay at the Santiago Bernabeu. The cost to Madrid of Chelsea's insistence was a pay rise considerably above what Madrid had hoped to pay him.

The fact that Chelsea can bid for such players disturbs Madrid. The

Spanish giants are used to having things their way. Every summer for the past 4 years, it is they who make football's biggest transfer. The names in the hat for their big signing next summer – Ruud Van Nistelrooy, Thierry Henry, Pavel Nedved – reflect that ambition. The fact that the players in question don't necessarily want to leave their current respective clubs doesn't matter: Madrid are convinced that they have the means, and the prestige, to entice them away. And indeed, they had been successful as they were the only club that could deploy such means.

Until now. And that's what hurts Madrid so much. When Madrid talk of signing a player next summer for €30 to €40 million, how can they possibly compete with Chelsea, who suggest that, if they identified the right player, they would be prepared to pay £100 million: In short, that at the same time as Madrid are reducing their budgets, Chelsea are suggesting that they could double the world transfer record. And the players that Madrid had identified as possible targets next summer (Henry, Van Nistelrooy, Nedved) are precisely the same ones who have been linked with Chelsea.

Real Madrid like to specify that many players go to the Bernabeu because of the club's magnificent history. That is undoubtedly the case. However, for all that pride, it is also a fact that Madrid – like Manchester, Juventus or Milan – have got where they are due to greater financial means than their rivals. Zinedine Zidane certainly wanted to play for Madrid. But that desire counted for nothing compared to the fact that Madrid were prepared to pay Juventus some £52 million for him. The big clubs' success was built upon the fact that they could afford to buy the very top players. And in doing so, excluded other clubs from taking such players.

Chelsea are now in that league, and beyond it. They can now afford players that are beyond even Madrid. They could, in theory, afford to buy the star players that have made Madrid what they are, and they could also afford to deprive Madrid of the players that they need to sign, every summer, to keep up their momentum. Chelsea are a major spanner in Madrid's works. The Madrid press likes to disparage Chelsea. We aren't one of the 'big' European clubs – nobody seriously wants to join Chelsea for reasons apart from the money. In a poll in the other pro-Madrid daily 'As', more than 60% of readers consider that Abramovich will not be able to transform Chelsea into a great European side. Yet there are rumours every single day in the Spanish press linking Chelsea with some of the best players in the planet, many of whom ply their trade in Spain.

Madrid, and their fans, like to consider that because their side is the best in the world (arguably), any other club simply doesn't make the grade. When a club comes around that threatens Madrid, mainly in the area that Madrid hold supremacy (the financial power to buy the world's best players) you can see that they don't like it. That Saez hoax was a good indication: Chelsea, apparently, make purchases on a whim without thinking about where the new member of staff would fit in. That would include taking on a coach who has no success to his name. Funny joke – but clearly designed to rattle Chelsea and Claudio Ranieri in particular.

We're only a small club in London? The insistence with which Madrid publishes rumours about us and puts us on the front page of their newspapers says the opposite. We are, in fact, one of the biggest in the world right now.

EuroBlue

*****

Bring Back The 70's Lion!

Most Chelsea supporters who care about the club crest will tell you that the reason that Ken Bates replaced the 'Mears' 1970's Lion was because the symbol is un-copyrightable. This meant that while Chelsea Football Club continued to use it as their club symbol, others could use the crest on merchandise and memorabilia without the club's permission, thereby denying Chelsea revenue. Looking at the situation from Chelsea's perspective, one can – to a degree at least – understand their reasoning. That said, the club 'own' the 70's Lion as a registered trading mark that gives them the potential to use and exploit the badge in any way they can.

However, Bates has in the past made it clear that he does not like the fact that the traders who sell goods on the Fulham Rd prior to Chelsea matches are, in his opinion at least, preventing potential customers from buying their goods from the club itself. He thought that by changing the club badge to a design that was covered by copyright, he would put the independent Fulham Rd traders out of business. He did not however, reckon upon the popularity of the 70's badge, and he was totally unprepared for the fact that the crest he wanted to dispose of became one of the symbols that would mark an opposition of sorts to his Chelsea Village regime. He has, without any shadow of a doubt, severely miscalculated.

Should Chelsea decide to bring the badge back, there is an easy solution that would enable the club to maximise the potential that the favoured symbol has. When marketing a product that uses the 70's badge, all the club would have to do is add the words "Official Chelsea Merchandise" somewhere on the item in question. Potential customers could then make their minds up as to whether they wanted official or unofficial Chelsea products.

Please utilize the centre page pullout that has been included in this edition of cfcuk. It is easy to use. All you need is a pen. Ask those in your pre or after match pub to sign it, or even take the pullout into the ground and ask 12 people either side of you to sign the petition. Once you have collected 25 names, you can either send it direct to Roman Abramovich/Ken Bates yourself, or return it to the cfcuk stall (or see one of our sellers) and we will ensure that it is delivered to Stamford Bridge.

This could be your chance to make a difference, or at least let the club know how you feel about the subject. 10 completed petitions equals 250 signatories. 100 completed petitions equals 2500. 200 is 5000. We're not promising that we will achieve anything by taking this course of action but at least we are trying. Please, if you think anything about this cause, please try to help by collecting signatures yourself. 25 for every person who buys the fanzine would bring a petition that would total 10s of 1000s of signatures.

Come on Chelsea…let's see if WE can make a difference. It is, after all, YOUR Chelsea!

Chels Guevara

ISSUE 33 February 2004

The Thoughts Of Chels Guevara

This fanzine doesn't do a lot of boasting but if there has been one underlying theme that has been constant throughout the life of MATTHEW HARDING'S BLUE AND WHITE ARMY and this, it's continuation in the form of cfcuk, it has been the belief that one day, CHELSEA FOOTBALL CLUB will play in a 'proper' stadium and that the hotel, restaurants and other 'extras' would be replaced. With the arrival of ROMAN, our hopes and dreams are as close now to becoming a reality as they ever have been but, until they have been achieved, we will continue to press the case.

Meanwhile, I'm pleased to hear that the 'BRING BACK THE BADGE CAMPAIGN' is doing well and completed petition forms now boast numbers of signatories in the 100's. Those who have signed include some West Ham and Arsenal fans who, although not exactly agreeing with our choice of club do, however, have an empathy with CHELSEA SUPPORTERS as far as the subject of the reinstatement of the club crest is concerned. I'm also pleased to report that Ralf Little - one of the stars of BBC TV's highly successful comedy series "The Royle Family" - was also good enough to add his name to the petition when he was spotted at January's LONDON CALLIN gig. There to watch highly rated band Badge, he too, although admitting to being a Man U fan, was only too pleased to help fellow football supporters try to have their say on a matter that to them, is crucial to the side they follow.

All associated with this fanzine were saddened to hear of the death of STEVE SALMON. Aged just 39 years, STEVE, a MATTHEW HARDING season ticket holder and life-long CHELSEA SUPPORTER, died suddenly on Wednesday 21st January 2004 after a short illness.

Those at his funeral were numbered in the 100's, a large proportion of them being CHELSEA SUPPORTERS. Following the service and the burial, many went to give STEVE a final send off by way of a drink and inevitably, the main topic of conversation was about his love for CHELSEA FC. Thanks from this fanzine go to MARK G and MARK W for enabling our representative to attend, while a special mention must go to RORY, who brought along a collection of photographs that recorded many of the games that STEVE and his friends had been to when following CHELSEA, thereby enabling everybody to remember the good times.

STEVE, a friend of this fanzine and website www.blueandwhitearmy.net will be sadly missed by many at CHELSEA.

R.I.P. STEVE SALMON – CHELSEA SUPPORTER

Chels Guevara

*****

A Fair and Balanced View

In the interest of providing a public service, and in the spirit of fairness and objectivity that all true football fans possess, I have decided to write an easy to follow guide about the other clubs in the Premiership.

This totally fair and balanced view of our opponents in this "the Greatest League in the World" could become an indispensable guide for all those wishing to know about more about the other clubs in English football, but were afraid to ask.

Arsenal Bastards. Truly deplorable team from somewhere in North London. Arrogant, French twats for whom hanging would be too good. Sure, they can play a bit, but so what, a bunch of cheating, diving thugs with an arrogant manager who suffers from selective blindness. Shit ground, no atmosphere. Nearest underground station: Hell.

Aston Villa This team play in Birmingham. This means the locals speak in the most annoying accent in the world. Their manager, although not from Birmingham, also has a very annoying accent, and a piggy nose.

The chairman is known as "deadly Doug". He is friends with Ken Bates, so I will not comment as I want to keep my season ticket.

Birmingham City As you will probably guess, this team is from Birmingham as well. Their manager hasn't so much got an annoying accent, as is just very annoying. And quite ugly. He seems to think that because Alex Ferguson used to scream at him in training, now he will be a good manager, of course he is wrong. Their owner has something to do with jazzmags. And they have Mikael Forssell on loan, let's hope they don't do anything silly with him.

Blackburn Rovers Once did what Chelsea are now trying to do and bought the title. I have never been there, but I imagine the bleak terraced houses will look the same as in any other northern shithole. Graeme Souness is now wasting away and doesn't really look scary anymore which is why his team are now inexorably sliding down the table.

Bolton Wanderers Sponsored by Reebok, loved by Mr Spock. Actually that's just me being silly: Mr Spock supports Bayern Munich, this is just one more of those Lancashire teams that only got in because about eight of them formed the Football League originally. Managed by "Big" Sam. The big presumably refers to his mouth out of which he utters some of the most inane rubbish. Full of ageing foreigners, a fact that no one seems to pass judgement on whilst Chelsea provide half the England team and still get labelled "overseas mercenaries". Any team with Ivan Campo in it deserves nothing but relegation - for that haircut alone.

Charlton Athletic One of those teams regularly described as "plucky". In other words a shit team doing better than expected. Basically teams like this act as a feeder club for Chelsea, or somewhere to farm out the youngsters on loan. There is no other reason for them existing.

Everton Hold on to your wallets, it's the Scousers part 1. This mob have lived in the shadow of their neighbours ever since anyone can remember. This means they have finished runners up in a quite a few competitions. Incredibly now their neighbours are shit this lot are even worse. Wayne Rooney will undoubtedly save the club however, as they should be £20m better off for his sale. That's just in savings on their annual Clearasil budget.

Fulham If you've ever wondered who the press are going on about when they talk about the homeless, well this is them. How happy they were when the shopkeeper took them over and the ever excitable "King Kev" brought them up. Now every time they lose Al-Fayed blames a plot by Prince Philip. Their fans hate us, but personally I don't think any of us can be bothered to hate them back. Like all vermin they long to be by the river.

Leeds *'We all hate Leeds and Leeds and Leeds Leeds and Leeds and Leeds and Leeds Leeds and Leeds and Leeds and Leeds We all fucking hate Leeds'.* I hope they enjoy playing West Ham in the Nationwide, assuming they're still in existence of course.

(and) Leicester Their new stadium is named after a crisp packet. They have Frank Sinclair in the centre of their defence and L*s F*rdinand upfront. It would be unfair, and rather cruel, for me to comment further.

Liverpool Hold on to your wallets, it's the Scousers part 2. They say all ManUre fans live in Surrey. Well, all Liverpool fans live in the past. Their manager lives in cloud cuckoo land. For all young Frenchmen of African descent with a penchant for diving, uncle Gerard has a place for you to play. I am always amazed that Phil Thomson's mouth has grown so huge considering it has always been in the shadow of that enormous nose.

Man City I feel quite sorry for City fans. Not only do they have to share a city with the forces of evil at Old Trafford, they currently have to put up with 'King Kev's unique style' of management. Well I say unique, but there are lots of crap managers out there, he's just got the biggest profile. Still, they're not doing too well at the minute so it's only a matter of weeks before he walks out on them.

Man Utd Evil, evil, evil, evil. The footballing equivalent of Microsoft. In Star Wars they would be the Empire, Ferguson would be the Emperor and Roy Keane would be Darth Vader. Let's hope that Obi One Abramovich and Adrian "Skywalker" Mutu can defeat the forces of darkness.

Middlesbrough At one time this club's destiny was to provide easy pickings in cup finals for the mighty blues. However, these days their sporting spirit shines through by their attitude of steadfastly refusing to score a goal against anyone. As if that wasn't enough, at the time of writing they were rumoured to be after Emile Heskey, so they obviously don't want to change this no-scoring attitude. This lack of goals means they'll never get anywhere near a final again.

Newcastle There is a myth that this lot have the best supporters in the land, who will follow them through thick and thin. This assertion ranks alongside Roberto Carlos's success at free kicks as one of the great lies of our time. I think it comes about because as no one understands a word they are saying, we are just assuming they are being loyal to their team. Everyone in Newcastle wears a replica shirt, this is because they have absolutely no dress sense whatsoever.

Portsmouth Hello sailor. This lot are sinking faster than a submarine with a hole in its side. Managed by H*rry R*dknapp, who bizarrely thinks that West Ham rejects are the answer to stave off relegation. That and T*ddy Sh*ringham, who is 103. Will also be playing West Ham next year.

Southampton The excitable ginger midget they call a manager is quitting at the end of the season. All their goals are scored by the same player, their chairman is called Rupert and the stadium is named after a virgin. Their nickname is "the Saints". Peter Osgood is still their best player. What is the point of this club? Answers on a postcard to the usual address.

T*ttenham HAHAHAHAHAHAHAHAHAHAHAHA....Oh sorry, hang on....let me get my breath back.............HAHAHAHAHAHAHA.........Sorry, it's just when I think of T*ttenham....HAHAHAHAHAHAHAHA. They nearly signed Rivaldo you know, and only last week they missed out on D*vids. It was only last week that I myself missed out on the lottery jackpot. Anyway, this club is growing ever more bizarre and insignificant (amazingly, they don't make the scientifically compiled top 350 clubs in the world compiled by the Institute of Football History of Statistics). Apparently it's lucky for Sp*rs when the year ends in 1, maybe 2011 they will get promotion back to the First Division. But only through the play-offs.

Wolverhampton Wanderers A typically dour West Midlands town.

Midlanders say they are neither Northerners nor Southerners, and are duly despised by both. Fleeting visitors to the top flight. Their ineffectiveness might be the only thing that delays the relegation of one or another of my other tips to go down, but only by a season. Paul Ince still thinks he's the Guvner, and he's still wrong.

Quique21

ISSUE 34 March 2004

The Sheditorial

Although Ken Bates finally admitted defeat and fell on his sword on March 2nd, 2004, he had, effectively, been 'dead in the water' since 2nd July 2003 when Roman Abramovich stepped in to buy Chelsea, thereby rescuing the club from bankruptcy. While it is common knowledge that, along with paying off the crippling debts that had accrued under the flawed vision for a 'Chelsea Village', Roman paid Bates a figure in the region of £17.5m for his shares in the PLC, thereby gaining overall control of the company. Many suspect that Chelsea's Russian saviour was, when giving Bates his wedge, too polite to add, "Now fuck off!"

On the evening that Bates resigned, a writer for this fanzine was at Stamford Bridge and had a conversation with a member of the Chelsea Village staff. The Village employee maintained that Bates had done wonders by saving Chelsea and, if it was not for him, the club would probably not now be in existence He said that buying the club for £1 and taking on the debts was, at the time, a brave move by Bates and he should be given due respect by every Chelsea fan for what he'd done. The cfcuk writer, however, replied by asking how he could possibly admire the business acumen of Bates when, at the end of his reign, he had left the club with debts in the region of £140m and was forced to sell. The employee then asked what the Chelsea supporter would have done had he been given a chance. The reply, put simply, was, "Built a club upon which, the main business focus would have been football."

Bates' resignation should, in theory, leave the way clear for the new regime to make their own mark on Chelsea and, from what our sources at the club tell us, those making the decisions as to the future direction that the club will take are ruling nothing out and nothing in. It wont take regular readers of cfcuk long to work out what most of us here at this publication long to see - the reinstatement of the 70's badge, the demolition of the hotel and apartments followed by the rebuilding of The Shed and, of course, to compliment the 'new' 55,000 / 60,000 capacity stadium, an equitable pricing structure.

However, according to the London Evening Standard's report on Bates' decision to walk, he made clear his intention to continue to occupy his penthouse apartment. Asked what price he'd accept to vacate his home, he was quoted as saying, "Half of Siberia." The clear inference is that Bates will move - but only if the price is right.

During his period as chairman of Chelsea, Bates often maintained that he took nothing out of the club by way of a salary yet he was, at one time during his tenure, one of the highest paid football 'consultants' in the country. After Bates sold the club, he was graciously allowed the privilege of continuing as chairman by the new regime. He was, after he stepped down in 2005, due to become life president. According to the Standard, Bates would, because of his position, receive 'generous expenses', although a salary would not be provided.

During his resignation speech, Bates said of Roman, "He has bought the toyshop and lets hope he respects the toys." From where we're standing, it appears that it is in fact Bates who has not looked after 'the toys' and, after his latest outburst, has thrown them out of the pram in good style. He has turned his back on Chelsea.

He bought the Chelsea Football Club for £1 and, after revelling in the limelight that came attached, sold it some 22 years later for a personal profit of £17.5m. He now wants a settlement to leave Stamford Bridge once and for all. The question surely has to be, as Chelsea supporters, how much more do you think Bates should TAKE OUT of your football club?

The Guy who Blagged Me

*****

The Thoughts Of Chels Guevara

Although some people might well consider it a shift in position, I will, nevertheless, give a big 'thank-you' to DAVID MELLOR, who was kind enough to give £10 toward the 'BRING BACK THE BADGE' campaign. The long-time recipient of this fanzine made the donation when receiving his copy of issue 33 after a recent CHELSEA home game. While admitting that I have not always agreed with his opinion - especially when it came to what was happening at CHELSEA under Batesy - I was in total agreement with an article concerning the ex-MP that appeared in the February edition of FSF News - the Football Supporters Federation newsletter.

Written by Federation Chairman Malcolm Clarke, the article highlighted what he saw as the demise of BBC Radio Five's "6.06" phone-in show since the departure of the former head of the now defunct Football Task Force. Clarke highlights how, when MELLOR was hosting the show, he allowed the show to be used as a forum to draw attention to some of the issues confronting fans that were, very often, swept aside by the clubs they supported. Although managing to keep the main focus on the game of football itself, MELLOR maintained a constant theme that dictated that the game of professional football belonged to the supporters who invested their love and commitment in their chosen teams.

This meant that issues such as ticket pricing and problems attending matches were high on the agenda, as well as the mistreatment of fans by the clubs, stewards and police. As Clarke wrote, he, "...allowed the programme to be used as an effective voice for fans."

One CHELSEA SUPPORTER who has tried to get 'airtime' on the "6.06" programme to make a point about what he sees as ridiculous kick-off times to suit the purposes of television (ref; Scarborough, Bolton etc, etc) has contacted me to let me know that he has regularly been refused a platform to raise his point. He is in total agreement with key point number 8 from the FSF 'Fans Blueprint', a statement of intent, to try to establish a principle to ensure, "Prior consultation with supporters on broadcasting contracts to ensure a fair deal for the matchgoing fan and an end to TV overkill."

However, although successful in his attempts in 'getting through to the switchboard' and leaving his question with the 'researchers', those running the "6.06" have consistently decided not to allow his concerns to be raised. This might well be because the question put to the "6.06" people mentioned the fact that since they regained the rights to broadcast live FA Cup football, the BBC have been as guilty as SKY ever was of a total lack of consideration for travelling supporters when scheduling games.

While not directly affecting CHELSEA SUPPORTERS (although the Scarborough KO time was hard work for those travelling from the South of England), the worst example of this was when the Geordies were forced to travel to the South Coast to watch their side play Southampton in a 5.30 pm kick-off. OK, they might have had all day to make to journey down from the grim Norf Eastern wastelands but, as far as getting back after the game had finished was concerned, I'm sure the trip home was horrible, especially for those unfortunate enough to have to rely on the less than poor rail services. While I am able to print the point the CHELSEA SUPPORTER wishes to make within this column, the Five Live listening public is not destined, it seems, to have the chance to hear the grievance on air.

Clarke ended his piece within the FSF News by writing the following, "I don't know how much influence the presenters have in the types of callers put through or the approach taken by the programme, or whether it's all down to the producer. Either way, for me it's a case of come back Mellor, all is forgiven, and I never thought I would say that!"

Mr Clarke... you might be pleased to know that I'm total agreement with you!

Chels Guevara

*****

"I Take Thee Kenneth..."

The melancholic whimper (it wasn't really an aftermath, was it?) which greeted Ken Bates' decision to step off the board of Chelsea Football Club implied a whole lot more than has been said or written since, especially in relation to the voice of the pre-H*ddle Blues fans.

Even amongst our most anti-Greybeard brethren there has never been enough of a deep-set hatred reasonably to stop people from acknowledging his enormous contribution to present day Chelsea. And inside the minds of the small minority of delusional pro-Kennethites there will always be the wonderings of what might have happened, should a certain rich Russian (Roman to my faithful following of blind readers — thanks for the puppy Mr Blunkett) never thought up the idea of buying an association football team. Thus, within the grouping known as 'supporters of the famous CFC' there appears to be a broad happy medium concerning ex-chairman Ken; a sort of "good meal, average service, no tip" reaction, if you will. 'Wot Ken did for us' has been done to death; joining us for our parachuting expedition in 1982, he kindly lent us his umbrella on the way down. It worked, and barring a few bruises and bumps we survived, landing in the rather tatty barn known as Stamford Bridge.

It already had one great wall and Ken broke a lot of sweat rebuilding the other three (as well as a few unnecessary extensions), although his proposal to keep the animals out with a motion detecting rocket launcher was eventually discarded - an electric fence would have been much more fitting... However, we later found out that Mr Bates had borrowed most of his wood from an opportunistic lumberjack down the road, and that the milking wing of Barn Bridge Village Group PLC (used solely by two local cows) was not going to be able to pay for it. In the meantime, loyal workers on the farm were impressed by the quality of the hay present, and also by the fact that this hay was going to top continental hay exposure shows. Even though the bumpkins employed to drive the tractor were occasionally lynched (sometimes causing peasant revolt), employees remained grateful for the continuation of the traditional 'proper haymaking with a stylish swagger' which had been locally renowned for decades.

Err, where was I? Oh yes, whilst most people found Ken's barbarous comments beyond good taste and sense, he was always admired for his headstrong determination to smash and grab in the name of Chelsea. His programme notes were always worthy of a read and although a large proportion grabbed headlines, many highlighted many worthy charities and issues concerning the local community.

Whatever his detractors may say, Chelsea FC will always be in his heart and although he was a modern despot, he was often an enlightened one. All of this, rather belatedly leads me to the core of what I have to say about the man, and what I propose should be done in his name; his attitude is reflected in all of us – in his opinionated, heart-on-sleeve rants and jubilant celebrations – but also in his real world restraint, a vision of assets built in stone, not overpaid flesh, and a desire to leave a long term legacy for our future Blues fans.

May I ask what would be more of a fitting tribute than to rename the West Stand the Ken Bates Stand? Wait a second - before you start using this page as bog roll please consider and reason with what I am saying; first off, the revelations of a change in name would not be vast, after all, it is only that: a change in name; secondly, for those sceptics out there, please realise the parallels in naming the at-times-controversial western side of the ground after the at-all-times controversial Ken – it houses the extortionately priced and silent upper and lower tiers, and the underused corporate boxes sat in by the same underused hotel goers.

Who can forget the pre-Villa Park semi-final taunts aimed at those much despised prawn sandwich munchers, threatening to take the seats deserved of going to the MHL Lower? However, it also mirrors Ken's achievements in more positive terms; it stands out as the beacon of what is now a supremely world class ground, largely built on the back of Bates' endeavours to make us a world-class outfit. It is something which, above all else, reminds of us what we used to be before Ken and his £1 came visiting and it is, more specifically, something that reminds us of Ken himself.

Consider the ironic appropriateness of Ken gruffly being forced to sit next to Matthew for all eternity; between the latter and the new Shed, we will always be able to shout genial abuse in Ol' Greybeard's direction. In a generation's time I would like to be reminded of the guy who originally saved our farm. Would you?

Chelsea 'til I die!

El Russo

ISSUE 35 April 2004

The Thoughts Of Chels Guevara

April 9th will see the 38th anniversary of our very own SMIFFY'S first CHELSEA game. It was at STAMFORD BRIDGE and he was privileged enough to have watched the BLUES demolish West Ham 6 - 2 in a First Division fixture (CHELSEA scorers included BOBBY TAMBLING who notched a brace and RON HARRIS who not only scored for THE BLUES, but also scored an own goal!!).

I'm pleased to let you know that his love and support for CHELSEA FOOTBALL CLUB is still as strong as ever and, if all goes according to plan, he will still be following his side in another 38 years time.

Good on you SMIFFY! Now, if only those in charge CHELSEA realised and appreciated the devotion of supporters such as SMIFFY. If they did, the relationship between the supporters and the club itself might be somewhat better.

Chels Guevara

*****

Substance, Not Style… Please

The likelihood is that Claudio Ranieri won't be manager of Chelsea next season. The press, media and "sources" at the club have confirmed this rumour more than enough times for it to be denied with much confidence. Sadly, I believe that when we examine this period of Chelsea history this incident will be seen as a time when Chelsea abandoned reason for madness. When Roman (bless him) decided that it was about time

Chelsea were talked about in the same breath as Real Madrid, AC Milan and others, he was sensible enough to realise that this was a project that would have to be completed over the long term. Indeed, in one of his rare direct comments he said; "It is hard to say if it will be the most successful season in the history of the team. The internal structure of the team has been destroyed and time is needed for the players to play together and only then can you hope for a result."

Ultimately, the club's goal is to be as successful as Real Madrid. However, one of the incomprehensible aspects of the current situation is that the club appear to be thinking as if it is Real Madrid without having achieved anything like as much as the Galaticos. As a result such careful and cautious thinking as exemplified by Roman at the start of the season has not been followed, something that has become apparent when you look at some of the rather surprising comments made by Peter Kenyon: "Roman wants exciting, good football. It is not just a case of winning it (the championship) with more draws than anyone else or fewer goals. He does understand from a real fans' perspective that you all want to romance about the fifth goal that got knocked in from 30 yards."

I was staggered when I saw this comment. The first point that comes to mind is the fact that we haven't won the Championship for 50 years. When you consider this point, it seems that Kenyon's remark is rather disappointing. I praised him in an earlier article as being a man of pragmatism, but the more we see of him the more disappointed I am. Our efforts should be concentrated in winning the title first, how we do it is not my particular concern so long as we've won it. Do you think Liverpool fans cared when they won those 3 trophies with some fairly ugly football? Do you think Milan fans cared that they won the Champions League despite scoring one the fewest goal totals in the competition? The answer is no, because as everyone knows you have to complete your objectives first before you can worry about what style they are done in. Our objective this season was to show that we can at least improve and show signs of being able to win something in the near future. A trophy would have been nice but not essential - it was the first season of the new era.

As Ranieri says: "I had to take Chelsea forward, to the point where we could be among the top three clubs challenging for the title."

That was Roman's stated aim and now the manager is to be sacked for achieving it. Arguably, if Liverpool had stuck to their guns in playing the effective football that won them the 3 trophies in 2001 they might have won the league and they might now be in a position to say that they want to play in a certain way.

We've not even won the Premiership yet and we have Peter Kenyon telling us that he wants the fifth goal being knocked in from 30 yards. Cart before the horse? I seem to remember T*ttenham fans complaining about St*ffen Fr*und and the fact that G*orge Gr*ham was playing negative football. Well where are those Sp*rs fans now? The answer is moaning on phone-in's complaining that they don't have a defensive midfielder and that they can't defend. Lessons are not being learnt.

It been said before but it needs to be said again for some people to understand. At time of writing, we have kept 17 clean sheets. This means that the opposition have failed to score against us in half of our games in the Premiership. You cannot be lucky for nearly ¾ of a season. We have also won the most amount of away games in the Premiership and have not conceded a single goal away in the Champions League, and are 1 game away from the record of clean sheets in the competition. We have achieved this with the attacking players who, rightly or wrongly, Claudio wanted to build his team around (Veron, Duff and Crespo) out for a sizeable portion of the season.

Of course you shouldn't make excuses for injuries and of course we should be able to cope with the squad we have. This is the theory we all like to repeat like a mantra. However, the reality is somewhat different. The loss of key players hurts. You want evidence? Look at how Arsenal fell apart when they lost Campbell and Ljungberg for just a few games last season.

Whatever people may say about Claudio's tinkering (as if no other manager ever makes a substitution or changes their line up). No one can say we haven't improved in the league, No one can say that we haven't distinguished ourselves in the Champions League. Neither can anyone say that this has been achieved in the midst of his own club failing to give him the support and the confidence to manage his own team and to go about putting Chelsea on the World map. It cannot feasibly be argued that this Chelsea team is not on the right track to becoming an effective one and that is what we should be concentrated on. Effectiveness is not always pretty but it works. We're likely to finish second in the league bar a crazy run of form and could yet make the semi-finals in the Champions league. I'd take that over and above being a Utd fan at the moment.

It seems that the club want just throw it all out of the window because we're not flashy and don't have a flashy manager. I just can't make any sense of it and I worry that we'll go down in history as screwing up the best chance this club has ever had to become a force in World football because of it.

Football is not like a vending machine; you don't just pour money in and get guaranteed results. The reality is it takes patience and takes time to create a great side. It always has and it always will. It's somewhat ironic that we hear the club's top brass going on about how we want to be like Real Madrid and play football like Real Madrid. The fact of the matter is that Real will go down as a great side, but they'll also go down in history as the side who never truly took the chance they had to become the greatest side of all time because they had a president who chose not to buy defenders despite the warnings of the manager. This was their downfall last year in the Champions League and could well be their downfall in the same competition as well as in their own domestic league. What will happen to them when a now 31 years old Zidane calls it quits? When Figo decides his ankle injury is too much?

We have the chance to be greater but the way things are going at the moment we're not going to take it because we're being blinded by the same impatience and lack of understanding that could ultimately scupper them and that did scupper Inter Milan. Instead of looking at the example of Ferguson's dynasty and (choke) Arsene Wenger at Arsenal and seeing the way in which they were allowed to build and mould teams over time, we want instant success. Well I'm sorry but it just doesn't happen that way. Ask yourself this: Surely the new manager will come from abroad? Won't he have to buy his own choice of players? Won't then team have to learn how to play to his style? Meantime, Arsenal get stronger and their players will build even more of the understanding that comes from having a manager that has been at the club for more than a few years and players who've been with him for most of that time.

So what will happen if we don't win anything as a result? He'll probably be fired too. Then what?

I was also interested to see the second part of Mr Kenyon's comment: "He does understand from a real fans' perspective that you all want to romance about the fifth goal that got knocked in from 30 yards."

I find it interesting to note that Mr Kenyon knows so much about "the real fans perspective" when, allegedly, Chelsea supporters who have written to him with their views, ideas and suggestions for the club, have had their mail unanswered. I, for one, know that my ideas and those of several other Chelsea fans don't concur with his. My "perspective" is to first have a side that is capable of winning a title by winning games. I don't really care how it's done, so long as it's done.

When I've seen the title being held aloft by John Terry, I'll then bother myself about whether the 5th goal has been scored from 30 yards or even 2.

The Chelsea Advocate

*****

The Football Factory – The Review

"It is a face of Britain that won't be seen in the travel brochures, but it is nearer the core and culture of the nation than many will admit".
Chris Nelson, The Times
The Football Factory is set to become the new and long reigning heavyweight champion of football-orientated cinema. Bloodier than The Firm and smarter than ID, this Brit flick is the dogs bollocks.

Based on the best-selling cult-classic book penned by John King, the film centres around Tommy Johnson (Danny Dyer), a die-hard Chelsea fan that lives for the weekends of class A powdered drugs, easy lays and "occasionally kicking the fuck out of someone". We follow Tommy through the preceding weeks to the climatic match where Chelsea play their arch-rivals Millwall at the Den in an FA Cup tie. This is one meeting that is sure to sort out the men from the boys. However, through a series of run-ins with members of the rival firm, Tommy has set off a chain of events that will culminate around this fateful game and he will be forced to ask himself, "C'mon really... IS IT WORTH IT?"

Dyer is supported by a stellar cast spanning four generations of firm stalwarts- Tommy's best pal Rod (Neil Maskell) his partner in a number of crimes, Bill Farrell (Dudley Sutton) his veteran grandfather, Billy Bright (Frank Harper) as a psychotic fan who gets a real kick out of giving people a good kicking and Zeberdee (Roland Manookian) who is a "thieving little c*nt" and the new blood for the firm. The naturalistic performances from the main cast cannot be faulted, while the complexity, warmth and ferocity of male relationships are portrayed commendably by all the actors. This is especially true of Billy Bright, and his relationship with Fred, leader of the rival Millwall firm (played by a menacing Tamer Hassan) which is a fabulous representation of the hypocrisy and tribal nature of the football hooligan. Danny Dyer proves himself as a great lead actor in his role as Tommy. He is funny, cocky, sympathetic and identifiable – it is although the part was truly made for him to play.

The star player behind-the-scenes is Director Nick Love – responsible for cult classic film *Goodbye Charlie Bright*. Love has crafted this tale using a real knowledge and understanding of football subculture. *The Football Factory* is well-directed, eliciting cracking performances and spinning a fast-paced storyline in its 90 minutes with as much excitement as you can find on any pitch.

The Football Factory provides an intelligent and critical representation of the phenomenon of English/British hooliganism and, rather than condemning or celebrating this world you, the viewer, are left to make up your own mind. Moreover, 'it is as it is'. The end result? A firm favourite that packs a proper punch.

Emma H

*****

It's Time For Chelsea And Claudio To Part Company

The season had been progressing well. We were 2nd in the table, and through to the semi-finals of the Champions League. Indeed, there was also a groundswell of support for our Manager, Claudio Ranieri, as the Chelsea supporters – as well as the supporters of other teams – considered that he was the architect of Chelsea's success. Moreover, there was some sympathy with Claudio at the way the genial man was being treated.

I was, in fact, one of Claudio Ranieri's staunchest supporters. Even at the beginning, when he seemed confused, and he was mocked for his idiosyncratic command of English, I was convinced that his tactical nous was invaluable – and that he was doing a sterling job in restructuring our squad for the future. Indeed, before a fateful Tuesday evening in Monaco, I considered that there would have been no shame in going out of the Champions League in a semi-final. I'm sorry, but now I realise that there is actually considerable shame if we are ejected on the back of such a poor showing. And that the blame for this, and for an end of the season that seems to be heading down the toilet after a highpoint just before Easter, has to be laid at the feet of Claudio Ranieri.

It was difficult to gather any coherent thoughts after the abject performance in Monaco, so stunned were many of us by what we had witnessed. However, one thing was clear: in terms of lessons learnt, there must be some cold and hard assessment of Claudio Ranieri as the Chelsea manager. For if the victory at Arsenal was the high-point of the season, everything that he has done subsequently suggests that he is determined not so much to blot his copybook as to redecorate it Jackson Pollock-style.

After all, a certain rot didn't set in only on Tuesday. It had already been festering in the weakness that we showed in the previous 3 League games. There is clearly a motivational problem - as if the team is playing out the rest of the season from the Highbury High. More fundamentally, however, is the feeling that Claudio has lost the plot, and can't contain some of his instincts to fiddle.

Ah Claudio. We wanted to continue to love you and to support you through thick and thin until the end of the season. But you've made that impossible now. It's as if you've been doing your utmost to provide as much ammunition as possible to all your detractors, the people who considered that your constant tinkering was a handicap to Chelsea's progress, the fact that you haven't worked out what is your best 11 yet, or the notion that, frankly, if we deserve the best, surely we could bring in someone even better than you. To be brutal, Claudio, being a thoroughly nice bloke is no longer good enough to have our support. Neither is the sympathy that you deserve for being treated in a shoddy fashion by the Chelsea bosses.

There's an uncomfortable feeling dawning that maybe actually those cold-hearted suits were right. They can feel vindicated by your performance over the past 2 weeks.

Many of us, however, are having to come to terms with the unpleasant realisation that we might well have let our emotion and empathy cloud our judgement. Because, let's face it, Ranieri's tactical choices in the second half of that Monaco game played into the hands of all those who don't have any qualms about producing a headline as crass as 'Tinker has a stinker'.

His substitutions were all wrong - from placing Veron on the left, to switching the strikers around, to bringing off one defender in order to shore up the attack, and then to bring on another defender who was asked to play out of position.

Many other people have analysed just how poor these substitutions were. We can only add that each substitution further removed the shape and coherence of our side. Each substitution was followed by a moment of instability when our team had to adjust to a shape that was unfamiliar.

By the final whistle, there were a good 5 or 6 players who were on the pitch outside of their natural positions. How on Earth could that have been a tactic to win the game? That's before one considers the imbalance brought to the side.

There are rumours of players on the pitch desperately looking to the bench as they were seeking for instructions. They were as confused as we, the spectators, were. There are also reports of the players' anger spilling over in the dressing room. "What the fuck was that all about?" an international is said to have asked, whilst another's text message to his father, saying that Claudio was a dickhead, was also leaked. It is very dangerous when the coach has lost the confidence of his players. The very same players who had, until now, been very supportive of Claudio Ranieri.

When Claudio gets the tactics/substitutions right, he does so with mastery. One has to ask how he got them so spectacularly wrong. But the charge hanging over him cannot be limited only to tactical ineptitude. It is also the case that he could not prevent himself from fiddling with the squad. Up until that point in the match (and in the season), to be honest, Chelsea were doing well. They were increasing in confidence and the team formation was gelling.

There was a feeling that, as time passed, that coherence would only increase. Come the half-time break, Chelsea could feel confident about the second half. Despite the dubious circumstances in which Monaco went a man down, that surely would have been a boost. Yet it was Claudio who pulled away the supporting beams in Chelsea's shape. Our formation was good; it should have been up to Monaco to adapt to having 10 men on the pitch, rather than Chelsea, who had the perfect opportunity to continue as they were.

Bringing on extra strikers doesn't actually guarantee more goals. That kind of tactic must be the last gasp attempt of a manager who realises that, at that point, the team has nothing left to lose. That was not Chelsea's case as, effectively, we reduced our supply to the strikers. In any case, the strikers were being asked to play in roles that were unfamiliar to them.

Claudio Ranieri managed, in 45 minutes, to fritter away all the goodwill that he had accumulated. In truth, the seeds of that wastage were planted already several matches ago. They were being nurtured by the frustration that fans and players had seen at a lack of direction seen in the 3 League matches since the Arsenal high. The 22 changes to the squad that had been witnessed, and which resulted in a failure to win 4 consecutive games, were a clear indication of having lost the road map. All this came to a head on a Tuesday night on the Mediterranean coast, as there was a feeling that even if we couldn't possibly win the League, we would have a clear crack at the Champions League. Even that crack seems to be on the road to failure after the first leg.

In addition to that, there is a major motivational problem. We could have believed that the Champions League was the challenge for all the players (and, apparently, we can't even get that right). However, how is it that the League slipped so quickly from our grasp? We were within touching distance of Arsenal. Suddenly, after the famous Highbury game, we let it all slip, reaping only 2 points from 9. Of course, it is one thing to have got the tactics wrong and to score a dismal no-score draw against Middlesbrough. But was it really necessary for Claudio to concede the Premiership there and then? The day after, he stated that. "I said Arsenal could only lose the title but after the Liverpool match I say well done, they are the champions. They are the champions because they showed - not quality, because they are full of quality - but fantastic reaction and fantastic character. Well done. In my opinion, they are now the Premiership champions."

Many fans were stunned. What was Claudio doing? It is one thing to be polite – we all like and appreciate that. It is another to recognise the qualities of your opponent. But it is something else completely to lie down and let your rival tickle your tummy. Claudio could well have simply stated that winning the title was even harder after that draw, but that he fully intended to fight until the very final whistle. Indeed, that the Premiership title is only awarded only when it is mathematically awarded. Not before.

There would have been nothing impolite, nothing ungracious about saying that Chelsea were still in the race until they were clearly out of it – and that Claudio would be battling on. For the fans, that particular declaration from Claudio was completely out of synch with what we were feeling. We can barely imagine what the players were feeling when it appeared that their efforts would be fruitless.

In that dismal 45 minute spell, Claudio Ranieri managed to lose the support of the Chelsea faithful. Of course, I'm only showing the bitterness of the disappointed, those who realise that their faith has been misplaced. But for me, it is clearly time to start the process of bringing in a new coach. Not anyone, mind. Not Sven, not David O'Leary, not Steve MacLaren: if Chelsea are to have such ordinary cloggers, frankly I'd prefer to stay with Claudio. But there are other coaches out there who could ensure that, with all the player talent that we have on our books, we can do better

EuroBlue

ISSUE 36

The Thoughts Of Chels Guevara

This edition of the column starts with a 'Was That You?' appeal. One of the cfcuk contributors happened by chance to strike up a conversation with an American who was also standing in the same queue for the EAST STAND prior to kick-off sometime circa 2001/2002. Employing his observational qualities to the maximum, our man noticed that the gentleman in question was in possession of a season ticket for the MIDDLE TIER. Seeing that his ticket had been spotted, he said, "I bet you're wondering what a guy from America is doing here..." The CHELSEA SUPPORTER, genuinely pleased that someone from the States had fallen in love with THE BLUES, said simply, "I'm glad you enjoy the game." If you are reading this column and you are the American gentleman in question and, if cfcuk's informant is correct, would you, Bruce Buck, please get in touch with this fanzine asap, re; CHELSEA FOOTBALL CLUB. I guarantee that striking up a dialogue with the support in the 'early stages' will save a lot of bother in the long run.

Anybody who is thinking about messin' with any of cfcuk's matchday sellers had better think twice! RORY BEN KING, aged nine-years, weighing in for the 38k class and fighting out of the BLUE corner, made a winning debut in his first ever boxing match. He wore the colours of Chichester Boys Club against an opponent from Marlow Boys and beat him over three one-minute rounds. Perhaps we'd better think about sending him down next time anybody we know has any problems with the ticket office.

Sharp-eyed CHELSEA SUPPORTERS might well have noticed RORY, alongside another product of the cfcuk youth system, namely URCHIN D, on the pitch at half time during the recent game against Everton. They were there helping a CHELSEA SUPPORTER receive a Pitch Owner's share certificate and were introduced to CHELSEA legend BOBBY TAMBLING. THE BLUES' leading all-time goal scorer was, according to reports, 'feeling humbled, honoured and privileged to have met a couple of the cfcuk staff.'

Chels Guevara

*****

You Must Be Joking

Choose overbearing arrogance. Choose to see yourselves as one of the giants of continental football when you've never even reached a European Cup semi-final in your entire history. Choose systematic dirty play and calling it "competitiveness". Choose the most staged, contrived, up-your-own-arses goal celebrations ever witnessed. Choose having the ugliest man on earth as your centre-back and the second ugliest as your manager. Choose winning three Championships in twelve seasons and acting like you've won seven in nine. Choose drawing 99% of your fan base from the ranks of the suburban English middle classes. Choose Patrick Vieira whinging about having to play too much football even though he gets six games' rest every season due to suspensions. Choose paying £9 million for Francis Jeffers. Choose being "The Bank of England Club". Choose Dennis Bergkamp and his carefully timed elbows into the side of the head. Choose deliberately disrespecting and belittling the other team by playing keepy-uppy in their half with a few minutes to go. Choose forcing merchandise vendors out of business because they might deprive you of a couple of hundred quid on match days. Choose fancying yourselves as better than Real Madrid, then having Auxerre run rings around you at home. Choose Sol Campbell continually tripping over himself. Choose turning the sports section of The Observer into a Gunners fanzine. Choose getting away with light or delayed punishments at FA disciplinary hearings because you've had every possible string pulled by David Dein. Choose a persecution complex nonetheless and never shut up about it. Choose gamesmanship. Choose embarrassing yourselves in a Renault "Vava-voom" ad and then disgracing yourselves further at the World Cup Finals. Choose watching an opponent miss a last-minute penalty against you, then running after him and jeering him. Choose George Graham grinding his way to the dullest championship win of all time. Choose stepping forward in a four man line with your right hands all raised in the air, then screaming abuse at the linesman when he has the audacity to keep his flag down. Choose picking Ray Parlour for over a decade. Choose having the quietest stadium in the world ("The Library") as your home ground, and then having the cheek to slag Man Utd about their fans… Choose having Nick Hornby as the mouthpiece of your supporters. Choose making umpteen lists of reasons why Arsenal are so great, and then admitting you didn't bother following them for a few years in the 1980s when they were getting sh*te results. Choose Tony Adams coming out with his usual dreary "I am a recovering addict" spiel every time a premiership footballer blots his copybook. Choose pretending that five or six years of playing in a watchable fashion makes up for inflicting over a century of ultra-defensive dogsh*te on English football watchers. Choose Igor Stepanovs, Nelson Vivas, Kanu, Pascal Cygan, Davor Suker, Gilles Grimandi, David Grondin, Remi Garde, Kaba Diawara, Junichi Inamoto, Jeremie Aliadiere, Oleg Luzhny, Luis Boa Morte, Richard Wright, Stefan Volz, Christopher Wreh, and all the other turkeys that nobody ever mentions when creaming themselves about how great Wenger is in the transfer market. Choose 58 red cards in seven years. Choose lying to the media that you didn't see a single one of the incidents that caused all these red cards. Choose being a bunch of smug, self-regarding w*nkers who are well on their way to being even more unpopular than Man Utd in less than half the time. Choose Arsenal.

A man is driving a car down the road in an erratic manner. He gets pulled over by a policeman, who says, "I'm sorry sir, but I'm going to have to breathalyse you."

The man promptly produces a card, which reads, THIS MAN IS ASTHMATIC. PLEASE DO NOT TAKE BREATH.

The policeman says, 'Well in that case sir, you'll have to accompany me to the station for a blood sample.'

The man again produces a card, this one reading, THIS MAN IS A HAEMOPHILIAC, PLEASE DO NOT TAKE BLOOD.

To this, the policeman says, 'well, in that case, we'll have to take a urine sample.' With that, the man produces yet another card, this one reading, THIS MAN IS A T*TTENHAM SUPPORTER. PLEASE DO NOT TAKE THE P*SS.

Hocus McPocus

ISSUE 37 August 2004

The Thoughts Of Chels Guevara

Meanwhile, it seems that the cfcuk staff are probably amongst the hardest fanzine sellers in the country. Following the mention of RORY BEN KING'S boxing debut in issue 36, the FULHAM ROAD'S best salesman HARRY MOSS (as featured on the cover of this book) was pictured in the Daily Mirror delivering a punch to former World Boxing champion Frank Bruno. So punters, you know what this means ... don't mess us about or else!

Chels Guevara

*****

Mourinho – The Man

According to Brian Glanville, the doyen of British football writers who has been covering the game for nearly 50 years (it just seems like longer), the knives are already being sharpened for José Mourinho, even before Chelsea's new manager has seen his expensively assembled side kick a ball in anger.

"Schadenfreude," Glanville says in dire warning, "as we used to say when I was at The People."

For one thing of which Mourinho could never be accused of is false modesty. After leading Porto - poor, unfashionable, under achieving Porto - to the UEFA Cup and European Champions' League in successive seasons, Mourinho has a finely attuned notion of his own abilities and worth (a rumoured £5 million a year contract to take over at Stamford Bridge).

"I have been coaching only a short time," Mourinho told the assembled journalists at his first press conference as Chelsea manager, "and I have won the Champions League, the UEFA Cup, and my team has dominated its national league. Ranieri has been in football for many years, and he won nothing."

If Mourinho's accuracy was not perfect - Claudio Ranieri, his predecessor at Chelsea, had led a team to the Spanish Cup, once - his point was well made. In buying Chelsea in 2003, Roman Abramovich clearly had no intention of buying failure. Yet Ranieri, the manager he inherited, was unlikely ever to give him success. Even last December, with five months of the season to go and his side at the top of the Premiership, Ranieri publicly conceded the Title to Arsenal and Manchester United.

Then, at the climax of the season, with victory at Monaco in the Champions League Semi-Final within his grasp, the Tinkerman tinkered crassly. With rumours that Abramovich wanted to hire Sven Goran Eriksson, the England coach, swirling around for months, Ranieri took to calling himself "Dead Man Walking". Only the European Cup itself might have saved the amiable Italian's job.

Yet in Mourinho, Abramovich may have hired a better coach than Eriksson. Time will be the judge of that, but at least Chelsea enter the club's centenary season with a man at the helm without the inferiority complex of his predecessor and capable of playing mind games with Wenger and Ferguson on equal terms. Mourinho, though, might disagree with that. He considers himself the superior of the managers of Arsenal and Manchester United: he has, after all, called himself "The Special One".

"Please don't call me arrogant," Mourinho said. "What I am saying is true. I'm European champion, so I don't want to be 'one out of the bottle'; I want to be The One."

At 41, Mourinho has clear objectives in terms of selecting his squad ("23 players, including three goalkeepers. No more than that"). Nor would he allow the likes of Hernan Crespo and Seba Veron to be foisted upon him, as Ranieri did. The Argentineans were quickly shown the Stamford Bridge exit when Mourinho arrived, and other, older players on large contracts, such as Jimmy Floyd Hasselbaink, also left. "I work with short squads in a very specific, intense way, and we must communicate".

In his first weeks' training, in early July with those members of his squad that had not played in the European Championships, Mourinho showed himself to be ruthless in other ways, bringing in his own backroom staff at the expense of other, established figures. Then came the twice-a-day training sessions, followed by a 10-point code of conduct that legislates for everything, from the players' bedtime to the food that they eat. And whatever salary level a player might be on, under Mourinho they will play their share of reserve team games if it is necessary in the interests of the squad. "He's different, it's hard work, lots of running, but always with the ball," said Joe Cole. Despite having been in England's squad in Portugal, Cole returned to Chelsea early, eager to prove himself for his new boss. With Mourinho favouring a 4-3-1-2 formation at Porto, with the Brazilian-born attacking midfielder Deco in the "hole" behind the two forwards, Cole, too often a peripheral figure in Chelsea's midfield under Ranieri, may have at last found a role. "He's been very encouraging," said Cole.

And yet, all indications are that Mourinho can also be very discouraging, too. Abramovich, having hired his own man, did so on the clear understanding that Mourinho should be allowed to get on with the job in hand. The key moment in Mourinho's recruitment came during a meeting on board the Abramovich yacht off St Tropez, when Mourinho produced a dossier that told the owner what the prospective club manager - not team manager, but manager over all playing matters - expected and wanted and would give.

"Sometimes, I can understand his desires," said Mourinho of Abramovich. "He had some very good moments when he could smell the European Cup Final – and I had the taste of it. I think I'm a winner because I'm good at what I do and I am surrounded by top people. I prefer to say 'we', and not only in relation to players, but people who work with me and understand my philosophy."

Players, according to Mourinho, do not win trophies. Teams do. Thus, after bids to land Steven Gerrard and Wayne Rooney broke down, Mourinho's first signings as Chelsea manager, in another summer spending spree of almost £100 million, were good, capable professionals, but hardly Gallacticos – more Gary Neville's' than David Beckham's'.

From Porto, he brought defenders Ricardo Carvalho (for a seemingly extravagant £20 million - Real had offered only £7 million) and Paulo Ferreira (£13 million), and he plucked from Dutch football the promising winger Arjen Robben (£12 million) and Mateja Kezman (£5 million). Only by spending a club record £24 million for Didier Drogba, did Mourinho seem to go down the superstar route.

"I have a big impression of players and I am the defender of team spirit," Mourinho said, "so I should not tell you, 'I love this player, I want to change this one'. What I love is players who want to win, not just in matches, but day after day."

And so players on his existing staff who he admires. Frank Lampard and John Terry, were both swiftly given generous new contracts, with Terry taking the captain's armband from Marcel Desailly, who was another to leave during the summer.

"I can say we have top players and - I'm sorry - we have a top manager," he said. "But we have to work, we have to be on the pitch together 15 days before I can say if they are ready to work with my methodology or not. I accept the word 'failure' will be used if I do not win something in the first year. It is nothing to be afraid of. It is wrong to say that Didier Deschamps is a failure because he lost the European Cup Final; I think he deserves as much prestige as me. But as motivation, I catch with both hands that we have to win something."

To win what Abramovich really wants, the European Cup, entails "beating every shark - and every shark is there," Mourinho says.

"I don't want protection from this fact, and I will tell the players that the first ambition is to win the first match of Chelsea on August 14; the second ambition is to win the second match on the 21." Already, Mourinho is becoming attuned to the English game: he just wants to take each game as it comes.

Chopper

*****

No Tears Goodbye

I've spoken to a few Chels over the close season, fans with a markedly similar viewpoint, the same deep sense of regret at the passing over of Claudio. Only Big Brother and Euro 2004 have pulled some through their self-induced lethargy of the summer, after the sad demise of their Mr Tinkerman. How could he not be allowed at least another season? How can we do without him?

There was even a letter in that sad excuse of a rag, the club's official mouthpiece, Onside, bemoaning another loss - 'the sad and untimely departure of Ken Bates.' That was not a widely expressed view. Perhaps his latest dummy-out-of-pram tantrums have finally convinced some of his erstwhile supporters that Ken was not, in fact, that in love with our club. His £17 million pay off was insufficient. He came back, suing for more. He said he wouldn't give up his penthouse above the shed for all the oil in Georgia i.e. it will cost yet another huge packet to be able to build a proper stand where he built his ridiculous money-draining-Village. Yes Ken. All you are doing is proving what many knew all along, you were only in it for the money. Now stick your £17 million dummy back in and .... off.

So what is the issue here? Bring back Ken, bring back Claudio? Is this really what some people want? What are they on? Are they for real? Do they have just a little inkling of sanity left in their obviously under-developed little minds? How nuts can one be, someone who obviously once had a little taste and style to choose the Blues?

One thing I find very odd with the pro-Claudio brigade (forget the pro Ken, a lobotomy is the only sensible solution for these poor lost souls) - where were you in the three odd seasons before the home leg of the Arse game? You certainly never sang for him, you never made your affection and undying support clear back then. Not once did his name ring out like it did that night of the Champions League.

All it showed was how easily little minds can be bent by a few choice words in the tabloids. After ridiculing Tinkers for years, for his poor English, for his poor selections, for... all of it, they decide in a typical-English-press way, to build up a hero. And so many fell for it - hook, line and sinker. Don't you have your own minds to make up?

The last issue of cfcuk was full of articles writing his obituary, most laying the final straw on that night in Monaco. For me, Claudio had to go way before then, a long time before that much derided night of tinkering. Claudio is a nice man, without a doubt, with honour and humour, attributes rare in the Premiership. But he lacked many, many more qualities which are necessary in a successful manger.

Many will wonder what I am on, whether it is I who need the lobotomy. We came second, our highest finish since 1955. We were just a tinker away from a Champions League final. We were great. Well, if that is what you think, you didn't see enough matches. Yes, we won, and occasionally won well and with great style. The 4–0 against Lazio, and that night at Highbury are up there with the greatest Chelsea nights of all. But those nights only showed the paucity of the majority of our performances last year.

Anyone with such a great collection of footballers as we undoubtedly hold, could have cobbled together at least a few good games with that squad. And I mean, anyone. The fact that Claudio managed it so infrequently showed how poor his tactical awareness and man management was.

There were far too many first halfs at Bolton, or first 80 minutes at Man City throughout the year. Games where we got points, but played some of the worst football I have seen for years. Winning is not all. If it was, we would not have been Chels fans for the last XX years (insert as appropriate, 33 for me.) One thing you cannot take away from him was his defence building. Bringing in JT was inspirational. Last year we had 21 clean sheets. Fantastic, unbelievable. Compare that to Manure's and the Arse's 15 and 16. But that is the Italians all over, get a great defence, and then bore us to death. Claudio, you were the man to take on an ageing team with huge debts. You simply weren't the one to take us on with Roman's riches.

As to whether José is, only time can tell. If you didn't get that lucky goal disallowed at Old Trafford, and Porto went out as they should have, I doubt you would be in charge now. But Napoleon liked his lucky generals. And I like his good looks, arrogance and self-belief, all classic Chelsea qualities. You can see he fits in at once.

I like how he went to call in on Eidur as well as the England Chelsea boys in that pre 2004 friendly. Attention to detail. I like cutting the squad, though the numbers brought in, loaned out and sold seem to have been playfully rejigged.

I am not so sure about the criticism of Van Gaal at Barcelona for bringing in 9 Dutch players as showing a distinct lack of self-confidence, being surrounded by fellow countrymen, and then proceeding to bring in more Portuguese players to these shores than any team since the 66 World Cup. £13 mill for a right back who can't even get in their team?

But best of all, I like the fact in our centenary year, when winning the title would have such a sweet ring, you are not Claudio. The Emperor is dead, long live the Empire. No regrets, and certainly, no tears goodbye.

Norvern Muppet

ISSUE 38 September 2004

The Sheditorial

It's great to hear that José Mourinho is intent on making Super Frank Lampard into Europe's greatest player. When he joined Chelsea from West Ham, many scoffed at the £11m transfer fee that was paid. After taking time to settle in, Chelsea supporters can now only marvel at the player Frank has become, not only for Chelsea Football Club, but for England as well.

After Chelsea's defeat to the Gooners in the 2002 FA Cup Final, I was one of the few who went to Fulham Broadway to welcome the team back. The players, although bitterly disappointed, were good enough to walk along the barriers holding back the crowd and meet and talk to all who were there.

As Frank walked the line towards me, I held out my hand to shake his and asked, "Are you glad you came to Chelsea, Frank? Do you like it here?" Grinning broadly and looking me in the eye, he replied, "I love it here!" Well, Frank, I think I can speak for everyone at Chelsea Football Club when I say that we love having you here too! Good luck for the rest of the season, Frank.

When this fanzine, then known as Matthew Harding's Blue And White Army, was first published, the intention was to keep alive some of the ideals that we felt were dear to Chelsea supporters. We set out to oppose the then chairman Ken Bates' plans for a 'Chelsea Village' and his desecration of the history and artefacts that were, to many, the embodiment of what Chelsea Football Club is all about.

While we were vilified by many, and misunderstood by many more, our aims were always based upon principles with which no 'true' Chelsea supporter could argue. Despite the fact that the general overtone of the fanzine and the BlueAndWhiteArmy.net website was almost exclusively against Bates, we always gave people the opportunity to defend him. Unfortunately, our efforts to give a 'balance' to both the fanzine and website often went un-noticed. Instead, we gained a reputation for being against the club and labelled as 'wreckers'.

However, we held our ground and, over the years, have found that we now have a loyal following of regular readers and website patrons who are, judging by sales and kind comments, more than happy with what we are doing. Perhaps one of the reasons for this is that we are now seen as somewhat less confrontational than we were when we were at odds with most of what Bates stood for. That said, we want to make it clear that we wish to support and help those now charged with running Chelsea. We are definitely not out to cause any trouble with the Board but instead, seek to further develop the relationship that we now have with those at the Club who know us. I will though, for the sake of clarity, again outline the basic fundamental principles of the cause we seek to champion.

The restoration of, and belief in, the '70's crest; The demolition of the 'Village hotels/apartments and a rebuilding of a stadium at Stamford Bridge that would allow a sixty, possibly seventy thousand capacity; An equitable pricing structure; A supporter representative on the Board of Directors; No shirt Sponsorship; The club should stress to those concerned, the importance of supporters being able to travel to and from games at reasonable times, as opposed to having to cater for the mass ranks of the armchair supporter via live televised broadcasts; A recognition that the club's 'bread and butter' is earned within the structure of the English League and FA, and as great a prominence as possible should be placed upon Chelsea's responsibilities, as part of the English system, to the other 91 League clubs; Chelsea Football Club is a worthy and up-standing concern that will not only put something back into the local community but will give that community a sense of pride in the club.

After more than two decades of Ken Bates, Roman Abramovich gave each and every one of us a new found zest for Chelsea Football Club. After years of mistrust and concern for the future, Roman's financial input and his obvious love for the club gives us hope that one day the above aims might be achieved. It's what we, as Chelsea supporters, want and we know it makes sense. The period of doubt is over… it's now time to sow the seeds of possibility.

The Guy Who Blagged Me

*****

Don't Worry - Be Happy!

At the time of writing, we are a few weeks into the season and still have a 100% record (that's the kiss of death!) I can't remember a time in living memory where Chelsea have had such a great start - thank goodness Coventry aren't in the Premiership these days! Yet apparently winning is not good enough for some fans.

I can just about understand pundits and rags laying into us. After all, it's become fashionable to bash Chelsea these days if you're not a supporter. This is one of the pitfalls of being a top side, and something we've had to come to terms with over the past year or so. Though some would argue that it's always been fashionable to bash Chelsea!

What I do find it a bit strange, is hearing some of our own fans grumbling. Seemingly not placated by the team winning matches, some have deemed fit to moan about the style of our play. It isn't just the prawn sandwich/Sky armchair brigade either, but some supporters who have been going for years. You'd think that long time Chelsea supporters would be a bit less hasty when making negative comments. Sadly, the expectation level has been raised so high nowadays, that even getting three points (and doing so comfortably, which I believe we have done in pretty much all of our games so far) isn't good enough!

José Mourinho has been the first to admit that we haven't played "beautiful football" so far, but after such a short time in the job, it is a tad unreasonable to expect his team to replicate Brazil 1970. It's been all about getting points on the board, something which the Portuguese fella has so far delivered. He is a winner, and would rather win games by defending than play entertaining football and lose 4-3.

People will point to Wenger's Arsenal as proof that it is possible to play exciting, attacking football, and still win games in the Premiership. This is true – but the French boffin has had years to mould his team into the slick, finely tuned outfit we see before us today. If you fast forward a few years, I've every confidence that this young, promising squad can deliver exhilarating performances as well as results. It's all about being patient. In the meantime, let's get behind the players and the manager, and be happy that we are winning games and are at the right end of the table.

If you want to watch all-out attacking football, go up to the City of Manchester to watch Kevin Keegan's Mancs. I'm sure the Sky Blues would swap places with us in a flash. In the modern game, a lot of winning is all about how well you defend. Real Madrid have arguably the most impressive array of attacking players in the world, but without a strong back line, they failed to win any silverware last season.

It may not always be exciting to watch, but I for one am thrilled with the start Mourinho has made at the club. Look at the bigger picture, and we have a lot to look forward to with this man at the helm. Inconsistency has been our biggest pitfall over the past decade or so, where we have always just fallen short of challenging for the Title. There is a real feeling that everything the team does now is meticulously planned, which has inspired a confidence in me which I don't think I have ever had before with Chelsea. You won't hear any moans from me! Come On Chels!

Carefree!

Famous CFC

*****

ISSUE 39 October 2004

Be Chelsea, Be Proud!

They say in adversity you know who your friends are. Certainly the supporters of this Club would be able empathise with that statement. The yo-yo period of the late 70's and early 80's saw the club lurch from one disaster to another, yet still the Shed remained proud in the Blue of Chelsea Football Club. The likes of Doug Rougvie, Joe Allon and Gareth Hall, with all due respect to their efforts, were no Osgood, Zola or Cooke, yet still Chelsea fans remained firm in their loyalty to the club in spite of dwindling attendances, a decaying ground and failure on the pitch. We've always got to be proud of those times, those who were there proved their worth as supporters and realised their love for the club.

However, no matter how defining those times were, I don't think it's right that we dwell on them to the exclusion of the rest of Chelsea Football Club's illustrious history. The time has come for us to stop romanticizing those dark days of the late 70's and 80's as characterising the entire history of Chelsea Football Club, because quite simply this isn't the case. Every club has its dark days – indeed, the only side never to have been relegated is Arsenal and those who know their history have serious questions as to the validity of that "fact".

Yes, I realise some of you are going to accuse me of sabotaging the history or denying the truth or even being patronizing, but I take issue with all of you who do. I want to use this article to broaden both your perspectives on our club's history so the picture of the past is complete. I also want to get the message across to the newer fans so they don't get warped by this perpetual image of Chelsea as some back water club that suddenly appeared out of the ether upon the arrival of (God bless him) Roman Abramovich.

219

I want them to know the parts they haven't been told in the TRUE history of Chelsea Football Club and be proud of them.

Why? Because for every 8,000 at home against Grimsby in the old Second Division in the Eighties there were 60,000 against AC Milan in the old UEFA Cup (ironically the second highest attendance in English Football history is our home league match against Arsenal in 1935 - 82,906). For every relegation three pointer against Bolton there was a victory over Real Madrid in the Cup Winners Cup final. Chelsea sides under Ted Drake in the 1950's (Champions - 1955), Tommy Docherty in the 1960's and, of course, Dave Sexton in the 1970's, were amongst the finest in the land. Those three eras saw us win and regularly challenge for the title, win both domestic cups and beat the previously invincible Real Madrid for our first European trophy. Those great sides, featuring the likes of Bonetti, Venables, Bentley, Osgood, Cooke, Hudson and co, were spurred on by the famous Shed End under the direction of Mickey Greenaway. The Shed was widely regarded by both Chelsea players and managers and people in the footballing community as one of the most passionate and intimidating quarters of any football stadium in Europe.

Even the period of the club's decline attests to the ambitions of the club in times past. The Club's attempt to build the first 60,000 all seater stadium in all of Europe as a fitting arena for potentially THE outstanding side of the era, ultimately fell apart for various reasons and cost us about 20 years of our development. So came the famous late 70's and 80's yo-yoing as the club struggled to pay the cost of it's previous ambition. Relegation scraps and even a near miss in avoiding relegation to the old Division 3 (The now League 1). Make no mistake about it, times were hard and things seemed a million miles away from the days of Bentley and Osgood, but after years of pain, blood and "Save the Bridge" buckets we fought our way back to our rightful place in the top division.

So we come to the 90's, Matthew Harding and Ken Bates. Hands up how many of you realise that we've now qualified for European Competition for 10 consecutive years? Not even Liverpool can boast that in the 90's. Chelsea used the era to invent "Sexy football" for it was Ruud Gullit who coined the phrase of the football we played. Two FA Cups, a League Cup, another Cup Winners Cup also defined the Nineties era. Since 1995 we have not finished out of the Top 6. A great and proud club Liverpool may be, but again not even they can boast that fact and as for the supposedly "Massive" Newcastle... I'm not trying to say we're the biggest club in England, because we're not. Undeniably there are clubs with more trophies and sustained records of success. However, that it is not to say that we do not have our own history that we can be proud of, our own culture as a club that played its part in Football's glorious past.

It is our duty as Chelsea fans to remember that past in its full good, bad and everything in between, not just the parts that suit the media or the press or even our own conceptions of what Chelsea Football Club is about. Chelsea supporters – be proud of our club, because you have every reason to be.

The Chelsea Advocate

*****

FIFA Don't Know FA!!!

Football's changed. Remember the days when you'd get home from the game, wait hours to see the action on Match of the Day, only to end up watching half an hour each of Man United and Liverpool with the Beeb squeezing the Chelsea goals on at the end, just past midnight? I do, quite vividly!

I'm one of the first to have a pop at Rupert Murdoch's Sky for ruining Saturday 3pm kick offs and showing no regard for fans who actually go to the games. However, I have to take my hat off to them for this Football First lark. If you haven't seen it, essentially its aim is to give viewers the chance to see as much of the day's games as possible. They show one game for 90 minutes, then for the rest of the night you can choose to watch an hour's action of whichever of the other fixtures takes your fancy.

One of the advantages of this is you can finally see for yourself what other fan's meant when they used to moan that highlights on MOTD didn't reflect what truly happened. I can now truly give opinions on opposition sides and players who I might otherwise know little about. Another upside is I can see just how bad officials and refereeing in this country is. But some of their decisions can be excused when you take into account that they are expected to simply be robots, who aren't allowed to use any sort of common sense.

You'll no doubt have seen Everton's Tim Cahill sent off at the City of

Manchester Stadium for putting his shirt over his head in celebration at scoring the winner for the Toffees. This is now seen as a bookable offence (removing your shirt that is, not goal scoring – how long before we see that abolished?) and referee Steve Bennett applied the apparent letter of the law. FIFA brought this ruling in during the summer, yet their bungling embarrassment of a Chief Executive, Sepp Blatter, contradicted his very own rule change by suggesting the caution for Cahill was "unfair". If the men who make the rules aren't sure what the law is, how are the players and officials meant to know?

More recently, Aston Villa's Lee Hendrie scored a belter to level the score in his side's clash with Crystal Palace. This was an important moment for the little midfielder. Not only was it one of the goals of the season, it was a massive relief for a player who had been the target for boos and much criticism from his own fans. In the moment of jubilation after seeing the ball flying in the net, he went over to the crowd to take their acclaim and naturally he was mobbed by his now adoring public. However, that moment of adrenaline fuelled happiness was tainted by the referee awarding Hendrie with a yellow card for 'over celebrating'!

What a ridiculous term. How can anyone over celebrate a goal? As someone who grew up dreaming of scoring for Chelsea, I can only imagine what my reaction would've been had I been fortunate enough to do so. As we all know from years watching in the stands, the few seconds following the ball hitting the onion bag sees us do some crazy things. Be it hugging the bloke next to you or jumping and screaming like a madman, something takes over and we are unable to control our actions. Unfortunately, people like Blatter are not passionate fans of the game, and none of them have played it at the top level either.

They don't know what it's like to experience such joy, so how can they judge how players should react?

After watching this Hendrie incident, I switched games onto Liverpool vs Norwich City. A seemingly innocuous pass into the centre of the park saw Pool's German midfielder lunge at the ball only to put his studs directly into the outstretched leg of Canaries counterpart Damian Francis. Had Francis have angled his leg slightly differently, we could've seen a career ending injury at Anfield not unlike the challenge from D*an S*unders on our very own Paul Elliot all those years ago. You'd think that compared to such minor offences as removing shirts and celebrating with the crowd, challenges like this should result in not only a straight dismissal, but also a hefty fine and suspension on top of that. You'd think wrong – Hamman got away with a booking.

What is wrong with our game that silly incidents get treated with the same disdain as serious, foul play? Nobody's ever had their career ended by over celebrating, yet the powers that be want to see this type of enjoyment and natural human emotion eradicated. As City boss Kevin Keegan rightly said in his post match interview for the Everton match, soon crowds will not turn up to games, because the passion will have gone out of football and games will just be contested by 11 robots against 11 robots.

Famous CFC

*****

Eddie McCreadie's Blue And White Army!

I read an article in the paper a few weeks back about that seven-year-old kid from Brighton who has signed for Real Madrid. His family are packing their bags and moving to Spain to live in a flat close to the stadium and he'll go to school there while training with the youth squad. Hang on… it got me thinking! What's happened to our youth policy then?

I know that Chelsea have set their stall out now with a 'why spend time growing the talent when we can just go out and buy it" attitude…and hey, I'm not knocking that! It's great to have the money! But it just seems a pity that this kid's talents (and others like him) won't be nurtured by our club. Hey, and lets be honest here, apart from the likes of John Terry we have had very few players pushing through our own youth squad over the past few years. Yes, I know there will always be room for the next Osgood or Hudson to come through the youth ranks but I feel that since the end of the decade we have seen fewer and fewer players rising from the juniors. Some players have had a chance to shine but it has only been for the odd game or two!

In the Nineties, we had the like of Duberry, Hughes, Nicholls, Morris. Burley, Myers, Newton, Sinclair, and Shipperley to name a few. The Eighties saw Stuart, Lee, Hall, Matthew, Cundy, Bumstead, Pates and Rhoades-Brown. OK, no world famous names here you might say… and only a few of them went on to greater things when they left the Bridge…

but they were all talented home grown (100% Blue) youngsters who held down a first team place at Chelsea!

It doesn't seem that long ago since our team was full of young home grown players. I remember the days of 1975 to 1977 well. Eddie McCreadie was our manager in those days. He had taken over from Ron Stuart with just three games of the season to go. He made wholesale changes by dropping the more experienced players who he considered being 'past their sell by date' and replacing them with boys; and even made the 18-year-old Ray Wilkins team Captain.

His bold gamble failed and we went down to the Second Division. We all knew deep down that it had been left far too late but through the pain of relegation we could see what McCreadie was trying to do at Chelsea. No money was available to bring in new players during the summer and a massive financial crisis threatened the very life and soul of our club. We struggled in our first season down, as some youngsters failed to perform on the field. McCreadie knew his boys had the talent and the following season we found the winning blend and raced to promotion. In that season, 76-77, I went to every game home and away (yes, even the 3-0 away defeat at Millwall!) and the football we played was exciting and flowing! If we lost one week we knew that we would bounce straight back the week after. The team sprit, skill, commitment and determination shown by these youngsters was excellent.

There were times during that season when every member of the starting line up had come up through the youth team set up. This will never happen at Chelsea again! Ray Wilkins, Gary Locke and Ray Lewington played every league and cup game that season. Finnieston led the line and his fellow youngsters like Swain, Britton, Stanley, Sparrow and Steve Wicks (to name a few!) all contributed to this excellent season. McCreadie said "We are going into the first division to liven it up - not looking to consolidate, but to cause a stir!' I believe that he would have done just that if they had just given him the chance!

BlueBear

ISSUE 40 October 2004

The Thoughts Of Chels Guevara

Finally, I have been asked by those selling cfcuk to again reiterate that the 1970's LION will be returning and I'm sure that it will be in place for the next season. Apparently, everywhere they go, the said sellers are being harassed by prospective customers asking, "Is it true that the BADGE IS coming back?" As I have said before and no-doubt will have to say again, IT IS COMING BACK!

I have staked my reputation on the premise that it will be reinstated and, dear reader, what, may I ask, reassurance do you need other than the words printed below..?

"Trust Me... I'm A Chelsea Supporter"

Chels Guevara

*****

Give Us A Song

Dear cfcuk,

How times have changed. From the eager anticipation of what would have happened under the Chairmanship of Matthew, through the agony of October 22nd 1996 when that bastard helicopter went down and, believe me, he would have been spectacular as leader of the Blue Army... then the elation of May 17th 1997 – I am sure I am not the only one of us who can safely say that was the best day of my life so far, followed by the trophies and the great football under the Vialli/Rix combination. Meanwhile, though, on the quiet, the club was quietly going skint. Then, along comes a billionaire with very little time left before Chels got into remarkably deep corporate sh*t financially. What does he do? He puts his money where his mouth is for a start, signing what looks like a very good and very determined manager, some great players and a corporate team to run the show.

It is, however, the off the field changes that are catching my attention. It is beginning to sound increasingly likely that our beloved badge – or something similar to it – is on its way back. I cannot personally work out if something close to it is fair enough – particularly before seeing it – but anything is better than the current badge. What would be really good would be if the board made the decision to change the badge because they know what it means to us. That might just be the case.

I am also delighted to hear that the former Chelsea legends are now being welcomed back and that the Board have begun to create real forums for supporter representation and there are some real supporters involved in it. This looks to me to be more than a token gesture and very welcome it is too. Then there is the growing rumour that they want to tear the hotel down. Delicious though it would be, I for one cannot see it yet. There is one resident at least whom I doubt would move out without a fight but you never know... It occurs to me that we may well now have the sort of people running this club that we true Blue supporters richly deserve. Judging them on what they have done and said they will do since taking over, you have got to hand it to them. I have read every issue of Matthew Harding's Blue And White Army/cfcuk and all the specials – and I would not mind betting that Peter Kenyon has read most of them by now. It is my firm belief that some – if not all – of the positive vibes coming from the club now are due in part to the fact that your fanzine has been consistent and dogged in publishing it's views which represent the views of the majority of true supporters, despite sometimes being very difficult indeed for it to do so and for this you deserve thanks from every supporter, so here are mine.

Of course there is still much to do but I urge you to continue the positive dialogue that you have begun with the club as this is definitely the way forward.

I totally agree with the final paragraph of True Blue's piece in issue 38. The whole adventure of the last decade began with the two H men, Harding and H*ddle – they should both be respected and loved by us for their contribution. Finally, can only imagine the awful time Juvenile and

Doris D must have had when their daughter went missing and I am delighted that she has safely returned. Supporting Chelsea means belonging to a wide family and Juvenile D is right when he says that Chelsea supporters really are the best in the World.

Stay carefree!

Regards

Local Boy London SW10 Via email

Cheers mate, Up The Chels!

*****

From Stamford Bridge To Imperial Fields

I am sure that there are many other Chelsea supporters like me who have stuck by the club for many years through thick and thin but, now the club has turned it's fortunes around, we have been priced out of Stamford Bridge and priced out by the Johnny come latelies, while we are confined to only seeing our games on TV.

Well, the likes of us who are no longer good enough for the club that we saved from going out of existence should take our loyalty to clubs who will be more grateful for it and really appreciate it, such as our local clubs in the non-league.

My local club is Tooting And Mitcham Utd. They have got a terrific stadium at Imperial Fields in Morden and I fully recommend that the local Chelsea fans in the area, like me, who are surplus to requirements at Stamford Bridge get along to Imperial Fields and support a club that the local people are really proud of. Those real fans who unfortunately now find their 'football days' free, should give the non-league a try.

The situation at most non-league clubs is the same. At Tooting, for an entrance of £7 for adults and £3 for juveniles/OAPs, you can once again stand on the terraces, have a pop at the referee and enjoy some banter with opposing fans without being dragged out by 17 stewards, see some great games of football and some great battles from 22 players who play for the love of the game and not for the money that ends up in their pockets. All for a pittance compared to the fortune that people have to pay to enter a Premiership ground.

Whereas we at Tooting have the added advantage of having our new stadium featuring two immaculate terraced stands behind both goals and a superb new main stand. Some other club's facilities are sometimes a bit more basic but, with extra support coming through the turnstiles, things will only get better. Tooting's website is excellent and can be found at: www.tumfc.co.uk and it tells you all you need to know.

It's great to have such a good quality non-league club so close because it means that, as a passionate football supporter, I can still enjoy a 'live' game. I'm certainly not new to the non-league scene as I've supported Tooting for many years from the time they played at their great old ground that was Sandy Lane and I used to watch them regularly when Chelsea were away. There are no Charlie Cooke's or Gianfranco Zola's in the non-league but there is a lot of superb talent and many youngsters playing for such teams as Tooting might well have a professional career ahead of them.

In essence, there are plenty of great little clubs out there and, if your bank balance isn't big enough to allow you to get to Stamford Bridge, your local side might be grateful of your support. Chelsea's loss should be their gain!

Martin W

*****

Bring Back The 70's Lion... Keep Up The Pressure!

Most Chelsea supporters who care about the club crest will tell you that the reason that Ken Bates replaced the 'Mears' 1970's Lion was because the symbol is un-copyrightable. This meant that while Chelsea Football Club continued to use it as their club symbol, others could use the crest on merchandise and memorabilia without the club's permission, thereby denying Chelsea revenue. Looking at the situation from Chelsea's perspective, one can – to a degree at least – understand their reasoning. That said, the club 'own' the 70's Lion as a registered trading mark that gives them the potential to use and exploit the badge in any way they can.

However, Bates has in the past made it clear that he does not like the fact that the traders who sell goods on the Fulham Rd prior to Chelsea matches are, in his opinion at least, preventing potential customers from buying their goods from the club itself. He thought that by changing the club badge to a design that was covered by copyright, he would put the independent Fulham Rd traders out of business. He did not however, reckon upon the popularity of the 70's badge, and he was totally unprepared for the fact that the crest he wanted to dispose of became one of the symbols that would mark an opposition of sorts to his Chelsea Village regime. He has, without any shadow of a doubt, severely miscalculated.

Should Chelsea decide to bring the badge back, there is an easy solution that would enable the club to maximise the potential that the favoured symbol has. When marketing a product that uses the 70's badge, all the club would have to do is add the words "Official Chelsea Merchandise" somewhere on the item in question. Potential customers could then make their minds up as to whether they wanted official or unofficial Chelsea products.

Please utilize the petition forms that has been included in some previous editions of cfcuk or get copies of the pull-out from either our matchday stall or via our postal address. It is easy to use. All you need is a pen. Ask those in your pre or after match pub to sign it, or even take the pullout into the ground and ask 12 people either side of you to sign the petition. Once you have collected 25 names, you can either send it direct to Roman Abramovich / Peter Kenyon / Bruce Buck yourself, or return it to the cfcuk stall (or see one of our sellers) and we will ensure that it is delivered to Stamford Bridge. This could be your chance to make a difference or at least let the club know how you feel about the subject. 10 completed petitions equals 250 signatories. 100 completed petitions equals 2500. 200 is 5000.

We're not promising that we will achieve anything by taking this course of action but at least we are trying. Please, if you think anything about this cause, please try to help by collecting signatures yourself. 25 for every person who buys the fanzine would bring a petition that would total 10s of 1000s of signatures.

While we ARE at this stage confident that the Board will be making the correct decision soon, please ensure you let them now EXACTLY how you feel about it now!

Come on Chelsea…let's see if WE can make a difference. It is, after all, YOUR Chelsea! This is a word for word repeat of an earlier article

Chels Guevara

*****

"69, 69, 69!"

Chelsea 1 – 0 Liverpool. 03rd October 2004.

"Justice, Not Charity." Sir Bob Geldof.

I'm on a walk for justice with CFC Andy and Seagull Si. We're walking 100 miles of the Thames Path in 5 days, 20 miles a day, raising money for a project in Kenya that works with the street kids. On Saturday 2nd October we walked 20 miles from Oxford to Benson. On Sunday we walked 20 miles from Benson to Reading. The last 4 miles were a killer. I had two blisters an inch square on both feet, my knees were swelling up and I have never been so grateful to reach a pub – getting there at 3.45pm with time to spare until kick off – brilliant timing! But bad news was to follow – the SKY TV was broken.

Devastating. We asked how far the next pub was – the fella behind the bar tells us it's a mile and a half further on… It felt like the longest mile I'd ever walked. The rain still drizzling down. The rucksack cutting into my shoulder blades. My feet throbbing. My head swimming with exhaustion. 40 miles in 2 days and we've got to dig deeper. Andy starts singing: "Wherever we go, we follow our team" – he's been chatting on about making a pub in Reading in time for kick off for 2 whole days, though I never felt as optimistic as him!

Seagull Si drives me on, and he's not even bothered about Chelsea, he just needs to recover with a few pints. Somehow we got to the pub and ordered drinks just before kick off. I have never, ever enjoyed a Guinness as much as the one I drank in front of the big screen. Of course, we won with a brilliant goal by Joey Cole – what a sweet result. My feet and knees were battered, but Chelsea ensured my spirits were lifted high.

The Red And The Blue Battles.

"DAY-OH, DI MATTEO! VIALLI SCORES AND THE SCOUSERS GO HOME. NOT ONE, NOT TWO, NOT THREE, BUT FOUR! VIALLI SCORES AND THE SCOUSERS GO HOME…"

In recent years there have been some massive matches with Liverpool. Season 1985/86 when Dalglish scored and they won the league. The programme for that match has 2 players modelling "THE CHELSEA COLLECTION", I think my brother in law has a copy. Then there is a 4-2 victory when we were 2-0 down on our way to winning the 1997 FA Cup, and the last game of the season pre-Roman when we pipped them to the final Champions League place. As me, Andy and Si's Thames Path Charity Walk continued, we shared our Chelsea and Brighton stories. With Liverpool in the forefront of our minds after Chelsea's latest victory I recalled a couple of matches from yesteryears.

Liverpool 1-0 Chelsea. October 16th 1999.

"Quite Good! You Used To Be Quite Good!" The Chelsea Choir. While this match was still at 0-0 we serenaded the Scousers with this little tune. Even though they eventually won and took the 3 points, the tables had definitely turned in terms of power and success. We had won the FA Cup, Cup Winners Cup, League Cup and Super Cup. The Scousers had nothing to celebrate. It was brilliant singing that song! They used to be quite good, now they were shit and we were better than them. The night before I had dreamt we won 4-0 with Frank LeBeef scoring first, so of course I had to put the bet on! The next match we beat Galatasaray 5-0 away from home in the Champions League, while Liverpool probably signed another player who was a pile of sh*t. We were going places and it was great to be a part of it – even though it was standing room only on the train up there which really pisses me off when that happens! You stand up for hours, run out of booze, get to the match, Desailly and Wisey get sent off, and Flo registers our only poxy shot on target. It's a right pain in the a*se following Chelsea sometimes.

Chelsea 4-2 Liverpool. May 04th 1991.

Let me refresh your memories. It's the last game of the season, George Graham's Arsenal are top and Graeme Souness' Liverpool are second – Liverpool must beat Chelsea and hope Arsenal lose (Arsenal only conceded 18 goals all season, and lost one match – TO US!). A Chelsea victory over Liverpool would mean Arsenal will win the league coz Liverpool won't be able to catch them. I think The Shed gates closed by 2.30pm – Liverpool obviously filled the away terrace and there were loads more in the West Stand and at the front of The Shed – I didn't notice them until R*nny R*senthal's equalizer.

We had been 2-0 up so they were understandably jubilant. Once they celebrated, I don't think they lasted too much longer in the Chelsea end… I checked on a couple of websites to try and clarify the scorers. In my mind R*senthal scored both goals, but a Liverpool site said Speedie scored first. I couldn't find any info on the Chelsea scorers, but I think

Kerry Dixon got the 1st and 4th, with Gordon Durie and Kevin Wilson in between. Can anyone 'shed' any light? I can clearly remember Liverpool singing at the final whistle "One Team In Europe" – as the European ban for English clubs had been lifted.

The 1991 Nostalgic Bit…

I want to take the Fulham Broadway stairs two at a time, but there's too many people in front of me. I've got a brand new Nike Air Cross Trainers on. I hook a left. Chelsea Independent stall. "Hats, Scarves, Badges and T-shirts!" Smell the horseshit and hamburgers. The Deathburger! Rough, but I'll be buying one after. I don't want to get locked out this match. I'm nearly there. Last game of the season. C'mon Chelsea. Past the West Stand. Railings on my left. I can hear singing. That beautiful sound. There's that sh*tty club shop. The resounding choruses are beckoning me. Yes! I'm nearly there.

I've been waiting all week for this. I'm showing my membership card to the bloke in his box behind the clear plastic. Beyond there is laughter. Beyond there is community. Another song is starting as soon as the last one fades away. The grey haggard bloke in his box behind the clear plastic is glancing at my membership card. Yes mate, I am a juvenile. However quickly I throw him my seven pounds, the turnstile always seems to jam before I push it again. I'm closer to getting there.

Now I'm through. I'm off the street and inside the Bridge. I'm so very nearly there. I'm running up the long steps. The singing sound is stronger. Finally I am at the top of the steps. I'm a little late. But I am there. I am in. Look left with me. See the huddles of coppers. Breathe deeply with me. Smell the mixture of Bovril and booze, horse shit and hamburgers.

Stare down with me. Survey the thousands … now push through the people and stand crushed at the last game of the season in The Shed.

At half past two someone said they'd closed the gates. Everyone crouching and squatting down for One Man Went To Mow. It's a mental sight, hundreds of geezers all bobbing on the terracing. Someone says "Why isn't it like this every week?" We sing and taunt the Scousers until the teams jog onto pitch. We sing the names of our heroes. Come on Chelsea. "John Barnes is a homosexual" starts up, and gets higher and faster and faster and higher until everyone starts laughing, then a spontaneous round of applause breaks out. "We're The Middle, We're The Middle, We're The Middle Of The Shed!" Then The West Side reply, then The Whitewall. *"We're The Shed End, We're The Shed End, We're The Shed End Stamford Bridge!"* On occasions the Middle would turn ninety degrees and point at the Left Side singing: *"Middle, Middle, Middle, Middle, Middle, Middle, MIDDLE!"* One time I remember them replying: *"Middle run from Left Side, Middle run from Left Side, la la la la, la la la la!"*

Liverpool win the toss and swap ends, so Chelsea are attacking The Shed end in the first half, rather than the second which we all prefer. Bruce Grobbs is getting booed and slaughtered as he jogs towards the goalmouth, but he laughs and waves at us and wobbles his legs a bit. Chelsea go 2-0 up, Kerry Dixon and Gordon Durie. Second half, R*nnie R*senthal scores once, then beats a few players and equalizes. The scousers go up all over the place. Different Chelsea boys ease out the terracing and jog down the yellow gangways ready to confront.

Chelsea somehow go 3-2 up. The Scousers are bricking it. Souness is doing his nut. He substitutes the substitute – Jimmy Carter, Millwall reject. Fucking Liverpool. I'm sick of them. Everyone is. They win everything. But not the league now – not this year!

Above the away end is a massive scoreboard showing the teams, the score and the time. Whenever the clock showed 69 minutes, someone would notice and shout: *"69!"* and everyone would sing *"69, 69, 69!"* to the tune of *"Here We Go!"*

We are 3-2 up, it's the last minute and Chelsea have a corner in front of the Liverpool fans. Kerry Dixon near post header. We go mental. Loads from the West Stand are on the pitch, jumping in front of the defeated, deflated Scousers. Arsenal have won the league. Liverpool's dominance broken. Hundreds storm the pitch at the final whistle.

I jog down the yellow gangway with Paul and climb over the advertising board. There's Gary laughing at me – they were higher than I thought! I should have taken a running jump. It feels great to be on the pitch. Looking up at the massive East Stand. Liverpool fans are chanting *"One Team In Europe"* – trying to muster something from their defeat, but they are locked in and going nowhere for at least forty-five minutes. We stand gloating. I can't see any of them coz blokes taller than me are in front. Hundreds, no thousands, of Chelsea stand on the hallowed turf facing the away end and sing over and over and over and over with glee…

"WHERE'S YA TITLE GONE? WHERE'S YA TITLE GONE? WHERE'S YA TITLE GONE? WHERE'S YA TITLE GONE?"

On the way back towards the emptying Shed, I pull a handful of Stamford Bridge turf and put the grass in my pocket. The season is over. We finish 11th in the table. This has been a day I wish I could live again.

Right Here, Right Now.

We have had some great battles with Liverpool. There is no doubt that now we have overtaken them – remember when they used to win bloody everything? After Manchester United dominated the 1990's, it seems power now has swung to Arsenal – though Chelsea are fighting hard. You never know, one day we might be able to taunt those passionless, spoilt Gooners: *"Quite Good! You Used To Be Quite Good!"*

Wally Otton

ISSUE 41 November 2004

The Sheditorial

Using a combination of natural ability, skill, determination and grit, Adrian Mutu became a professional footballer. As a child in Rumania, he worked for countless hours, perfecting the skills that would eventually allow him to become a world star in the world's greatest game. He became an icon and a beacon of hope to thousands of young boys in his homeland who saw that, if they followed his example, they too might one day be able to live the fantastic life that their hero enjoys.

When he joined Chelsea, he signed at a time when the club was making world headline news, following the financial input of Roman Abramovich. As soon as our benefactor had rescued our club, Chelsea supporters knew it would only be a matter of time before the silverware and honours started to come. It didn't happen in the first season and, following the departure of Claudio Ranieri, José Mourinho was appointed as manager.

As soon as he arrived, he made it clear that he meant business. He gave every player the chance to talk to him and discuss their futures and he gave every player the chance to show him what they could do. Mutu was one that Mourinho decided was worthy of selection.

Once the players had been chosen, Mourinho gave them clear advice as to what he expected from them as individuals and underlined exactly the standards that he intended to set as well as defining the rules to which the players would have to adhere. Recreational use of cocaine strictly off the menu.

Acting within their remit as an employer, Chelsea asked for Mutu to undertake a drug test. The player failed and was promptly sacked, a decision that was unanimously endorsed by Chelsea supporters.

Immediately, PFA boss Gordon Taylor sprang to Mutu's defence and accused Chelsea both of not doing enough to 'help' the player and using the fact that he'd admitted to taking drugs as an excuse to sack him because 'things were not working out on the playing side'. Taylor also accused Chelsea of 'snubbing' a visit by the Sporting Chance organisation, which had planned to meet the Chelsea playing staff and give a lecture on the danger of using drugs, whether performance enhancing or 'recreational'. However, subsequent fixture obligations meant that when the actual day came, both the first team and second XI had been given the customary day off, a practice that is the norm following a match. Sporting Chance did meet with Chelsea's youth players but were annoyed that there were no senior players present.

Despite the fact that the date for this meeting had been arranged while Chelsea was being administered under the old regime, Taylor took the opportunity to attempt to smear Chelsea and Peter Kenyon for their stance in standing firm against the use of drugs in football by inferring that the club had 'pulled the plug' on the said meeting. As leader of a Trades Union, Taylor has an obligation to play by the rules. We here are disgusted by his behaviour and hope the PFA Rep at Chelsea voices his concerns directly.

For the record, all associated with this fanzine, the BlueAndWhiteArmy.net website and all the readers and patrons that we have spoken to about this subject, are 100% behind both Chelsea and Peter Kenyon in their actions.

Chelsea supporters are also 100% behind Peter Kenyon et al after they announced reinstatement of a redesigned version of the 70's crest as the Chelsea emblem from the beginning of next season. While some still yearn for the 'classical' Earl of Cadogan badge, all are happy that the symbol of Chelsea will once again be a proud lion rampant instead of the mess of a crest that was installed by Bates.

At the press announcement, Paul Smith spoke of the constant stream of letters and correspondence that the club received about the subject of the badge and, credit to him and the rest of the Chelsea board, they listened and magnanimously acceded to the wishes of the people to whom Chelsea Football Club means the most - the supporters.

While many have offered their congratulations to us here for our efforts in keeping the profile of the subject of the badge in the spotlight, we in turn must thank all those Chelsea supporters who bothered to fill in our petition forms or contact the club directly on the matter. Although we still have several thousand signatures in our possession (we are still receiving them!) , they will, in due course, be forwarded to the club. This last batch will, however, also have a note of thanks attached.

The Guy Who Blagged Me

*****

The Thoughts Of Chels Guevara

With CHELSEA remaining high in the Premiership and with all well on the pitch, the instincts of the low-life journalists remain strong. A couple of Fleet Street toe rags named Neil Syson and John Kay thought they'd make a name for themselves by 'exposing' the 'betting practices' of JOHN TERRY, WAYNE BRIDGE, EID*R GUD*OHNSEN and SCOTT PARKER. Accusing the players of being "gambling crazy", the gutter reporters then went on to claim that the players had spent over £2m on their 'habit'.

The Sun newspaper has subsequently retracted the story and, although he would prefer them to spend their time doing other things, according to CHELSEA MANAGER JOSÉ MOURINHO, the players can gamble if they want to. While the overwhelming majority of CHELSEA SUPPORTERS can only dream of earning the money that CHELSEA'S FOOTBALLERS earn, I'm sure that there are not too many that, despite the fact that they might say they earn a little too much, begrudge the players their wages. Good luck to you lads and spend your money how you want - you earned it!

Although I have just finished writing the above paragraph, I will nonetheless, continue with a story that happened to me that concerns placing a bet in a bookmakers. Taking a break from writing this column the Sunday before publication, I was thinking about the cause of CHELSEA FUNDAMENTALISM when I happened to pass a betting shop and wandered in. I'd intended to have a couple of bob on the football but, as I entered, I heard the announcer say that a horse called FUNDAMENTALIST was running in the soon to called 2.05 at Cheltenham. Having my 'football' money in my hand - it was nowhere near £2m - I placed my money on the horse. It romped home at a very good price of 2/1 and was, according to the commentator, "strong, resilient and full of running." Says it all really...

*****

Gianfranco Zola – OBE

On the day that Adrian Mutu was officially, and quite rightly, sacked by Chelsea Football Club, it was very uplifting to be greeted by the news that Gianfranco Zola, the legend, has been awarded an honorary OBE. In a strange sort of way it put things in perspective and proved that good does sometimes eventually triumph.

Normally, I don't pay much notice to these awards. I convinced myself long ago that they never really went to those that deserve them. Too often they were awarded years, sometimes decades, after the recipient actually carried out the duties that merited a nomination. Also, too often I held the belief that some of those awarded them had been given them by employees simply paying lip service.

Therefore, it makes it particularly pleasing for Gianfranco to receive his award whilst his talents are still giving football supporters, albeit in Italy, magical moments that make this little Sardinian so special.

Gianfranco received his award in Rome on Monday 1st November from the British Ambassador. Unfortunately, the ceremony came hard on the heels of Cagliari conceding five goals against Roma. Whilst it proved impossible for me to be there, I'd like to think that Gianfranco accepted his award knowing that there were several thousand Chelsea fans looking on from a distance. His award officially came as recognition for probably being the most memorable foreign player to have graced the Premiership. In a statement issued by the British Embassy, the following accolade was annotated; "The most enduring and popular foreign player in the history of Chelsea Football Club. The 2002 / 2003 season was his last with Chelsea, and he left the club with style, scoring 16 goals. Despite the pleas of the fans to remain, he decided to return to his native Sardinia in 2003, having made a remarkable contribution to English football."

Sadly, this monumental event only received minimal media coverage. Instead the media preferred to concentrate on a similar award bestowed upon the former Manchester City goalkeeper, Bert Trautman. Whether this is indicative of my earlier statement of awards being given out years after a player has retired I'm not sure. A little whisper in my ear tells me that Bert continued to do a great deal of charity work after he retired from the game.

However, the next time you're supping a pint; please take time out to toast our favourite legend, Gianfranco Zola OBE. Who knows, in a few years time we may even be raising our glasses to Sir José Mourinho!

Merlin

*****

John Terry's Barmy Army!

If you know anything about football, you will know that the greatest asset that Chelsea have is the one and only John Terry. In order to pay homage to this great man, a few individuals who are all old enough to know better, decided to paint a flag and dress like idiots at all the European away trips. Why? Why not!

Suddenly premiership football, and Chelsea in particular, is sexy. So out of the woodwork come 100's, no 1000's of people who would not know who Micky Droy was if he came up and jumped up and down on their balls. In fact I would not be surprised if many of them think that the Matthew Harding Stand is named after some construction company rather than the great man himself. I don't care when and how people start to support the Blues, I do care about the passion they show - or don't in so many cases. I will put my hands up and admit that at times during a game I lose it, totally. I have never understood how others can sit their calmly and clap politely in that cricket kind of way when a goal goes in. The atmosphere at the Bridge is too often non-existent, at least in the past we had away games to go to. Now it appears that the corporates have started to take that bit of fun away from us as well.

What's the point of all this waffle I hear you ask? Well it is from here, out of the ashes, that John Terry's Barmy Army was born. It all started in the pub before the 4-0 win at Leicester last season when we were talking about the trip to Stuttgart. We thought that dressing up for the occasion might be fun, and actually get a few more people involved in backing their team. So dress up we did, as Vicars, Vicars with fez's. Why a fez? Why not, they were kind of thrown in with the Vicars outfits and made us look even odder than before, if such a thing were even slightly possible.

Since then we have been Pirates and members of the Sgt Peppers Lonely Hearts Club Band. What comes next you might ask? Well I would tell you but then I would have to kill you. *Why?* is the big question behind it all, and the answer is simple. We want you, each and every one of you, to get behind the team, our team, and shout us to the top of the League. And it can be done. Years ago, Anfield was a really intimidating place to go. Not just because the Scousers would rob you as soon as look at you, but because of the noise their fans generated. It was often worth a goal start to the team. We want that atmosphere at the Bridge, and wherever we go on our travels. Wearing stupid clothes might not be enough, carrying a daft flag that most sad clubs (our own included) wont allow us to put up might not either. But if it gets you thinking, then our job is half way done.

Chelsea Football Club is the most important thing in so many of our lives. We should all enjoy it, and show our passion in the only way that matters, making lots and lots and lots of noise. You know you want to, sometimes you maybe do it without even thinking. Possibly you think you might look daft if you stand up and give Graham Poll what for. But will you look any dafter than a group of idiots wandering around Islington in pirate gear and not being allowed in pubs because they have a, "no fancy dress policy"?

So the next time a song starts, join in. When you hear the strains of "Zigger Zagger" or "10 Men Went To Mow", give it some throttle. You could well be the difference between success and failure. The alternative? John Terry's Barmy Army are gonna get you, wherever you might be hiding…

John Terry's Barmy Army

*****

Give Us A Song!

Dear cfcuk,

Thank you for sending me copies of cfcuk which I'm enjoying enormously! I would like to become a subscriber and enclose a cheque for £23 (large size tshirt please).

Let's hope that the results keep rolling in!
Best wishes,
Right Honourable Peter Hain MP
C/O The House of Commons Westminster
London SW1

Cheers Peter, your t-shirts etc will be in the post soon. By the way, we know you're very busy helping Tony run the country but, if you do get a moment, is there any chance of 'having a word' with someone influential in order that Chelsea get the planning permission for a 60,000 all-seater stadium at Stamford Bridge?

*****

Mutuuu Who?

There have been a few significant events at Chelsea since I last sat down to etch out my contribution to cfcuk. At the time of writing my last piece, we were five points behind Arsenal at the summit of the League and Adrian Mutu had seen more first team football than the injured Arjen Robben.

Since then, the flying Dutchman has emerged as one of the finest young talents I've ever seen at the club. Just 20 years old, his arrival has coincided with us leapfrogging the Gooners in the Premiership, and we've also already qualified for the knockout stages in the Champions League. In a team with such influential attacking players, it's high praise indeed to suggest Robben has had such an important influence. But as well as chipping in with vital goals, the excitement when he gets the ball is felt all over the stadium; he fearlessly takes defenders on and has the required strength and pace to beat them.

Not wanting to jinx it, but if he and Duff can stay fit (the Irishman's injury record is even more extensive than the unlucky Robben's) then you get the feeling that there's no team we need to be afraid of. Didier Drogba returns in December, and with his attributes you can see him plundering a few goals alongside the Wide Boys.

Let's hope that Robben's career doesn't go the way of another player who enjoyed a fantastic start to his life in SW6. Adrian Mutu couldn't stop scoring in the opening weeks of last season, and was rapidly tipped to become a Stamford Bridge legend by the fans who had taken him to their hearts instantly. He had his own cult chant, and all the kids had his name and number on the back of their replica shirts.

Although the goals dried up somewhat, one of his most notable traits was his hard work ethic. This is what made his appearance at Villa Park towards the end of the season all the more puzzling. I've rarely seen a player look so disinterested, and this stood out all the more considering how enthusiastic and hardworking he was in the first half of the season. Rumours of off the field antics overshadowed his intermittent performances on it, and it was clear something was not right.

Ranieri perhaps wasn't the right man to handle such a wayward pro. Despite arriving with a reputation for being a scholar, the Romanian idol let the money and adulation change him. It's something that happens to so many young players. But let's not kid ourselves that these were the acts of a youngster starting out in the game – Mutu's 25 years old, and the captain of his national team. At an age when most players are starting to approach their peak, Adrian was acting like a spoilt, star struck kid.

Some sections of the media have criticised Chelsea for sacking Mutu when news of his failing a drug test emerged. Peter Kenyon insisted this was in line with the club's zero tolerance drug policy. The critics claimed the club should've stuck by the player, but our management are trying to run a football club, not a drug rehabilitation clinic. The Romanian has plenty of his own money to spend on that, despite only playing a handful of games this year. The wages that us fans help pay has gone up his hooter, and his behaviour has disrespected the club, supporters, the manager and his former teammates.

Indeed, when Mourinho questioned Mutu and his agents in pre-season about rumours of a drug problem, the claims were laughed off. Thankfully, José retained his suspicions and we are now rid of a player who threatened to cause disharmony in an otherwise united dressing room.

I've no doubt that if a player suffered a serious injury, the club would stick by them. Illness isn't something voluntary, it is unfortunate and players who get them deserve our sympathy. It may sound like I'm taking the moral high ground, but when I see people being paid thousands to represent a team I'd give my right arm to play for (best not go in goal then!) only to consistently take advantage of that privilege, I can safely say he doesn't deserve a second chance with Chelsea; let's face it, with his previous misdemeanours he's lucky to have had so many chances here already. The joke seven month ban handed out by the weak FA (who don't even have a chief executive at the moment) doesn't perhaps directly affect us any more, but after all the cash wasted on Mutu since his arrival, it would be galling to see a Bolton pick him up on the cheap and resurrect his career. Whilst I don't wish bad luck on him, I hope he doesn't remain in this country and goes back to Italy to ply his trade. If you believe the stories, this is what he has wanted all along.

I don't care when people say a two-year ban would ruin his career – HE is the only one who has done that; nobody forced him to take an illegal substance. People must take responsibility for their actions. It remains to be seen whether his remorse is genuine. For such a clever man, he's been very stupid boy.

This may well be a blessing in disguise, with youngsters Carlton Cole and Mikael Forsell waiting in the wings to take Mutu's place in José's 24 man squad. It's always great to see youth team prospects make the grade in the first team, and their impressive performances in Brummyland show that they have the talent and willing to do just that. Hungry players that have the desire to play in the Blue of Chelsea - that's what's taken us to the summit of the Premiership, here's hoping the next month can go towards mounting a real claim to staying there come May.

Famous CFC

ISSUE 42 December 2004

With this issue of cfcuk being the one to appear over the festive season, we have regular reader and occasional contributor MM to thank for sending us the following...

Feed The Sp*rs

It's Christmas time, The Sp*rs are so afraid, It's Christmas time, They've not got enough points from games they've played, But in our world of plenty, Jol spreads no smile of joy, Throw your arms around a Sp*rs fan, At Christmas time, But say a prayer, Pray for lilywhites, At Christmas time, It's hard when your team is playing sh*te, There's a world outside your window, and it's a world of T*ttenham fear, Where the only water flowing, is a whining Sp*rs fan's tear, And S*ntini's mobile ringing was the clanging chimes of doom, Well tonight thank L*vy it's them instead of you, And there won't be many points for them this Christmas time, The greatest gift they'll get this year's a draw, Where no pass ever goes, no flick or long ball flows, Do they know how 3 points feel at all? (Here's to you), 3 points for everyone (Here's to the Sp*rs) Travelling to Gillingham Do they know how 3 points feel at all? Feed the Sp*rs (Let them know how 3 points feel) Feed the Sp*rs (Let them know how 3 points feel)
    (Repeat until you either die laughing or pee your pants!)

*****

The Selecter at Club Ska 13/11/04

And so it was that - on the back of a 4-1 thumping of Fulham – all thoughts turned to the mighty 2-Tone label. Off to the brilliant Club Ska at the Rayners, Rayners Lane to celebrate our triumph and to acknowledge 25 years of 2- Tone music. The label that gave us The Specials, Madness and The Beat – this was gonna be extra-special. For those that have never been to a Club Ska night – let me share this with you – you are missing out! This show was a sensation.

I arrive in the side bar with 20 minutes to go before the main doors open – the place is already heaving. From the stage we can hear the roar of the Club Ska Sound System warming up. Pint in hand, I walk round to the entrance to be met by the Genial Geno Blue – proprietor of Club Ska and his side-kick Dave. Duke Dale – the legendary Ska DJ is dropping some wicked rocksteady and Ska tunes on the people.

Geno introduces me to some fellow Chelsea supporters from Chessington – cheers Roger – and before we know it, Geno is putting on the support act. The Goldmaster All Stars hail from Southend. 13 white Rastas who kick up a brilliant Ska beat. They got the house rocking in double quick time with a selection aimed to please.

Next up, Geno calls The Duke to the stage for a presentation to celebrate his new job as a Revive FM (98.3) daytime DJ. The Club Ska crowd is also treated to a personal message from Jerry Dammers. To a large cheer, Jerry tells us to "Keep the faith!" More news – that Shed End favourite Laurel Aitken is coming to Club Ska for a special show on the 8th of January (huge cheer).

Then the main order of business.

The Selecter - in three words – they were awesome!! It is amazing how Pauline never seems to age and with about 300 fans in the crowd the band launch into their anthem – the Selecter (original 2-Tone style). Next up – 'Missing Words' and the serious skanking begins. Pauline observes to the crowd that "it's really nice to play to people who love ska" and she ain't wrong. Special mention must go to Martin Stewart (ex- Bad Manners) on keyboards who pushed the band to the limit. The Selecter hits keep coming – *"James Bond", "Celebrate the Bullet"* – a manic version of *"Last train to Skaville"*.

Already this show has surpassed expectations when up steps the lovely Rhoda Dakar. Rhoda was lead singer with the Bodysnatchers and then joined the Specials AKA. Dressed in a great black and white 2-Tone one piece dress Rhoda gives us a top rendition of the Bodysnatchers classic " *Do Rocksteady"*. Pauline and Rhoda power on with a great version of *'Three Minute Hero'* and a storming *"On My Radio"* The crowd are ecstatic – demanding an encore they return with a roof busting *"Too Much Pressure"*.

An incredible end to the show. 25 years old and still wonderful – thank you. On the way out – with *"Night Boat"* and *"The Liquidator"* cranking out of the PA – the dulcet tones of Rayners Blue are heard in the car park *"Top of the league, we're having a laugh!"*

Nuff Said.

Jack Slade

*****

Stand Up If You Love Chelsea!

Happy times down in SW6. Top of the League, looking unstoppable in Europe and domestically, and we've got our badge back! Next on the agenda, it's our atmosphere.

Our away support has been, for the most part, excellent this season. One reason for this may well be that supporters who follow the team around the country tend to be of a very passionate nature. It's become the norm at most Premiership grounds for the visiting section to be louder, and Stamford Bridge is no exception. The position of away fans helped contribute to José Mourinho's calls last month for the Chelsea home support to get behind the team more, much like we did at the Valley, Craven Cottage and the Hawthorns (with a special shout to those who made the trek to Moscow. You did the club proud!)

The manager, the board and indeed the club's official media have all called for the home crowd to be more vocal. But, with respect to them, they don't know what it's like for us who sit in the ground. For a start, the club operates a strict no-standing policy. Most games, we see the stewards asking fans to sit down. Plenty more are shouted at to sit down (or SIDDDAAAHHHNN!) by someone sitting behind them. This irritates me so much, their argument being that they pay their money so they deserve to sit down (why these people can't save their money and sit at home or in the pub, I don't know) but we also pay our money. Why can't we stand up if we want to?

One solution would be to have an area of the ground where fans are free to stand. Whether this is currently allowed by the rules of the

Premier League I don't know, but it's a question worth asking. In the long term, a solution could be installing seats similar to those in Rome's Olympic Stadium or even following Schalke's example by having seats which can revert to terraces if needs be. What could be better than recreating the atmosphere of the 70's/80's Shed than having a loud, terraced Shed again! It could happen. Pretty much every popular Chelsea chant only works if the supporters stand while singing it. So how can we be more vocal when we are not allowed to be on our feet? It's no coincidence that the prawn sandwich brigade who moan about people standing are the same people who are always quiet.

Another key part of creating a good atmosphere is banter between supporters. Sitting near the East Lower, I often see away fans being warned and sometimes ejected for doing next to nothing. I feel that all too often the reasons for doing this are harsh. Indeed, word has it that it was a steward's over-reaction that sparked the trouble at the end of the West Ham game. Understandably, when incidents like the Porto follower spitting at Mourinho occur, the offenders have to be dealt with. But fans should be allowed to stick a finger up, or swear. This isn't provocation or inflammatory, it's normal behaviour at a football match, and always has been. What the powers that be have to realise is, that not all of these people are trouble makers. They have to understand that what goes on in the ground stays there, and we are responsible enough to forget about it after the match when we walk out amongst the very same people who've been winding us up for 90 minutes (and vice versa.)

If Chelsea are truly serious about asking the fans to sing more, they need to look at the situation of standing. And if anyone reading this has ever told the person in front to sit down, think twice next time! This isn't the Library, this is Stamford Bridge. Let's sing our hearts out and start making it feel more like home!

Carefree!

Famous CFC

*****

José Mourinho – Simply Unbelievably Ace

José Mourinho proclaimed himself "A golden God of Managerial Nous" as Chelsea topped the Premiership's most cocky Manager competition for the first time this season. Bringing a tough, uncompromising style to post-match commentary, Mourinho's revolutionary "everybody but me is wrong" tactic has shaken up the footballing establishment.

"It'll take a lot to bounce back from this," admitted second-placed Arsehole Whinger yesterday. "He's certainly raised the bar. My once-innovative 'I could not see from zer dugout' routine appears rather dated now." The Secretive Whines Panel made the unprecedented step yesterday of delivering their first ever month of full marks for a manager. "We couldn't fault Mr Mourinho for indignation, selective blindness to facts or loudness, and his arrogance was particularly outstanding," said a spokesman yesterday. "Has he ushered in a new era of boot-room mithering? The panel certainly hope so."

Meanwhile, the upper reaches of the whining league are some way off for past master Alex Ferguson. Having only blamed three out of seven referees for results and even delivering a couple of back-handed compliments to opponents have seen his scores from the Whines Panel plummet. "Changes must be made. I can see where I've made mistakes in the hairdryer department," admitted Ferguson, hoisting himself with his own, particularly conciliatory, petard. "I need to start lashing out before I'm in a relegation dogfight with Kevin 'the lads did their best' Keegan."

Meanwhile, Mourinho goes from strength to strength. Upon learning of his league-topping success, the Portuguese upstart was in no mood for celebration. "Pathetic!" he roared while roaming the marble halls of his palace complex in search of a linesman to berate. "My scores for the season so far are still way too low. Your panel are corrupt, blind fools and I should be made King of the World for such slander."

Dave Mac

ISSUE 43 January 2005

Sing Up If You Love Chelsea!

For me – so far at least – the match at The Library has been the best away game this season. It was a passionate affair both on the pitch and within the ranks of the supporters, especially those at the Clock End of the ground. The Chelsea supporters were placed right next to the Gooners with just a fence and a few stewards separating them. Unlike the situation at Stamford Bridge, those in charge of policing the crowd did not make a big deal of the fact that both sets of supporters were standing for the entire duration of the game and they were allowed to engage in some good old-fashioned banter, as well as some good vocal support for their teams. No one (to my knowledge at least) was injured as a result of people standing and the atmosphere was definitely enhanced as a result of the liberal stewarding that took place.

Although a couple of people were warned for over excessive abuse and one or two might have been thrown out, supporters were generally allowed to support their teams without undue interference from stewards who would otherwise run the risk of verbal and physical abuse because of 'club policy'. The present regime in charge of Chelsea are, quite rightly, very concerned about the atmosphere (or lack of it) at Stamford Bridge. However, the malaise of the Chelsea support is due, in part, to the rules employed by the club concerning crowd behaviour.

While I will not condone en-masse singing of songs that involve swearing (a bit of a problem at Chelsea I know!), I don't mind a bit of banter between supporters. To me, one person giving the wankers sign to another who is on a similar wavelength is not that much to worry about and, in many cases, the exchanges between rival supporters are extremely entertaining.

249

However, at the moment, Chelsea supporters sitting in the Matthew Harding Lower are seeing supporters in the away section being allowed to stand during the game and are subject to abuse that, because of the over-excessive stewarding, they are not allowed to respond to. This is a point that is made often yet nothing is ever done about it. It is a clear case of one set of rules for one group (the away supporters) and another totally different set of rules for another (the home Chelsea supporters).

The time has come for Chelsea Football Club to consider the following proposals;

The complete middle three or the back halves of the middle five sections of the Lower Matthew Harding should have unrestricted seating but be available to season ticket holders only. This would mean that although anyone sitting within these blocks would, for the purposes of security and identification, have to produce their season ticket for inspection, they would be able to sit anywhere within the designated area. Those taking up a seat would purchase tickets with the knowledge that they would be in an area where other supporters might well stand or would otherwise be doing their best to create an atmosphere by singing in support of Chelsea and taunting the opposition players and supporters (I will always remember the 1997 FA Cup tie against Liverpool and the 2000 European Cup game against Barcelona where the whole crowd, not just the Matthew Harding end, were standing for entire match, such was the excitement).

Although some people might not get the seats they wanted, having unrestricted seating might well encourage supporters to get to the ground a little earlier in order to try to do so. If such an experiment were allowed to take place, I think that, after it had been in place for several matches, supporters would eventually, more often than not, start to sit in the same places week after week, especially if they thought that they might be at the 'heart of it'. All those who used to regularly stand in the Shed will remember having their 'own' little part of the terrace where they would go week after week and where, in many cases, friendships were formed that are still alive today.

One of the best places for pre-match singing is The So Bar. Just imagine if the several hundred who go in there were all able to sit in the same section of the Matthew Harding end and sing like they do in the pub. It has often been remarked that the atmosphere in that particular pub often matches or is better than in the ground itself. Without knocking the patrons of The So bar, that is indeed a sad state of affairs.

The regulars who travel away with Chelsea are amongst the most loyal of the Stamford Bridge supporters. Match after match at other grounds, they will when the need arises, stand for long periods in order to help them fully support their Chelsea side. Having spoken to many of them, I don't think I'd be wrong in saying that the consensus is that the current support given to Chelsea, especially at home, leaves a lot to be desired. Many agree with the proposal I have mentioned above and several have similar ideas themselves. While not everyone wishes for a return to the terraces, there is a growing section of concerned supporters who wish to see this situation remedied before it is killed off altogether.

Although what I have written relates to the current home end, I would, of course, long to see the redevelopment of the Shed End. I, for one, have signed the petition for a 60,000 seater stadium at Stamford Bridge and I hope that every reader of the fanzine will as well. A single tiered Shed End with a middle singing section, as set out above, is the obvious answer to all Chelsea's worries about the dismal atmosphere. A larger stadium, sensibly priced, is the only way forward. After all, as has been said several times in previous editions of this fanzine, if Chelsea are going to be the greatest side in Europe, they will need a stadium to match their aspirations.

It's not for me to tell other people how to spend their money but, if I was Roman, I'd put a little less towards buying players and a little more towards developing the ground. After all, Chelsea Football Club is there because of the supporters. If the right decisions are made on their behalf, the future 'well being' of the club will be assured.

While the club has started to listen to the wishes of the supporters through the Forum that has been established, those in charge must act sooner rather than later when addressing the issue of how best to create a decent atmosphere. I have read in previous editions of cfcuk that such people as Peter Kenyon and Bruce Buck read the fanzine. I hope they do take note of this article and consider its merits.

Chelsea Football Club is reliant on its supporters. While the club provide the facilities for us to come and support our team, it is time that they took notice of how we want to do it.

The Striker

ISSUE 44 February 2005

Dealing With The Envy

According to some members of the media and press, we are "Champions Elect". I, and hopefully other Chelsea supporters, consider this comment to be fairly worthless, given the fact that these same people will turn on us ruthlessly should we slip even just once. I would also remind Chelsea supporters not to assume the arrogant tone of our competitors in N5, who had the cheek to talk about the Champions League being a formality once the quarter final draw was made. Pride comes before a fall. It would be much nicer if we didn't sully any possible success with that kind of arrogance. However, it seems that many are already preparing the excuses and the vitriol given the seemingly relentless pace with which we seem to be heading for the title. Phone-ins on Talksport and Radio 5 live have been bombarded by people complaining about how sad it is that the title is being bought by Chelsea. Were these not the same people who took such glee in reminding us that you couldn't "buy the title"?

They were quite correct of course; you only need to look at how nearly $450m was wasted on players by Massimo Moratti's Inter to prove, what should be an obvious truth, that a lot of money is no guarantee of success in this sport. Perhaps this is one of the reasons why so many people must be upset. The intelligence with which Roman's investment has been spent both on and off the field (at a fraction of what Moratti spent on players alone) is cementing our position amongst Europe's top clubs. The abject failure of "Sweeney Investigates" to provide any tangible "dirt" on Roman probably makes our rivals all the more bitter, as must the knowledge that the likes of Peter Kenyon are working on making the club self sufficient.

That argument has failed, so people are now turning on the old chestnut of us having "no history" and our success being "fake". We are repeatedly lectured on our 15,000 crowds as if Chelsea History began and ended in the late 70's and 80's and then told we have won nothing. Well as many of you who read the website know, I'm not to keen on this sort of rubbish. You and I both know that it comes from the usual Man Utd-Liverpool-Arsenal axis who just can't cope with the fact that the door, which we have been banging on for a while now, is beginning to be forced open. These individuals have been joined by the supporters of other clubs, who despite having achieved staggeringly little for decades, feel the need to lecture us.

I'm going to list a few facts that every Chelsea supporter should know but, before I do, let me just say this. The history of Chelsea and our supporters is everywhere you look at Stamford Bridge, you just have to open your eyes to it. The Stadium itself tells its own and the club's story. Take a look at the East and West Stand, the former reflecting a period that took us into almost terminal decline for 20 years and the latter's completion reflecting our rise to prominence once more. When the Man Utd supporters took it upon themselves to say "You're not Chelsea anymore" they failed to spot the irony that we were sitting in a stand named after a fanatical Chelsea supporter, that has borne Matthew Harding's name through two successive ownerships: one that was at odds with him and the other from a man who will, hopefully, take the club to unparalleled success. As Brian Mears once said: "Chelsea FC will never lose its identity. Chelsea will be Chelsea for always and at Stamford Bridge."

We know where we've come from better than anyone else and we know where we are going. When the first Chelsea team of the new Chelsea century runs out at Stamford Bridge, their shirts will bear the crest demanded of the club by 20,000 supporters signatures. Can Arsenal fans say that when they run out at the "Emirates Stadium"? Can Man Utd fans say that when their shirts don't even bear the words "football club" on the club crest? I don't think so. Maybe they'll also be able to entertain themselves by learning the following facts:

No History? Despite being founded in 1905 only (well behind several clubs), Chelsea Football Club has the fifth highest average attendance record in English Football. Our average attendance over our entire history is 30,593. Man Utd, at No 1, have an average of 35,733.

Together with Newcastle, we have finished as the Football League's best supported club on 10 occasions. We are behind Man Utd, Everton and Arsenal on this list. Compare that to Liverpool's 7 and Spurs' 6. We also have the 2nd highest attendance record in England: 82,000 at home against Arsenal in 1935.

In this last decade, only Man Utd and Arsenal have surpassed our efforts in winning 2 FA Cups, a Cup Winners Cup and League Cup. All achieved before Roman.

We have not finished outside of the top 6 for 10 years and have played in Europe for 11 consecutive seasons. Only Man Utd and Arsenal can match this.

Since Heysel, only ourselves, Man Utd, Arsenal and Liverpool have won anything in Europe. The FA Cup record for the past decade repeats the same story.

We were the 4th best club in Premiership History (1992-2003) before Roman arrived.

Money Talks? Before Didier Drogba's arrival for £24m, Man Utd and Arsenal had spent the most on individual players. In fact, those two made up the top 5 most expensive signings. Try: Ferdinand £30m, Veron £28m, Reyes £20m, Van Nistelrooy £19m. Not to mention Rooney at a cool £27m.

In a Times newspaper rich list at the beginning of the season, not even one Chelsea player made the top 10. Even if Lampard and Terry's new deals, and their estimated salaries, are included they would be our only 2 representatives in the top 10.

José Mourinho is not even one of the top 3 best paid managers in England.

The Chelsea Advocate

*****

The Thoughts Of Chels Guevara

Following CHELSEA'S League double over Liverpool this season - the first time the feat has been achieved for years - it was interesting to learn that CHELSEA'S OFFICIAL CLUB STATISTICIAN RON HOCKINGS also notched a 'double' of his own. RON, who surely holds the record for attending CHELSEA matches (more than 2,500 and counting!) attended his first BLUES game on January 4th, 1947 and watched CHELSEA beat Liverpool 3-1 at STAMFORD BRIDGE. Some 49 years later, on New Year's Day 2005 (almost to the day), I met RON in a motorway service station while returning from the game at Anfield. While very happy that his side was top of the League and on course to give him his second glimpse of a Championship winning CHELSEA side, RON was feeling a quiet satisfaction that he'd achieved his own personal milestone. Good on you RON, see you at the party in May!

CHELSEA CAPTAIN JOHN TERRY is surely in line to become one of the greatest CHELSEA PLAYERS ever. He will, without doubt, also go on to captain ENGLAND. While people can see what he does on the pitch, the work he does for various charities often goes unnoticed, not that JOHN would ever want any plaudits, and his relationship with the CHELSEA SUPPORTERS is one that should be used as a model for other professional footballers. He is CHELSEA through and through. JOHN made the day/week/season for one particular band of CHELSEA SUPPORTERS, namely JOHN TERRY'S BARMY ARMY, when he called them and left a personal message for them on their mobile telephone. He had, of course, seen the chaps' banner at CHELSEA games and (hopefully) read about them in this fanzine. He called to thank the lads for their support and the message has, I suspect, been recorded somewhere by JOHN TERRY'S BARMY ARMY for posterity. As well as that, JOHN was also kind enough to give a CHELSEA SUPPORTER a lift to STAMFORD BRIDGE before the game against Scunthorpe. JOHN - while we here at cfcuk can only praise you for your admirable services to THE CHELSEA SUPPORT, we (respectfully!) want to know why we haven't had a call from you. After all, as JOHN TERRY'S BARMY ARMY were told in no uncertain terms, it was this fanzine that put them on the map and, the next time they come around to our stall and large it with their recorded message, we'd like to have one to let them listen to as well! The cfcuk number is in the fanzine (cfcuk BLUE) bit so, if you get a moment in-between scoring goals from corners, leading CHELSEA on to victory, playing for ENGLAND and generally helping to make this season the best ever in the club's history, give us call mate…

Chels Guevara

*****

"Top Of The League - We're Having A Laugh!"

Ten points clear and looking, quite frankly, unstoppable (at the time of writing) as we proudly gaze down on the rest of the Premiership in sheer amazement, with smiles beaming across our faces as wide as Wayne Rooney's waist line. It seems we are surely about to witness something the majority of us have never seen in our lifetime, Chelsea winning the league.

As we draw closer and closer to our first Premiership Title in fifty years, it seems the responses from our rival supporters, notably the Mancs and Gooners, are becoming worse and worse.

A few weeks ago we were all being told how a blip was just around the corner and that sooner or later we would hit a rocky patch. I'm one who doesn't like to count his chickens before they've hatched but, well, looking at it now it's going to have to be one hell of a rocky patch to knock us off our seemingly steady perch. But it seems apparent to me that perhaps we have already had our blip, at the beginning of the season. When we were struggling for goals and grinding out one nil's every week, wasn't that a blip compared with our current form?

Also, I've heard that we, Chelsea, the team with numerous European champions and league champions from all over Europe, have not got the experience for what it takes to emerge, come May, as premiership Champions. If this was the case and you could only win the League with players who had previously experienced doing so in this league I'm sure Mr Mourinho would have purchased a few players from the Gooners and Mancs in our bid to become champions. Alan Hansen once said, "You don't win anything with kids…" and look what happened there: a team with less experience than ours became champions. So that firmly puts that claim to bed.

Now the final claim that has been echoed by many in recent weeks, and one that seems to me as if it is might as well be written on a white flag with the words we surrender written underneath is, "You've bought the league". Lets face it - we Chelsea supporters couldn't give a damn if we have or haven't bought the League, but coming from the Mancs and Gooners you just have to laugh.

First of all, no matter how much money you spend it never guarantees success, just ask any Leeds or Liverpool fan. Yes, in today's world for any club to be successful money is probably a must have, but that doesn't mean you will win anything. Look at Real Madrid last season a team of hugely expensive self assembled superstars who came away with nothing. So this proves that it is probably almost impossible to buy the league just by throwing money around at players, as there are certain ingredients every team needs to have if they are to become champions and these are things that no amount of money in the world can buy: team spirit, luck, passion, determination and the will to want to win more than anything in the world. All things I feel we have in abundance and have probably had a fair bit of luck along the way. Now the thing that makes me laugh is when I hear a Man Utd or Arsenal fan dare to murmur the words, "You've bought the league," simply because the pair of them have won the league by not spending a penny haven't they... yeah right! Wiltord, Reyes, Henry (although a bargain), Ferdinand, Veron, Van Nistelrooy, Rooney, Saha, Ronaldo, just to name a few.

They have won the league the same way as we are surely about to, by spending money and with great, although annoying, managers at the helms of their clubs. We are just making up for lost time. Now with José and Roman united as one, it seems nothing can surely stop us from becoming league champions for only the second time in our proud history and all of us witnessing our wildest dreams coming true come May - if not sooner.

Up the Chels!

Luke Turner

*****

You Must Be Joking!

Batesy decided to take a short break in Australia. Before he went, he sent one of his goons down to the cfcuk stall to buy a "Trust Me... I'm A Chelsea Supporter" t-shirt. After receiving the t-shirt, he sets off on holiday and arrives a day and a half later. Heading straight for his hotel, he checks in and decides to go and have a drink in the beach-side bar.

He immediately strikes up a conversation with a guy who was drinking there, a local by the name of Bruce. As the day wore on, they'd each had their fair share of alcohol and they start to argue about, of all things, Crocodile Dundee. Batesy, being his usual forthright self, began to hurl insults about Australians at his drinking partner and, after one excess too many, made a particularly nasty personal remark.

Bruce's patience snapped and he informed Batesy that local custom dictated that, in such circumstances, a bare-knuckle three-rounder would be employed to settle any lost honour.

Batesy, looking at Bruce's muscular build and big fists didn't fancy a 'toe-to-toe' and, as he was cleaning himself up after his a*se went, he was thinking aloud, saying to himself, '"How can I get out of this one?"

'Being a sportsman, the Aussie felt a bit sorry for Batesy and said, "There is another way of settling it…"

"Anything, anything!" whimpered a relieved Batesy, clutching at any straw. Pointing out to sea, Bruce said, "See that coral reef out there? It's a mile out from the shoreline. Seeing as you slagged off Crocodile Dundee, you swim to that, mate, and we'll be square!"

Picking up his beach bag, Batesy ran towards the sea. As he dipped his toes into the water, he reached inside the bag, took out the "Trust me… I'm A Chelsea Supporter!" t-shirt and pulled it over his head. "No problem!" he shouted gleefully.

"No problem?" sneered Bruce, "Wait until those sharks get a smell of you!" Undaunted, and to the amazement of everybody who was watching, Batesy swam out, touched the coral, turned and was soon drying himself off after returning back to the beach.

Dumfounded, Bruce could only utter, "Stone me, cobber, how the heck did you manage to do that? I was positive those sharks would have you for a meal!"

"Easy," chuckled Batesy, "Have a look on the back of my t-shirt… what does it say?"

"Trust Me… I'm A Chelsea Supporter!", replied Bruce, "but what's that got to do with it?"

"Trust Me… I'm A Chelsea Supporter!" laughed Batesy, "Nothing on earth - man nor beast - would ever swallow that one!"

Hocus McPocus

ISSUE 45 March 2005

The Sheditorial

Following the exit to Newcastle in the FA Cup and the subsequent 1-2 defeat away to Barcelona in the Champions League, the harbingers of doom were predicting the end of Chelsea's season. However, as we all now know, José Mourinho's men lifted themselves to win the League Cup in an enthralling match against Liverpool in Cardiff's Millennium Stadium.

Then, some ten days later, Chelsea thrilled the world of football by beating the highly fancied Barcelona 4-2 in the second leg of their Champions League tie to go through to the last eight of the competition. However, while revelling in the glory of victory, this publication's sympathies must go to Wayne Bridge who, during the defeat at St James' Park, suffered a dreadful injury that not only put him out of the League Cup Final but also will see him miss the rest of the season.

We here at cfcuk and BlueAndWhiteArmy.net wish him all the best for a speedy recovery and we hope to see him back in a Blue shirt soon. Our thoughts also go to Car*o Cud*cini, who was suspended for the Final, and Arjen Robben, who missed the match at Cardiff through injury. Fortunately, in the case of the Dutchman, he should be back playing regularly in time for the final run-in at the end of this season.

While mentioning the League Cup Final and the return leg against Barcelona, I am personally very pleased at the progress that Joe Cole has made and it is clear that he is intent on repaying José Mourinho for the faith that he has shown in him.

Well done Joe!

The Guy Who Blagged Me

*****

The Thoughts Of Chels Guevara

It's nice to hear that despite their highly paid status, the CHELSEA FOOTBALLERS like to have a laugh while at work.

Apparently, masseur BILLY McCULLOCH is addicted to coffee and, to quote JT, "He drinks about a hundred cups a day!" In an effort to help him cut down on his habit, the CHELSEA CAPTAIN decided to play a prank on BILLY by hiding the coffee machine that is located in the home changing room at STAMFORD BRIDGE.

However, JOHN'S plan not only served to mess BILLY up, but also caused several hours of grief for the training ground manager PAUL DEAKIN whose responsibility also extends to the changing rooms at STAMFORD BRIDGE. It was only after he performed a frantic search of the stadium that the missing item was discovered, hidden in the away team's changing rooms. Tut tut JOHN! In future, please could you inform the management when you perform such antics…

Chels Guevara

ISSUE 46 April 2005

Chelsea Are Messing Up The Established Order

People in authority in football don't like Chelsea and José Mourinho. José has become the target of a crusade. He has been the subject of relentless attacks and criticism, not to mention petty kangaroo court-style proceedings in which every one of his actions are deconstructed, placed under the microscope, and charged. Was there ever a more ridiculous uproar than that at the Carling Cup final levelled against José for putting his finger to his lips?

José has, in short, become 'the enemy of football'. That's not my phrase, it's the label given to our manager by UEFA's referee boss, Volker Roth. UEFA's soggy attempts to distance themselves from such inflammatory comments contrast somewhat from the vigour and pedantry with which they are picking the nits off everything that José says and does.

José Mourinho clearly polarises opinions. He leaves nobody indifferent. Many people have been seduced by his winning ways on the pitch. He has been a breath of fresh air in a Premiership that had become the personal possession of Manchester United and Arsenal. There is no doubt that he is a supremely talented coach and that has attracted many admirers.

Indeed, the best testimony you can have of Mourinho is that given by his players. No Chelsea player has a bad word to say about him. On the contrary, all are effusive in their praise and their declarations of loyalty. They know that José will bring them to glory. He has made each of them better players. The sheer elation and joy at the end of some of Chelsea's more difficult games (and famous victories) says it all. Who can forget the passion shared between players and coach when Chelsea beat Manchester United at Old Trafford, when we beat Liverpool in the Carling Cup Final, or at the final whistle of the Barça home game? There is no question about the sincerity felt by the Chelsea lads and coach.

Pundits are also fulsome with praise. Chelsea were accused of being 'efficiently dull' at the beginning of the season, when we were grinding out a series of 1-0 wins whilst finding our feet. But to find fault with Chelsea nowadays is to split hairs. A team that plays both Robben and Duff cannot be accused of being boring; a patented 4-3-3 is hardly conservative. And that's without praising the magnificent defence.

Indeed, many managers (even those who have been at the receiving end of a spanking) have been effusive in their admiration for José. On the other hand, it is almost understandable – predictable even – that José Mourinho and Chelsea would end up winding people up.

Many in football are used to a cosy order that has favoured a number of established clubs. The best example of this is the 'G-14' organisation of Europe's larger clubs in the bigger Leagues. The G-14 (confusingly this contains 18 clubs) is a lobby within UEFA for the rights of the big clubs. Chelsea are not part of this organisation, which makes its very existence absurd. After all, Chelsea have become a massive club, one of Europe's biggest, both on and off the pitch. Chelsea give a certain importance to joining the G-14. As well as a recognition of Chelsea's importance, Chelsea want to be a member of an organisation which has a significant representation role for the larger clubs.

Apparently Liverpool, Arsenal and Barcelona are opposed to Chelsea joining, and since admitting new members has to be by unanimity, Chelsea are staying out for the moment. Each has a particular grievance vis-à-vis Chelsea: Liverpool's is about Steven Gerrard, Arsenal's for Ashley Cole, and Barcelona's concerns the way that Chelsea had the impudence to knock the Spanish side out of the Champions League. In truth, the grievance is about Chelsea's capacity to annoy the traditional elite.

The jury is still out as to what Chelsea did wrong other than what bigger clubs have always done. There is no evidence that, in trying to sign Steven Gerrard from Liverpool, Chelsea acted contrary to the rules. Much rumour and conjecture surrounded the Liverpool captain's aborted transfer last summer (most of it coming from Merseyside, it has to be said). But Liverpool have not complained to any authorities about what Chelsea did; whist it clearly annoyed the fading club that their captain and poster boy might try to better himself by playing for a bigger side, nothing Chelsea did was untoward. For Liverpool to bear such a grudge seems little more than bad faith on their part. In Arsenal's case, the

N5ers are clearly annoyed by the Ashley Cole saga. As I write this, the F.A. has yet to announce their verdict, not to mention the potential punishments for the guilty parties. Yet the astonishing aspect of this case is that, although it appears clear that Chelsea did meet with Ashley Cole, it was, in fact, the player who initiated the contact.

Our North London rivals can complain all they like about expecting Chelsea to behave in a more neighbourly fashion; they could also have expected, first and foremost, that their own player (and local lad) behave with more loyalty towards his employers and club. Ashley wanted to meet Chelsea (we would be naïve to expect that the meeting was not about envisaging a possible move across London), Chelsea agreed to such a meeting. Chelsea were in the wrong in accepting that. Yet was our club guiltier than Cole himself? Arsenal's anger stems more from the fact that they have lost their place in the hierarchy of English clubs. This season, they have been second to Chelsea on most counts (apart from goals scored). It must have irked them, having had such a magnificent season last year, that Chelsea are romping away with the title. Moreover, their continued failure in the Champions League, compared to the fact that Chelsea have progressed where they have stumbled, is infuriating for a club with Arsenal's ambitions. Arsenal have been quick to blame Chelsea and their money for 'unfair competition'. You have to laugh at that: it's easy for them to blame other people's excellence when they should be examining their own shortcomings. It is not the fault neither of Chelsea nor their money that Arsenal lost twice to Manchester United. Or once to Bolton or Liverpool for that matter. Chelsea's cash has nothing to do with Arsenal's poor defence, or the fact that Thierry Henry seems to go walkabout for key matches. Or that Patrick Vieira is a shadow of the player he was last season.

Formally, Arsenal are annoyed because of the Ashley Cole business. That's just window dressing: the real reason for their anger is jealousy that, despite having a great manager who has been admirably astute in the transfer market, this season they are second best not due to any unfair competition from Chelsea but, simply, because they are not as good as us.

Which leads us to Barcelona. For Barcelona, read also Real Madrid, one of the biggest clubs in the world, two clubs that have had a purchasing power that towered over the rest of Europe for the past few years. Now they hate the idea that somebody has barged to the top of the queue. Apparently it was a phone call to Barcelona by Peter Kenyon that caused Barça to offer Ronaldinho a new, improved contract … barely 12 months after the bucktoothed Brazilian had signed his first contract. In Madrid's case, Chelsea not only signed Claude Makelele (the club's decline can be traced to that precise moment) but we are always linked either with purchasing their galacticos, or with buying the players that Madrid would like to sign. According to the rumours, Madrid will have to fight against Chelsea for Joaquín, Vincent Kompany, Asier Del Horno, Robinho, Fernando Torres, Steven Gerrard. Oh the lèse-majesté.

The Champions League draw between Chelsea and Barça provided a unique opportunity to decide who was top dog in Europe. It pitched the runaway leaders of the two biggest leagues against each other. It was a chance to measure the young pretender against a doyen of the established order.

Chelsea eliminated Barcelona. In the process, we managed to annoy, severely, the venerable Catalan club, who protested vigorously to UEFA. UEFA took up their complaint, and added to it. Of course, a formal justification was given to the complaint: Chelsea suggested that Barcelona had leaned on the referee. Plus they didn't turn up to their press conference. It is unfortunate (and regrettable) that the ref in question retired as he was the subject of threats from Chelsea fans. But does anything in what Chelsea did really justify the crusade that UEFA seem to be waging against Chelsea?

That crusade is a protest from the established order. It's a suggestion that the traditional club hierarchy should not be reshuffled to accommodate, somewhere very near the top of the pile, the brash new upstarts from SW6 who don't have the 'history' of some of their more illustrious counterparts, but have almost limitless prospects. It's not surprising that the tenets of that tradition – Real Madrid, Arsenal, Barcelona, Liverpool – are unhappy at contemplating a more prestigious past than a future that seems to be weighed against them.

We're suffering from the obstacles thrown by the establishment and the cries of protest from big name clubs who, all of a sudden, see a pair of Blue heels in front of them. Chelsea are continuing to knock noses out of joint. It's the sign that we have arrived and we are here to stay. At the top. The others should get used to it.

EuroBlue

*****

So Why Can't We Stand Up?

Every week across the country fans are being ejected or even banned for simply standing up to support their team. Away allocations have been cut, parts of grounds are under threat of closure, and there is increasing conflict with stewards.

Stand Up Sit Down have met with clubs, local authorities, safety officers, football authorities and the FLA, but have found very few people who really consider this a safety issue. We are now left wondering just why such efforts are being made to prevent supporters standing.

Safety The FLA say that the movements that standing spectators make to follow play could lead to them falling and causing a cascade effect, injuring those in front. SUSD consider that whilst there may be some risk of falls in steep upper tiers, we simply cannot envisage such an effect in areas of relatively low gradient, which are present in virtually every ground. This is not just the view of supporters, but also some clubs, safety officers and local authorities.

A senior council official, who is threatening his local club with closing part of their ground, told us that he can see no safety problems with standing in that area. However he has to be seen to be doing his job, and is under pressure from the FLA. At their conference last year the gentleman charged by the Core Cities Group of Local Authorities to deal with persistent standing, was shouted down by football club safety officers, angry at his ridiculous arguments. He later stated that a majority of Football Safety Officers Association members seem not to consider persistent standing as a safety issue. The FSOA National Administrator said that they are opposed to supporters being permitted to stand within football stadia during passage of play, and their policy is to support the FLA document 'Standing in Seated Areas at Football Grounds'. He noted however that there is a difference of view within the FSOA, but that a number of Safety Officers support the policy.

It appears therefore that the majority don't.

It is accepted that the greatest danger from standing is at moments of excitement such as goal celebrations, so why are such efforts being made to stop passive standing during normal play – the time of least risk? Lord Taylor predicted that supporters would stand at moments of excitement, so knowing that this will occur, why did the FLA allow many new steep stands to be built? The FLA say that standing supporters take up more room so spread into aisles, but our experience is that this is rare and easily prevented. We believe that there is less risk of injury when a goal celebration is started from the standing position, a view unanimously backed by comments from numerous SUSD members, but the FLA say the opposite.

The Government's standard reply to supporters writing in support of SUSD's proposals states that there are more injuries at grounds with standing than in all seater stadia. This is misleading as the relevant figures would be injuries from standing in seated areas compared to sitting, but the FLA say these are not available. We know of one major Premiership ground where the injury rate is the same whether supporters sit for a major fixture or stand for a lesser match. Even in grounds with terracing the average injury rate is only 1 in 20,732 and the FLA admit that 70% of these are illness or pre-existing injures.

If safety really is a concern, why don't clubs minimise the risk wherever possible? Where away allocations have been cut, why are supporters packed into a smaller section, surrounded by empty seats, rather than taking the opportunity to reduce spectator density and hence the safety 'risk'. Lord Taylor said that standing accommodation is not intrinsically unsafe. His report did not specifically cover the issue of standing in seated areas, but said that he expected that after a period of time supporters would get used to sitting. So how well did he understand us?

Every year in London alone an average of 70 passengers are seriously injured and two killed in accidents related to standing on buses. The Health & Safety Executive says that standing on trains is not a safety issue. Meanwhile the FLA are determined to stop standing in even lower tiers of football grounds. Is this objective safety assessment or convenience? It would cost billions to provide seats for all bus and train passengers, but football clubs had to pay to alter their grounds, and of course we know the Government don't want us to stand.

Inconsistencies The most dangerous place for standing is steep upper tiers, so why are away fans often allocated these, whilst the safer lower tier is empty? At QPR, away supporters in the upper tier have to stand in order to see part of the goal. SUSD suggested that the pitch is moved forward to improve sightlines, but QPR showed little interest. We wrote to Hammersmith & Fulham Council, who said they would 'observe the safety implications of standing in the School Upper', adding that 'any action however will need to be balanced against what is reasonably practical to achieve, given the stand is over 25 years old.' They didn't explain why the age of the stand is relevant to moving the pitch forward.

So in some grounds supporters are being ejected from gently sloping lower tiers, which are under threat of closure. In some standing is largely ignored, but in others the club choose not to take simple action to prevent standing in more dangerous upper tiers. Does safety not demand consistency? We asked the FLA why spectators can stand at rock concerts held in football grounds. They said firstly that the action is in one place, so there is less chance of toppling over in straining to follow it, and secondly that those attending music events are a different 'profile' from football supporters. Do they really think rock fans stand quietly in front of their seats? If safety is paramount, why did the FLA wait until last year to take serious action? What has prompted the recent clampdown on standing? We have seen no evidence to suggest that the safety risk has changed, so is there another reason?

The FLA The FLA was charged to monitor local authorities' oversight of spectator safety at English and Welsh football grounds, and ensure through a licensing system that these grounds became all seated. In 1992 the Government decided to allow clubs in the lower two divisions to retain standing accommodation, however if a club is relegated back into a lower division, or if it builds a new ground, it cannot have standing areas. All seating by stealth? The FLA now appears to have broadened its remit, to include comfort and security of supporters as well as safety. It seems that they have to resort to using every argument against standing, no matter how weak. Is it right that a body who don't even agree that a significant proportion of supporters want to stand should have such influence over the way we watch our game? A recent report by 'The Efficiency in Government Unit' claimed that many quangos could be merged or abolished without anyone noticing a significant difference and included the FLA, along with such bodies as the Potato Council, in a list of the most useless quangos. Do we still need the FLA?

Crowd Control & Customer Care How relevant is the argument that allowing supporters to stand will lead to crowd trouble? Any disorder will almost certainly occur at a time of controversy or excitement, when supporters would be expected to be standing. A ground regulation banning standing is hardly likely to stop anyone who is sufficiently agitated as to cause trouble from getting out of their seat. Those who are unable or prefer not to stand, should not have their view blocked by others, however rather than a justification for making all supporters sit, this is a major reason for providing separate areas for everyone to watch the game as they wish.

Debate There appears to be reluctance for many parties to participate in an open debate on standing. Despite devoting considerable time to SUSD, the FLA are clearly tired of what they consider are the same old arguments. Few clubs have been prepared to talk openly, and whilst several have publicly stated support for standing areas, others have told us that they support our aims but cannot allow this to be quoted. Premiership clubs discussed our letter at a meeting and decided not to reply. The Premier and Football Leagues did not want us to make public what was said when we met. One club made a public statement in support of our proposals, but then wrote to us with a far more guarded opinion. It is almost as if there is a conspiracy not to allow public debate, as this would highlight the weakness of the case against standing.

Summary *Stand Up Sit Down* proposes the simple solution that in all seater stadia, at least one area of each ground is selected where supporters would be permitted to stand safely in front of their seats. It is clear that supporters will continue to stand, as they have since the Taylor Report, so by allocating only the most suitable areas, our proposals would actually improve safety. The deeper we dig the more it seems that a total ban on standing cannot be justified on the grounds of safety, crowd control or customer care. Lessons have been learned from Hillsborough, and major steps taken to improve our safety, but a total ban on standing is simply not necessary or indeed workable. So why is there such reluctance even for an open debate on the issue? Is the issue safety or social engineering? Is there a hidden agenda to move the game away from its working class routes and fill our grounds with middle class fans who will buy the merchandise, clap quietly in their seats, join in with the orchestrated singing over the PA, but disappear as soon as football stops being trendy?

Peter Caton Stand Up Sit Down

Note – We do not wish to misrepresent the views of the FLA and fullnotes of our meeting stating the views of SUSD and the FLA can be read on our website **www.standupsitdown.co.uk**

*****

Boom Time At The Bridge

I don't want to hear any more talk about "no Robben no goals". I'm sick of reading about it! Three goals against Barcelona booked our place in the next round of the Champions League!. Three against Liverpool the week before gave us our first major trophy for a few years! Four goals against Palace and three goals at Norwich put us clear again at the top! We are not a one-man team…sorry, just wanted to get that off my chest!

What a great captain and player John Terry is! He always plays with total commitment and has never flinched from a challenge. He has blue blood and loves this Club! In the League Cup Final after Riise had scored that first goal my eyes turned to Terry, as I needed to see his reaction to this early setback as our captain. He didn't let me down! There he was, fist clenched inspiring his troops, he was 'up for it' and there was no way he was going to lose this match! No one had their heads down and players were being positive. They had just scored but I didn't care! I had total faith in Terry to lead us to victory and felt that it was only a matter of time before we got one back, especially as Liverpool chose to defend so deep. I was a bit disappointed talking to some Chelsea supporters at half time that just couldn't see us getting back into the game. We need to have belief in our team and our manager. It won't be long before Terry takes over from Wise to become the most successful captain in the history of Chelsea Football Club. This is his first season as captain and he will be lifting the Premiership trophy at the end of it!

Barcelona in the Champions League and there he was again! After that three goal 'Wet Dream' start we were pinned back by the disappointment of those two Ronaldinho goals. Again at half-time I could hear talk of how we had 'blown it' and there was 'no way back from this'! Where has our belief gone, I just couldn't believe what I was hearing!! Terry was there in the second half willing us on as he led from the back. He won everything and didn't put a foot wrong. Hey, if ever a player deserved to score a winning goal that night! He wanted that header and he wanted the win.

John Terry has at last been given the chance to get a few England games under his belt. In his recent two World Cup qualifying games he was commanding, and organized the English defence as if he was the captain. He won everything in the air and apart from one minor 'cock-up' against Azerbaijan, his passing and overall defending was perfect. He also added extra power up front at corners and free kicks. It's about time that Eriksson put Terry's name down first on the team sheet ahead of Ferdinand and C*mpbell. We are still well in front at the top of the Premiership and at the start of the season if we had been told that we would have been just one point clear by April, we would have been happy with that! Yes, I know United are closing the gap but lets all show the same belief and determination that the players show on the field every week. United have been on a really good run over the past few months but this only helps to show how well we are playing when we went up there for the semi final and turned them over. We will win the Premiership this season. Have faith and belief………John Terry will not let us down!

Blood, sweat and glory! This is our year and we will be Champions!

BlueBear

ISSUE 47 May 2005

The Sheditorial

We've done it at last! After a 50-year wait, Chelsea Football Club are once more Champions of England. Just as Jose Mourinho predicted many months ago, Chelsea won the Title at the Reebok Stadium against Bolton. While it appeared that the club were Champions elect for most of the season, even when the results went our way and it was impossible for the chasing teams to catch us, there is nothing like final confirmation of the fact and I'm sure that every Chelsea fan still took time to check out the League table and work out the mathematics just to make sure. With the chance of glory still to come in the Champions League Final, this is the greatest ever season in the Club's history.

For many, just seeing Chelsea win the Title once is satisfying enough – it is for me, but rest assured, this honour in our Centenary year will be the first of many. That said, defending the Title next season will be even harder than winning the trophy was in this current one. Opposing teams will be redoubling their efforts to beat us when they come up against us next season. We, the supporters, must ensure that our support matches the valiant effort of those on the pitch. It is easy to support the side and sing up loud and walk tall when Chelsea are winning Championships, as was the case at Bolton. However, it is when the side goes a goal down or isn't playing as well as expected that your support is crucial.

While the football this season has been brilliant, at times, those in the stands have let down those playing on the pitch. While we are bound to be tagged 'glory hunters' and suffer the usual jibes that supporters of successful teams are burdened with, let's do our best not forget our roots, our history and our heritage. We, the supporters, are what this club is all about. We always have been, still are and always will be. We must never, ever forget our place and do our best to ensure that those charged with running our club don't forget us either.

Finally, I hope that you, the reader, will allow me to send, on your behalf, a message of thanks to Roman Abramovich, Jose Mourinho and the Chelsea players for everything they've done for us. Blue forever! Up The Chels!

The Guy Who Blagged Me

*****

The Thoughts Of Chels Guevara

Following my mention of LAURENCE McGEOUGH in the last issue of cfcuk, a member of the personal staff (hereafter to be known as MR X) attached to ROMAN ABRAMOVICH, contacted me with a simply brilliant offer of help. After reading about how LAURENCE was unable to make the CHELSEA v Man City game due to the kick off time being altered by Rupert Murdoch's SKY TV, MR X promised to get LAURENCE two tickets for CHELSEA'S game against Charlton Athletic. Not only that, he also promised to cover the travel costs that 84-year-old LAURENCE and his son-in-law would incur travelling down to LONDON from their home in Airdrie. The reason? It's because the mother of MR X hails from Airdrie and, as he himself said, "Us CHELSEA SUPPORTERS have got to stick together!" Good? It gets even better! Upon hearing about the arrangements being made for the two CHELSEA SUPPORTERS, CHELSEA'S Group Operations Director SIMON ARTHUR arranged for them to stay in the Village Hotel on the evening preceding the game. We at cfcuk would also like to pass on our thanks to both he and SIMON ARTHUR on behalf of the family of LAURENCE, all of whom were overwhelmed by the kindness shown by those at CHELSEA. We're also pleased that those 'at the top' at CHELSEA FOOTBALL CLUB are reading this fanzine and that we have, in some small way, helped make a 'special day' for LAURENCE.

Chels Guevara

*****

Enemy Of Football? You're Having A Laugh!

The witch-hunt against Chelsea appears to go on and on and it seems irrelevant which newspaper you read. Recent weeks have seen the press congratulate Barca fans for booing Roman and attack Chelsea for buying success, ironic really as the press is influenced by one man and historically Barca have been a buying club. However, there have been plenty of instances where clubs have spent heavily and not succeeded. Indeed, Chels have waited 5 years for silverware. Yes we have money but we simply now have the best manager around.

The transformation in one season has been absolutely remarkable and José hasn't had an injury free squad to choose from by any means. The team spirit, organisation and tactical awareness has been evident from the beginning of the season but there is now an important mindset from the fans, we now believe we are winners. However, success doesn't come without a price and it is time for the fans to stand up and be counted. Be prouder than ever to be blue.

With speculation around as to José's feeling on the club stance with UEFA concerning his ban and fine, it is important he knows exactly how the fans feel.

Shout his name with pride, he is on the verge of making dreams come true for us. Indeed, looking ahead there would appear to be areas were the squad can be further strengthened and with José at the helm the future can be blue rather than red.

The alleged comments from Guillard branding Jose an enemy of football is in my view an utter disgrace, particularly when they were made prior to any evidence being considered. The fact that Frisk retired in such dramatic fashion is no surprise to me as he officiated in that manner also. However, all decent people would utterly condemn the alleged death threats made to Frisk. The whole episode revolves around hearsay; surely it is time facts emerged to enable football to move on.

It would be interesting to know what most people saw as the enemies of Football: match fixing perhaps, ticket touting, diving, drug taking, racism, spitting, the list goes on and UEFA and FIFA should be working on such issues. A media highlighted incident without any apparent substance from either side seems to me a distraction. Indeed, a successful man, fully qualified for his profession, who took the brave decision to give his time to preach the football word to bring Israeli and Palestine children together cannot be an enemy of football.

RAISE YOUR VOICES FOR JOSÉ!

Be Proud - Be Chelsea

In the eyes of others over the years we've been the music hall joke and the under achievers. Now because of Roman we are the team who bought success and because of his proud successful record, José is arrogant. Fact – we have a functional and entertaining team that has dealt with serious injury problems and not blipped. How many other teams would have organised themselves so well that they could perform without recognised full backs and without the flying Robben for so long.

Fact – we have the best disciplinary record in the Premier. Fact – there is a real togetherness in the whole club. Fact – unlike some, we have not 1 but 2 great goalkeepers (I have thought about writing to Wenger and Ferguson to tell them how to spot a good keeper but bollocks). Fact – our support is better than most. Fact – the club are planning for success and self-sufficiency. Fact – we are developing a great training facility. Fact – we have established a charity partnership to assist cancer care in children. Fact – we now sell edible pies! Fact – the others are jealous. Fact – the media rarely deal with them. Fact – never been prouder to be Blue. Fact – boy am I going to enjoy it.

Win or lose, Up the Blues!

True Blue

ISSUE 48 Summer 2005

Stat Attack!

Number one: The number worn by the awesome Petr Cech, who set new standards of Premiership goalkeeping this season. The 22-year-old went 1,025 consecutive league minutes between conceding Thierry Henry's free-kick at Highbury on 12 December 2004 and Leon McKenzie's header at Carrow Road 83 days later - a new record. The Blues' title win was built on defence and anyone fortunate enough to get past PFA Player of the Year John Terry *et al was unfortunate enough to meet a keeper who kept a remarkable 24 clean* sheets. Some might say, however, it's the least the Blues should expect.

Cech's £7m price tag means he cost more than every other keeper in Chelsea's history put together.

Number two: The number which represents the longest run of league matches Chelsea have gone without a win. Appropriately enough, this sequence has happened twice - in September and April - and it is the closest Chelsea have come to a slump in form. A goalless draw at Villa Park on 11 September was followed by a similarly score-free match at Stamford Bridge against Tottenham - after which Mourinho infamously accused Spurs of "leaving the bus in front of the goal." And successive home draws against Birmingham (1-1) and Arsenal (0- 0) followed earlier this month - hardly, it has to be said, the stuff of football nightmares.

Number three: The number of Premiership records broken by Chelsea this season. Anyone at the club will tell you that the Title matters more than the record books, but, to put the icing on the cake, Chelsea have bettered Manchester United's record of 28 wins in a 38-game season by winning 29. They also beat United's all-time Premiership record of 92 points set in 1993-94 by earning 95. And Arsenal's proud record of conceding the fewest goals - 17 in the 1998-99 season - has also been beaten. Chelsea have set a new record by conceding just 15. OK, so we cheated on this one a little bit having broken more than three records as well as a real desire not to madden the Mancs and cheating Gooners too much. We were of course, the only Premiership side not to have a player sent off. Why not add, the longest ever sequence of consecutive away wins - 9 - the best goal difference in the history of the Premier League and so many, many more! Of course, three could have been the number of Barclays awards won, the Manager of the Year, the Player of the Year and the Goalkeeper of the Year. Embarrassing, isn't it?

Number four: The number of goals Chelsea have scored in seven separate Premiership matches this season - the most they have managed in any single game. Such striking prowess, however, left critics such as Arsenal defender Lauren less than impressed. "It seems a lot of the top honours are being won by defensive sides rather than ones who attack, like us," he moaned as the Blues stood on the brink of taking the Gunners' crown. Sour grapes? Perhaps. If not, Blackburn, West Brom, Fulham, Charlton, Newcastle, Norwich and Crystal Palace - who all let in four against Mourinho's men - must be mightily relieved that Chelsea did not choose to go for it against them...

Number five: The number of trophies won by Chelsea boss José Mourinho before moving to Stamford Bridge. Mourinho won a treble in 2002-03, his first full season at Porto - adding the UEFA Cup to the domestic league and cup. And the 3-0 Champions League final win over Monaco in May 2004 went alongside another Portuguese league title to confirm Mourinho's status as one of the world's top coaches. Two more trophies have already followed this season. The charismatic Portuguese may be seen as arrogant by his detractors - but no-one can argue with his achievements.

Number six: The number of different players to score a Premiership goal against Chelsea at Stamford Bridge so far this season. That compares with 29 players who have found the net at struggling Norwich, while even Arsenal have seen 15 different opposition players score at Highbury in the Premiership. Two Bolton players are in this exclusive club, Kevin Davies and Radhi Jaidi, who both scored in November's 2-2 draw. And the roll of honour includes Crystal Palace's Aki Riihilahti, Birmingham's Walter Pandiani, Fulham's Collins John and James Beattie, then of Southampton, although he rather undid his good work by netting an own goal later in the same game...

Number seven: The number of English players to make an appearance for Chelsea under José Mourinho. Although the Blues have been able to sign the cream of the world's talent, Mourinho's side beats with an English heart, defender John Terry and midfielder Frank Lampard forming the core of his team. Joe Cole has blossomed since the New Year and is now an automatic pick for England, while Glen Johnson has also been a regular starter in 2005. And Wayne Bridge and Scott Parker both featured under Mourinho before injuries struck and Anthony Grant made his debut in the 3-1 win at against Man Utd at Old Trafford. Meanwhile, strike up the bagpipes for Steven Watt, the lone representative for the rest of Britain. The Scot's solitary appearance came in the FA Cup win over Scunthorpe.

Number eight: The number of league games Chelsea won in a row from 18 December to 2 February to cement their rise from Title hopefuls to odds-on title favourites. Although short of Arsenal's Premiership record of 14 consecutive wins, the Blues' streak saw them pull clear of the Gunners and Manchester United in the table. The run was only ended when Chelsea's nemesis, Kevin Keegan, came with his Manchester City side to Stamford Bridge to grab a 0-0 draw, to follow up their 1-0 win in Manchester earlier in the season. That has made them the only team so far to take four points off Jose Mourinho's men - and the only side to keep two clean sheets against the Blues.

Number nine: The number of major trophies won by Chelsea in the 99 years prior to this season - an average of one every 11 years. It is 50 years since Chelsea's last - and only other - league title, and although quality silverware has been won over the years, it has not been on display at Stamford Bridge as frequently as it has at Old Trafford, Highbury or Anfield. Three FA Cups, two Cup Winners' Cups, two League Cups and one European Super Cup complete the Blues' haul before this season. Nevertheless, Mourinho's men have now added another two trophies to the list.

Number 10: The number of League games played by Robert Huth. This was the minimum number of games required to qualify for a Premiership Winners' medal. According to an insider, the German youngster was told by José Mourinho that he would definitely play in the last two matches against Man Utd and Newcastle once the Title had been secured.

Number 11: The number of different players to score a league goal for Chelsea this season. As if to prove Chelsea's team ethic, José Mourinho could field an entire starting XI of goal scorers - and maybe add James Beattie to the bench, after his own goal while playing for Southampton in August. The key to Chelsea's success is that they have not relied on any one man to find the net - top scorer Eidur Gudjohnsen has just 11 league goals, some way behind leading striker Thierry Henry. And, it seems, if you stop Gudjohnsen and 10- goal Didier Drogba, then the midfielders - Frank Lampard, Arjen Robben, Joe Cole and Damien Duff - will get you....

John Terry's Barmy Army

ISSUE 49 August 2005

Life In A Fishbowl

What a summer it has been. No sooner have we won the one trophy that most of us have ached to have for as long as any of us can recall, but we set about buying just about everyone who plays football both here and overseas. That's if you believe the papers of course, we nearly signed Michael Essien (might even have finally done by the time you read this!), we nearly signed Steven Gerrard, we nearly signed David Trezeguet.... Have I missed any out? Probably thousands if truth be told, and that's why we have to be a little cautious about exactly what we read over our morning coffee.

Fish live in water, but not everything that lives in water is a fish. What the hell am I on about now? Well put simply, as far as the newspapers are concerned if there is no news, then make the bugger up. You could easily think that no one wanted to come to us and that the world and his dog (maybe even his fish) hates us. Well maybe they do and maybe they don't, but just coz there is a huge story in the Mirror saying we are after Joe Bloggski does not make it true.

However, things have changed in beautiful, wonderful, West London. With Roman's money and Peter Kenyon's ability to entertain over dinner, the world really is our oyster. We could sign just about anyone we want to if we threw enough money at them or their current club, and it is here that I see a bit of a sea change, and a welcome one at that.

Firstly, you have to realise that the pool of players that we want to pick from has shrunk. We have reached a standing now where the sort of player we are after will, in all probability, have to pass three tests. He will have to be young with plenty of legs left in him, he will need to be a world superstar or the potential to become one, and most importantly of all he

279

will need to fit in with the family spirit that José has so cleverly created. That was why, from the very first moment the story broke, I did not believe we would be interested in Ashley Cole. True he passes part one and two of the three part test, but can you imagine someone quite so up their own backside fitting in with what we have? Not a hope. Should we risk any splits in the camp in order to strengthen the squad? The answer to that has to be a firm no. In any case, signing someone who does not fit in and looks nothing like a team player would not strengthen the squad, whoever they are.

José commented the other day that in many ways buying players at a filthy rich club like ours was much harder than at some other clubs with a much smaller transfer kitty. Of course the papers mocked him, their editors probably could not keep the journalists out of the boozer long enough to get them to understand what he was saying. It's that pool effect I was talking about. Who can we sign who is better than Frank Lampard? Or JT? Or Petr Cech? There are very few players on this planet who are going to add very much to the squad we have currently, and they are lusted over both near and far.

The best players in the world are assets that clubs will not want to give up to us. Why should they want to make one of Europe's best sides, which is what we now are, even stronger? The only exception to this is if we are prepared to make a totally stupid and ludicrous offer. At this point I do have to take my hat off to Peter Kenyon. He gets an awful lot of stick, some of it is possibly justified, but he is a bloody good businessman and I for one feel comfortable knowing that we have him on board. I think he, and we, have learned our lessons from previous seasons where we probably paid substantially more than we should have for certain players. Those mistakes are ones we have learnt from, and in future, clubs will not be able to hold us to ransom. Let's be clear about one thing: it is often going to be the case going forward that (a) players will be desperate to join us and (b) many clubs in need of money will soon realise that we are their best, maybe their only, chance of balancing their books.

Any player worth having, any player with half an ounce of pride or ambition, is going to want to play for a high profile and successful team. Despite Roman's wealth we are new players still, we are a young and growing club. The likes of Juventus, Real Madrid and yes, sadly, Manchester United have years over us. That is not going to be the case for very much longer however. Success breeds success, it is true in every walk of life. As the trophy room needs to be expanded, so will the list of players who will look at the Bridge with real envy. I sit back at last season and I smile. I think of the one just about to start and I grin, a bigger grin than you can imagine. Just think, not only do we have the squad from last season that served us so very well, but they have now been together for a year or more and will be even more aware of how each other play. That is ignoring the fact that we have Crespo back, who I still believe is one of the top three or four strikers in the world, have added SWP and in Del Horno, someone who looks like a truly world class left back. That's if he can stop the yellow cards that seem to flow whenever he sticks his foot in. If we were a class outfit last season, what the heck are we going to be this term? United are rowing with each other before a ball is kicked and the Gooners have sold one of their two most important players and are so strapped for cash (and no bugger wants to sign for them either, shame!). OK, so the Scousers have signed Peter Crouch, but he is only there in order to help clean the floodlights!

The season is yet to begin, yet it could be argued it is already over. Maybe we should declare, maybe we should give the others a head start, maybe we should only play with five men. One thing in my mind is certain... They ain't gonna stop us!!

John Terry's Barmy Army

*****

"Flying high …"

When it became clear that Chelsea were about to be proclaimed Champions of England for the first time for 50 years, it was decided that it would only be right and proper for Arsenal and Manchester United to be reminded of this fact whilst fighting over the scraps of the season. So, a plane was hired to fly a banner over the Millennium Stadium on Cup Final day to reaffirm; "Chelsea FC – Champions 2005".The cost was just over a grand, and following internet exposure, contributions came in from all round the world.

Thank you – a list of people who contributed is on the opposite page.

The cost was £1,078.65. Fears that the cost wouldn't be met were soon dispelled and there was a decent wedge left over.

Having emailed all the contributors, it was agreed to donate the balance of **£686.35** to Frank Lampard's and Chelsea FC's adopted charity, CLIC Sargent. (Editor's note; *It is the charity that helps children with cancer and the one that sponsored Lucy Hilton, the young girl who joined the players on the pitch for the Championship celebrations following the Charlton match. Tragically, she died the following day.*)

The banner was a partial success as the BBC didn't catch it, which is not what I pay my licence fee for; and Sky only caught it from a distance, but we got some good mileage out of it as there were articles in The Mirror, The Standard and The Times. It was also mentioned on Talksport several times and on SoccerAM on the morning of the game by the actor Johnny Lee-Miller, much to Tim Lovejoy's delight.

A Manchester Utd supporter tells me that a pub full of their fans disgorged themselves from the boozer thinking it was an anti-Glazer protest only to look up to see Chelsea proclaimed as Champions, then singing, "Have you aver won a treble, have you fuck…" to a Cessna disappearing into the clouds.

John Drewitt

*****

MARY FULHAM

I used to take Mary a strong mug of tea and steal a few minutes with her while another pensioner at the other end of the Lunch Club was probably waiting for me to take them some liquid refreshment too. Mary would ask me about my girlfriend and I would ask her how her weekend was, and if the weather was nice we'd stand outside and smoke a cigarette and even though I had my own packet of smokes she would always politely offer me one of hers and I would always politely decline because I didn't want to be disrespectful.

Sometimes I dared to tease her about her team, but then she would turn on me and waggle a finger in my face and spread her arms out and insult Lebouef before praising Tigana or Saha and I'd never hear the end of it, but I liked that – I loved her enthusiasm and the twinkle in her eye when her team was on the march up the table – especially the year they got promoted to the Premiership and tears were in her eyes as she clasped her hands together before waggling her forefinger towards me again, saying they would go to every Premier League ground and play any team off the park once the new season started and they were in the top division and staying there for good.

The Lunch Club for pensioners on the SW15 estate opened in January 2000, and back then Mary would come every day. The very first time I met her she scolded me for making her a cr*p cup of tea that wasn't strong enough and sent me back to make her another mug and ordered me to leave the teaspoon in this time as well. The way she said it made me laugh, and I probably called her fussy and after that I looked for Mary every day to come through the door and I'd make her the perfect cup and I always felt I connected with her. Then, one Thursday, she didn't come in, and on the Friday I asked where she was and she told me she was in bed because the journey back from Rotherham (or somewhere similar) had taken hours and hours, and as she told me the story I realised she had been watching Fulham away on a Wednesday night at the other end of the country and she must have been pushing seventy years of age and then I clocked that everyone called her Mary Fulham for that reason, coz she was Fulham through and through, and so it became her affectionate adopted surname.

She asked me how many matches I had missed that season, and I replied that although I had a season ticket, I could only afford the odd away game. Then I asked her how many games she had missed. She said she could count the amount of games, home and away, she had missed on one hand…. I assumed she meant that she had only missed a handful of games home and away that particular season. She laughed at me and said No, she didn't mean the current season, but dating back to (I think she said) the year 1956. Amazing.

After Chelsea beat Fulham in the FA Cup Semi Final at Villa Park, it never crossed my mind to dare mention the result to Mary. I took her a mug of tea and gently squeezed her shoulder and left her. A few minutes later she joined me outside for a cigarette and off loaded. She went completely ballistic concerning the referee's performance. I listened and nodded and felt for her as I remembered my teenage face-painted head shaking in shattered disbelief as Elleray destroyed my dreams at rainy Wembley in 1994 with that diabolical display.

I could write several pages about the stories Mary told me and the friendship I valued and the energy, enthusiasm and positivity she oozed.

I helped at the Lunch Club on the Estate SW15 for less than three years before moving away. I have popped back to the Lunch Club a few times over the last two years to meet and greet my pensioner friends. Before I left England to go travelling in February, I heard that Mary was ill so I sent her a 'get well soon' letter. While I was in Australia I dived into an internet café in a town called Mooloolaba on the Sunshine Coast and read an email from a Fulham supporting mate that told me the terribly sad news that Mary had died. This email included a link to the Fulham website that showed a moving article. I emailed the club my condolences and received a poignant message back from a lady called Sandra Coles a few days later.

Last month I took a train to Putney and a bus to the estate and I walked down the road past the huge grey tower blocks and thought of Mary all the way until I arrived at the Lunch Club.

I sat next to Bruce who was the Golden Gloves amateur boxing champion in the Fifties (once he boxed Muhammad Ali to the deck at a charity boxing match) and who used to be mates with Lenny McLean. Bruce gripped my hand and asked me if I had been away in prison, and I laughed and reminded him that I live down the South Coast now, so no, I hadn't been away in the nick.

I made Billy a cup of tea, he still takes two sugars and bites the butt off his cheap cigarettes before lighting them up and he entertains staff and peers alike at the Christmas shows when he dresses up in drag and sings Shirley Bassey songs followed by a speedy version of a hymn called 'The Old Rugged Cross' and Billy never denies his rumoured reputation of being an exceptional pick pocket.

Then I plonked myself down opposite Albert who used to tell me fascinating stories about going to Stamford Bridge one Saturday and then Craven Cottage the next – but as the years rolled by his allegiance stayed with Fulham and he followed them through thick and thin but never gets to the Cottage much now because he's had his hip replaced and he's saving his money for a world cruise – a truly magnificent adventure that he must experience before he passes away. He has his usual dig at Chelsea and I tell him that he hasn't changed a bit and he starts humming a Fulham chant which settles in my ear as I shake his hand firmly goodbye and move onto the table at the rear of the hall where Mary used to sit.

I kneel on the floor between Hilda and Janet and they take my hands and Janet tells me that Mary didn't want any visitors in the final weeks and Hilda agrees it was for the best, and these are tough old birds who kept the country going in the Forties and they make me proud to be English and I look around the Club and see faces that fought for my freedom and then I remember the measly state pension they're on and the pathetic accommodation that some of them live in and most of them are isolated and don't even have the energy to take their rubbish out some days and are too proud to ask for help, and none of them leave food on their plates because they remember the days of rationing and then Elsie sees me and calls my name and I go and give her a kiss and recall in my mind the day when she was teary and I asked her if she was OK and she showed me a photograph in her purse of a young man and it was the anniversary of the day when he flew away with the RAF one morning and never flew back…

Smiffy motions at me that it's time to go, I'm on part two of a mission to find some of the teenagers I used to work with who have aged a few years and traded the Sunday football team and Tuesday night training with a lethal partnership, combining crack dealing with serious intimidation. It's time for me to dish out some home truths. As I get ready to leave, the pensioners in the Lunch Club put their cutlery down and sing Happy Birthday to John who is 93. I tell Smiffy we should give him the bumps.

I started this article and I didn't know where it was gonna end up. I haven't talked about Chelsea much. The pensioners were priced out of Chelsea long ago, and the kids always have been. I think it was Juvenile D wrote an article last season about 'The Missing Generation' - and how right he is. None of the kids can afford to go to the football and never have done since the terracing was knocked down – and even then we were the most expensive club in the league. I read recently that the average Chelsea fan earns £48K a year. Wow. I work for a charity (my choice, I know) and it doesn't bother me to admit that I'm a member who picks and chooses my matches now. October 2nd is Liverpool away, and providing tickets go on sale to members, that will be the first game for me, and I'm not ashamed to admit it. I'll be there vociferous and proud.

Honour your elders, especially at the football. Show some respect.

Wally Otton

Joe Cole - He's Here, He's There, He's In cfcuk!

ISSUE 50 September 2005

The Sheditorial

Welcome to issue # 50 of this fanzine. It has been a long journey since the first edition of the then called Matthew Harding's Blue And White Army first appeared in 1999 and it falls to me, as Sheditor, to thank all the contributors and readers who have helped in reaching this 'milestone'. Whether we as cfcuk will be around for another fifty issues remains to be seen but, for as long as we're here, we'll continue to try to keep you up to date with the thoughts, opinions, news and views from and about the people at Chelsea who matter most - the supporters.

What a brilliant start to the season. Following on from Chelsea's Community Shield triumph, ten years after our last League victory against Arsenal in 1995, Chelsea finally broke the hoodoo that seemed to have cursed us every time we played them since. Thanks to José Mourinho and following on from Claudio Ranieri's last two games against them, our record for the last six matches against the Goons now reads won 3, drawn 3, lost 0. Now, with a League fixture at the Library still to play, should we be drawn against them in any cup games, the 'fear' that might have previously constrained our efforts will have been dispelled and we can look forward to going into the game in the ascendancy.

In the first of what we hope will be some high profile interviews, we welcome Chelsea star Joe Cole to our pages. It was brilliant of Joe to take the time out to be interviewed and as well as thanking him, we here at cfcuk would also like to extend our gratitude to both Pippa Hancock and Simon Gr**nberg for their help in arranging the meeting. Joe, a Chelsea supporter, could not have been nicer and, in our opinion, he is a credit not only to the Chelsea Football Club itself but also to Chelsea supporters in general. Well done Joe, and thanks again.

Following months of speculation, Michael Essien finally joined Chelsea from Lyon after what must go down as one of the most protracted transfers in football history. However, it seems the wait has been worthwhile. The player looks hungry for success, keen to have the ball and take it forward and, against the bitterest of our rivals, he shone in the 2-0 victory at Three Point L*ne. We look forward to Michael winning a League winners medal in his first season at Stamford Bridge.

While football pundits and certain sections of the press claim that having such a large squad will only lead to discontent, those employed amongst the playing staff at Chelsea should take some time to remember that they are in the most privileged of positions. OK, so it's obvious that they all want to play, but they all know that there are only eleven places up for grabs. Those players who have intimated that they're not too happy about their situation might do well to remember that they are extremely well paid, enjoy the adulation of us - the supporters – and if they stick around long enough, they should, under the brilliant leadership of José Mourinho, pick up winners medals somewhere down the line. If we can offer any advice to the players it is this; keep your heads down, work hard and give your all for Chelsea Football Club - your time will come.

The Guy Who Blagged Me

*****

The Thoughts Of Chels Guevara

While it was brilliant that CHELSEA beat the Goons to win the Charity (Community) Shield, it was a crying shame that the idiots who decide such matters chose those purveyors of not so fine cuisine McDonalds to be their charity partner. It's a sure sign that the powers that be will do anything for money. Anyone who has seen a film entitled "Super Size Me" will know about the detrimental effects that eating McDonalds products can have on people and, if they are wise, they will adjust their food intake accordingly. As well as that, the amount of litter generated by McDonalds related products is a disgrace (although this time, the blame can only be directed towards the idiots who can't be bothered to place their waste in a litter bin). Surely such a prestigious game as the Charity Shield deserves a sponsor that has higher ethical standards than a hamburger chain and we here at cfcuk hope that the next time the FA look for a sponsor, they consider their own public image because, as far as all the CHELSEA SUPPORTERS that I spoke to on the subject, McDonalds is a terrible choice.

Anyone who watched JOHN TERRY'S recent television interview, in which he was promoting his book, would have heard the CHELSEA CAPTAIN talk about the influence that JOSÉ MOURINHO has had on the squad of players. JOHN also mentioned that the manager has a great sense of humour. Imagine then, the following scenario. MR MOURINHO and various other CHELSEA officials have just finished eating a meal and are at their restaurant seats chatting. In walks MICHAEL ESSIEN who has literally just signed on the dotted line to become CHELSEA'S record signing. The player is summoned over to the table by his new manager and the conversation goes as follows; MOURINHO, "You want to play football for me?" ESSIEN, "Yes, I do!" MOURINHO, "You want to play first team football for me? ESSIEN, "Yes I do!" MOURINHO, "Then you must pay the bill for this meal!" With that, all in JOSÉ'S company - including MICHAEL - fell about laughing and, according to my sources, CHELSEA'S brilliant, fantastic, wonderful and very generous manager did actually pay for the meal. Nevertheless, as everyone is aware, MICHAEL has played in every game since his arrival and, the way that he's been playing since he got here, I think that he deserves to have HIS meals paid for...

Chels Guevara

*****

Joe Cole Meets Mickey Microphone And Juvenile D

You've always been a Chelsea supporter haven't you? Yes. My friend Rick Burton and his Dad used to sit on the benches. I know he still goes because I got him tickets for the Barcelona game last season. It must be strange for him because he used to take me to the games and now I'm out there playing. My brother Nicky is a season ticket holder – he's been Chelsea all the way and my sister Charlie also comes to watch me play. Nicky used to come with Michael Roche, who now works for Chelsea's

Security, and his son Michael junior. All in all, I've got a strong tie with the club. I've been a ball boy at Chelsea, a supporter, I've played for the Under 12s and Under 13s and now I'm back playing professionally – it does feel like home.

What was it like when you were a youngster here and you had to go to West Ham? I had trials with clubs all over the country but my dad (George) just said to me that I should go somewhere that I feel the most comfortable. The reason I didn't sign for Chelsea back then was because the kids used to train at Battersea and it seemed a bit distant from the youth and senior team – it just felt like a kid's side. At West Ham, things were more integrated with the youth team training with the 1st team. I know that there is a big rivalry between Chelsea and West Ham but being there has been a big part of my career and I wouldn't knock it. Having said that, I'm really happy to be back here now.

Not as happy as we are! When you got the call about a possible transfer to Chelsea, did it take you long to think about it? It happened in less than a day! There were three other clubs interested in me at the time – two from the Premiership and one from Spain – but then I got a call from Chelsea asking whether I'd like to sign for them. My first thoughts were 'yes!' I always go with my first instincts. It was my dad who called me and he said, "OK, I'll meet you at Stamford Bridge in an hour's time." I drove over with my mum (Susan). I did the medical the same day and the next I was training with them. It was so surreal. The two days just felt like a dream and I couldn't believe it was happening. But as far as my thoughts about the chance of joining Chelsea were concerned, it was an immediate "Yes!" In my first season, when things weren't going so well, I always remembered that moment. It was my gut reaction and the memory has always served me well – I'm well chuffed.

When you first signed for Chelsea, there was a story published that the club were going to loan you to CSKA Moscow. Was there any truth in that or was it just tabloid rubbish? No truth at all – it was a story that the papers made up. When I read it, it wasn't good. It's never nice to see things like that because sometimes things like that can make you feel like you're not wanted. I knew it was rubbish and I just carried on with my training.

You knew Frank Lampard and Glen Johnson at West Ham. Frank told me that he knew Alan Hudson when he was there and it was him who told him he should move to Chelsea. Did he ever give you the same advice? I never met Alan senior although I played in the same youth side as his son Anthony and I know Alan's other son Allen was also on the books there. Anthony was a decent player but wasn't a patch on his dad but, as I said, I knew myself that I should make the move to Chelsea.

When we played West Ham, Frank got a bit of a bad reception but you didn't. Neither of you left on bad terms so why do you think that is? I don't know. I couldn't really put my finger on it. It's never nice to go back to a club and get a bad reception. At the end of the day, I ran myself into the ground for that club. A lot of the time, I had to play out of position and things like that so it wasn't always that easy for me. At the end of the day, I've still got a lot of friends there to this day. I hope I get a good reception when I go back there but the most important thing is that Chelsea win the game. I've got to make sure that I concentrate on playing well and remove any emotional ties that I might have for them. When we go back there, Frank, Glen and myself will just be thinking about helping Chelsea to win the three points and nothing else and, as for any reaction from their supporters, whatever happens will happen. It's just great to be playing for Chelsea who I think are now one of the biggest clubs in Europe.

We've ALWAYS been the biggest club in Europe! Yeah… but now everyone else knows it!

Last season, when you got a regular start place in the Chelsea side, you also burst onto the England scene. The run in the Chelsea side must have helped you get international recognition. I've got the shirt now – it's been a long time coming. I've been in the England squad for a few years now and I've always seemed to been nearly there or thereabouts but I've always been overlooked. But I knew that once I had a proper start – my chance in a competitive game came against Northern Ireland – I'd take it. I've played in the last five games and it's up to me to keep my place. Its always special to play for England.

If you asked most supporters to choose between their club winning

the League or England winning the World Cup, they'd go for their club winning the League. **Would you rather win the European Cup with Chelsea or the World Cup with England?** Phew… that's a bad question to ask!

OK, scrub that one then but we're going to have the lot anyway aren't we? Yeah, we're going to have the lot!

How much of a buzz was it to win the League? It was fantastic! I can get a bit emotional and that day at Bolton I got a bit choked up.

I think we all did! After the Charlton game when we went to collect the trophy, I thought to myself, "Phew! We've done it!" It was a blinding day but I had to bite my tongue – it was a magic, magic moment!

Actor Ray Winstone was being interviewed on TV the other week and he thinks that you're going to help England win the World Cup. He's now adopted Chelsea as all his favourite players are now at Stamford Bridge… I like Ray. I've met him a few times at West Ham. He's a good bloke and a great football fan. I love all his films and I hope he's right about us winning the World Cup. It would be great for England to win it anyway but, if I was in the team, I think I'd break down for a good few weeks then – I would be choked up then!

We want you to win an FA Cup winners medal so that you've got the lot as far as domestic medals are concerned… I've got to say that it's something I've thought about. As a footballer, you want to win everything but, in the FA Cup, the furthest I've ever got is the quarter finals. I was at all the Cup Finals with Chelsea. I was there against Middlesbrough and against Man Utd…

That was horrible that, wasn't it? Yeah, it was horrible. I went with a coach load of Chelsea supporters from Battersea. My dad got my brother and myself a couple of tickets and we went with a fella who runs a fruit and veg stall there. It was a good day up until the game. I still remember the referee David Elleray and, every time he used to referee a game I was in, I used to tell him that he broke my heart giving them those stupid penalties.

He booked Erland almost at the start of the game which more or less put him out of the rest of it… I know, it was shoulder to shoulder…

What about José… he's brilliant isn't he… Yeah, he's brilliant!

He's brought you on leaps and bounds… I can't quite put my finger on what he's done but I think that one of the main things is that he gave me the chance to have a consistent run of games. Under Claudio Ranieri, my best performances were at the back end of last season when I played seven or eight games on the spin. Under José, I've had the chance to have a good run in the side. His tactics are great and he gives us a lot of freedom. I can't praise him enough. All in all, the whole thing is working well.

That goal you scored at Norwich sums you up. You battled for the ball, won it, took it forward and slotted it… That was a big goal for me because think it helped me get my place in the Chelsea side for the Barcelona tie. Both those two matches against Barcelona were massive games for me to play in. I've learnt a lot under José and he's definitely helped me to improve. This year, and I don't want to bore you, I've got to improve again.

You're not worried about the new signings? It's not something to worry about and I'm not going to lose any sleep about it. At the end of the day, if you want to be a top player, you have to play for a top club and Chelsea are the best club. At the best clubs, there is always competition for places.

Is it all about winning medals or being in the team every week or a drop of both?
It's a drop of both. We lost Scotty earlier this year because I think for him, the itch was too big and he felt he needed to play football. It was great to see Chelsea win the trophies and he helped us but it wasn't a big enough part for him. It was a disappointment to lose him because we all know what he can do. It's all about getting the balance right. With me, I want to play in the big games like the one at Stamford Bridge against Barcelona – it was one of the best days of my life – that's what makes playing football worthwhile.

What do you think about the fanzine… if you ever bother reading it?
It's a good crack! I like it… I always read it – it's a lot more interesting than the programme!

Cheers Joe, we were hoping you'd say that! We love you!

Mickey Microphone & Juvenile D

*****

Chelsea - The New Force Of English Football

The Championship celebrations have barely finished and already we're well into the new season and carrying on where we left off. The new signings have bedded in well and the squad is now looking stronger than ever.

The manager has to be applauded for his meticulous planning in pre-season. While other clubs dithered and waited until the last day of the transfer window before making new (perhaps panic) purchases, José had his squad sorted before a ball was even kicked. The only player to arrive after the start of the new term was Michael Essien, and even he has slotted in as though he has been playing in this side for years. Indeed, the time it took the transfer saga to unfold, it almost seems like he has been around for years!

This is my first article this season, as I was out of the country enjoying the sun when the previous edition was compiled. Strangely, it was that holiday more than anything that really ignited my hunger for the new campaign to kick off. During my time away, I noticed how different the other Brits abroad treated us when they found out we were Chelsea fans, in contrast to previous years. Admittedly, we were never really been liked in the past. But the feelings of hatred towards our club and its fans are growing to the sort of level I have only witnessed being shown to Man United in the past. And no matter what their apparent reasons are for disliking us, I can only come to the conclusion that the reason we're so loathed is because we are what United were ten years ago – the best team in the country. Simple as that; and don't we just love it!

With every three points gained, there is a sense that the media and rivals grow more and more despondent. They'll grasp at straws, claiming that Roman will get bored or that we're too negative and will be found out. But the truth is, we're only going to improve and it's looking truly ominous for the chasing bunch.

As we move forward on the pitch, the club continue to try and improve off of it. Unfortunately, I have been left (not for the first time) less than impressed with the Box Office. Clearly, the club need to either hire better summer staff or find a more efficient way of dealing with season ticket renewals, as some of the errors myself and friends have encountered recently are not acceptable. Already fearing the worst, due to the fact whoever processed my form decided to ignore the part where I entered a new address, I rang the ticket enquiry line last week to double check that my name had been put down on the waiting list of supporters hoping to apply for European away tickets.

Imagine my disgust (though, depressingly, not surprise) when the voice on the other end of the line informed me that my name was NOT down on the list. I wasn't the only one that the club forgot to put down on this list and it's lucky that I phoned up and checked in advance, otherwise I'd never have known or be able to rectify this act of gross negligence on their part. I dread to think how many people that are expecting invitations from Eddie Barnett to come through the letterbox will not be receiving anything. Are the box office staff really that incompetent that they cannot process our forms correctly? Why should we have to ring the club and wait half an hour on premium rate lines, just to double check that people at the club are doing their jobs right?

Ironically, the only reason I had phoned in the first place was to cancel my request to have European home tickets sent to me automatically. It turns out my name wasn't down on that list either, despite me requesting it on my application! For once, a bungling error of theirs had been advantageous to me.

I know I wasn't the only one who felt let down when it was announced on the club website that all Champions League group games would be as expensive as they are. The club has been great in the past two campaigns with allowing discounts for booking all three group games in one go. However, this year the average season ticket holder will have to pay around £12 more per game to watch Anderlecht, Betis and Liverpool at the Bridge than they do for league games. I feel the club misled us slightly by not announcing ticket prices on the ST application forms sent out in the summer and there were many cases of money being taken out of people's accounts without them even being aware of this season's price increases.

The club have seriously underestimated the effect this will have on attendances for the home group games. People pay enough whilst following the club across the country and Europe – so why not give us loyal supporters discounts similar to those given in previous seasons? I feel another bout of adverts in the Evening Standard coming on as too many season ticket holders cannot justify spending that much on top of the huge amounts they already shell out, meaning empty seats all over the ground on nights when the stadium should be full and buzzing.

On the plus side, at least the draw for the group stage has given us the chance to avenge that disappointing semi final defeat at Anfield in April. With a tough group ahead, what's the betting that fate will play its part again and we end up with the scenario that the Scousers have to beat us at Stamford Bridge to progress to the knockout rounds. I sure I'm not the only one who's noticed that more and more red shirts have reappeared on high streets up and down the country (not to mention on summer holidays!) since their freak victory in Istanbul. What better way to finally put the ghosts to rest and reaffirm the belief that Chelsea are the new force in English football than to slay the club who used to hold that very title.

Up the Chels!

Famous CFC

*****

Blue Tomorrow (From the eyes of a young Blue)

We all know that the support at the Bridge needs to improve. Being a part of the younger generation at Chelsea it is obvious that we need to get the kids coming more often so they can build up their support for the team. At the Community Shield recently and with my sister always telling me about the family section support, it seems that kids enjoy coming but need to get behind the team more often.

The open days at the Bridge, I think, have been a great idea to get the younger ones down to watch their heroes for free and hopefully this will encourage them to attend games at the Bridge more often. Also the reduced prices for cup games seem to have had the same affect.

The only problem is that we need to show them how to support the club. As I have been going to Chelsea home and away since I was 7 and have a season ticket in the MHL, I have and still do experience the best atmosphere at Chelsea, and this is something that the other young blues need to experience as it is obviously too quiet in the family section and other areas of the ground. Hopefully with the family section now being in the East lower they can feed off the MH for chants, as well as members now being able to purchase tickets in that area. I also hope that with the away fans in the Shed it will mean that the blue half of the Shed will become more vociferous.

I'm sure that some parents won't chant as much if they are taking kids with them and that is understandable, but surely until they are old enough to hear bad language you could replace the odd word.

So with cheaper ticket prices and open days etc. we are geared up to bring in the new support, but I also believe that the club needs to look at how it deals with kids when they are stepping up to adult price tickets. When I moved out of the family section at 16 I had to pay more than my dad who was still in the family section with my sister. Surely this is wrong, but the situation is still the same until my sister is too old for the family section. Once they leave the family section it will be hard for us to then all sit together in the MHL. Since I have been going to Chelsea the cost to go to games has more than doubled.

What I think the club should introduce is "student" prices. I have seen this done at many clubs. I will still be in education of some form for a few years yet and will only have a part time job and a student loan to help pay for the things I enjoy. Surely I should not be expected to pay more than my dad or the same as other people who have a full time job. But anyway I will continue to try and afford to go to Chelsea for as long as possible, but it looks like it will be very hard for me to afford it in a few years time unless something changes.

So raise your voices and show the kids how it's done, then the blue support should be guaranteed for another generation.

Win Or Lose - Up The Blues!

CFC Andrew

OTHER CHELSEA TITLES AVAILABLE FROM *GATE 17*

OVER LAND AND SEA
MARK WORRALL
GATE 17
ISBN: 978-0955745904
www.overlandandsea.net

First published in 2004, *"Over Land and Sea"* is Mark Worrall's wickedly entertaining chronicle of Chelsea's dramatic attempt to win the European Champions League during what turned out to be the most tumultuous season in the club's history.

Having qualified for the competition following a famous end of season victory over Liverpool, the Blues charismatic manager Claudio Ranieri, short on cash and resigned to losing his star player, Gianfranco Zola, looked like having little chance of success. Enter Roman Abramovich. The billionaire Russian oligarch purchased the club and financed a spending spree unprecedented in the annals of the game.

"Over Land and Sea" overlays the team's fortunes with the transient adventures of Blues fanatic Marco and his Chelsea Gate 17 cohorts as they carouse their way around the bars, fleshpots and football grounds of Europe.'Glorious unpredictability,' that's what the Gate 17 boys called it. 'Pure Chels,' you never knew what was going to happen next. Whatever it was, Marco, Young Dave, Ugly John, Ossie, Baby Gap Brian and the rest of the Gate 17 crew had no intention of missing any of it...they'd even planned a spiritual pilgrimage to Sardinia to watch their hero Zola playing for his hometown club Cagliari.

CELERY!
REPRESENTING CHELSEA IN THE 1980s
KELVIN BARKER
DPS PUBLISHING
ISBN: 978-0955346507
www.cfclegends.co.uk

Celery! – Representing Chelsea in the 1980s is Kelvin's story of supporting Chelsea during the most turbulent of decades, both on and off the pitch. In addition to his own memories of watching his beloved team from the terraces, Kelvin has gathered together the thoughts and recollections of the players he considers form the Stamford Bridge club's 'Team of the Eighties'.

Celery! – Representing Chelsea in the 1980s is divided into two parts. In part one, each season from 1979/80 through to 1988/89 is reviewed through the eyes of a passionate supporter, as Kelvin recalls the trials and tribulations … and there were many … of supporting the Blues during a topsy-turvy decade. Part two is handed over to the star performers, as the aforementioned 'Team of the Eighties' spill the beans on their experiences in the royal blue of Chelsea. The popular John Neal, manager at the Bridge from 1981 to 1985, also gives his thoughts on a dramatic spell in the Stamford Bridge hot-seat which saw the club rise magnificently from near-oblivion.

From Kelvin's own amusing tales of hugging skipper Colin Pates on the hallowed Stamford Bridge turf and serenading Bob Geldof in the King's Road, through to the incredible behind-the-scenes stories as told by the players themselves – the mysterious case of Mickey Thomas' disappearing gold chain, how a kick in the head made Joey Jones a fans' favourite, the role physio Norman Medhurst's hair played in David Speedie's departure from the club, and many more – this book lays bare the facts of representing Chelsea in the 1980s, as recalled by those who were there.

BLUE MURDER – CHELSEA TILL I DIE
MARK WORRALL
HEADHUNTER
ISBN: 978-1906085001
www.overlandandsea.net

Money, sex, illegal substances, nightclubs and Chelsea Football Club …
Johnny Nipper is deeply preoccupied with them all. For thirty years he's
had it all his own way, double crossing and dealing his way through life
without a care in the world … until a drugs deal he puts together to gain
revenge on an ex-girlfriend goes disastrously wrong.

In fear for his life, Nipper leaves London to begin a new life in Goa
where he encounters Chopper Lewis, an old acquaintance from the
Stamford Bridge terraces who persuades him to unburden himself of his
guilt and tell his story.

Recalled vividly with huge slabs of hip and sexy humour, Blue Murder
is the chronicle of Johnny Nipper's life. As the story unfolds, entwining
itself with a fascinatingly detailed account of the changing fortunes of
Chelsea FC, music, fashion and popular culture, it becomes clear that
there's no way Nipper can return home, he'd be signing his own death
warrant. But with Chelsea on the verge of winning the title for the first
time in fifty years, will the temptation of being there in person prove too
much?

ONE MAN WENT TO MOW
MARK WORRALL
GATE 17
ISBN: 978-0955745911
www.overlandandsea.net

It's July 2006, the World Cup has just finished in dismal penalty shootout failure for England and back to back Premiership champions Chelsea FC are preparing for the new season with a squad bolstered by the high profile signings of Michael Ballack and Andriy Shevchenko.

Surfing on a wave of optimism, buoyed by the outspoken confidence of manager Jose Mourinho, Marco and the rest of the Gate 17 boys return to Stamford Bridge in expectant mood, high on hope and talking about the Blues winning an unprecedented quadruple of trophies.

"One Man Went To Mow", the eagerly anticipated follow up to Mark Worrall's cult terrace classic, *"Over Land and Sea"*, chronicles the ongoing adventures of a colourful group of Chelsea supporters as they follow their teams quest for glory. In true gloriously unpredictable fashion, the season unravels against a backdrop of injuries, boardroom disquiet and growing media speculation about the future of the Special One, Mr Mourinho.

Having retraced his Gate 17 roots, Marco sets out to explain the mythical concept of 'Being Chels', the peerless state of true blue mind that followers of Chelsea's rivals struggle to come to terms with. Drawing his conclusions from impromptu encounters with Blues fanatics he meets en-route, including club owner, Mr Abramovich, Marco is left in no doubt that Chelsea Football Club is an association, a fellowship of mankind founded on the commonly shared belief that what goes around comes around and that when it comes around you should make the most of it because it might not come around again for years.

From Sofia to Barcelona, Bremen to Porto, Valencia to Liverpool and Stamford Bridge to Wembley, *"One Man Went To Mow"*, is a uniquely entertaining, vibrant and fascinating fly on the wall travelogue of one fans near religious quest for footballing redemption.

CHELSEA HERE, CHELSEA THERE
MARK WORRALL, KELVIN BARKER,
AND DAVID JOHNSTONE
GATE 17
ISBN: 9780955745935
www.overlandandsea.net

Picture the scene, August 25th 1984, Highbury Stadium, London. Thousands upon thousands of expectant Chelsea fans have congregated at the home of Arsenal to celebrate the return of the Blues to the old First Division.

A quarter of a century ago, Chelsea were a very different proposition to the club they are today. On the brink of financial extinction, they were represented by an inexpensively assembled team of relatively unknown players. Despite this, the Blues were able to command a phenomenal away support, inconceivable in the modern era.

Chelsea Here Chelsea There is a flawless time capsule for Blues fans seeking a trip down memory lane or those on the lookout for enlightenment in the ways of the old school. An assemblage of fascinating player interviews, rare and previously unseen photographs and the anecdotal recollections of a broad cross section of Blues fans present on that special day give *Chelsea Here Chelsea There* an endearingly nostalgic flavour.

Dixon, Nevin, Speedie. Johnny Neal's Blue and White army swathed in Le Coq Sportif. 'FRANKIE SAY' slogan T-shirts, Hi-NRG music and the lunatic hooligan fringe, *Chelsea Here Chelsea There* incorporates them all with gusto and provides a welcome shot in the arm for any fan seeking an antidote to today's sterile football environment.